Critical criminology

International Library of Sociology

Founded by Karl Mannheim

Editor: John Rex, University of Warwick

Arbor Scientiae
Arbor Vitae

A catalogue of the books available in the **International Library of Sociology** and other series of Social Science books published by Routledge & Kegan Paul will be found at the end of this volume.

Critical criminology

Edited with
contributory essays
by

Ian Taylor
Criminology Unit, Faculty of Law, University of Sheffield

Paul Walton
Department of Sociology, University of Glasgow

Jock Young
Department of Sociology, Middlesex Polytechnic

Routledge & Kegan Paul
London and Boston

First published in 1975
by Routledge & Kegan Paul Ltd
Broadway House, 68-74 Carter Lane,
London EC4V 5EL and
9 Park Street,
Boston, Mass. 02108, USA
Set in 'Monotype' Times type
and printed in Great Britain by
W & J Mackay Limited, Chatham

ISBN 0 7100 8023 9 (c)
ISBN 0 7100 8024 7 (p)

Dedication

No reason to get excited
The Thief he kindly spoke
There are many here among us
Who feel that life is but a joke.
But you and I we've been through life
And this is not our fate
So let us not speak falsely now
The hour is getting late.

Bob Dylan: 'All Along the Watchtower'

Contents

Preface

However desirable as a form of theoretical practice, collective work and its associated periods of self-criticism and argument require patience and support, not just amongst 'the collective' but amongst one's friends. In the process of producing *The New Criminology*, we leaned very heavily on our friends, and this volume has also been a trial on our colleagues. In various ways, our friends and colleagues at Middlesex Polytechnic (Ken Plummer, in particular), at Sheffield University (Tony Bottoms, Paul Wiles, Colin Sumner and Dave Wall) and at Glasgow University (Greg Philo and Ian Roxborough) have been helpful in ways they might not realize themselves. In London, Henrietta Resler has been an ever-patient friend and support.

We would like also to acknowledge the typing help of Joyce Keen and Lesley Corner; and also the permissions received to reprint the essays by Herman and Julia Schwendinger and Richard Quinney from *Issues in Criminology*, and the exchange between Paul Hirst and ourselves from *Economy and Society*. Once again, Peter Hopkins of Routledge & Kegan Paul has been of inestimable help.

Though there are differences in emphasis and direction in our work and that of our American comrades, we would like to express our appreciation of their work, and the radical scholars at the School of Criminology at Berkeley in particular. Without them, American criminology would be so much the poorer. We wish them, and their new journal, *Crime and Social Justice*, all success in the future. Without the continuing help and stimulation from our friends in the National Deviancy Conference, of course, none of this would ever have been possible.

IAN TAYLOR
PAUL WALTON
JOCK YOUNG

Notes on contributors

WILLIAM J. CHAMBLISS is the author of numerous articles and books attempting to systematize and explore the 'critical criminological' perspective. With Robert Seidman, he authored *Law, Order and Power* (Reading, Mass.: Addison-Wesley, 1971), and earlier he edited *Crime and the Legal Process* (New York: McGraw-Hill, 1969), an initial attempt to apply a conflict approach to the sociology of criminal law. He is currently engaged in producing a monograph on organized crime in America, and on a book on the political economy of crime. He is Associate Professor in the Department of Sociology, University of California, Santa Barbara, USA.

PAUL Q. HIRST was born in 1946 in Devon, studied at Leicester University and Sussex University. He is the author of a variety of articles in the Althusserian tradition, mostly in *Economy and Society*, and is currently Lecturer in Sociology at Birkbeck College in the University of London.

GEOFF PEARSON studied at the Universities of Cambridge, Sheffield and the London School of Economics. He trained and practised as a psychiatric social worker and currently holds a lectureship in the Department of Social Administration, University College, Cardiff, where he teaches Human Socialization. His main interests lie in the relationship between deviancy theory and politics, and his publications include a number of papers on this, and a book *The Deviant Imagination*, to be published by Macmillan.

TONY PLATT teaches criminology at the University of California (Berkeley) and is a member of the Union of Radical Criminologists. His political practice, shaped by the New Left, includes work in the anti-war movement and community control struggles. He has written three books (*The Child Savers*, *The Politics of Riot Commissions* and

Policing America) and is presently working on a book about the 1935 Harlem riot. His essay for this anthology reflects the collective ideas and practice of the Union of Radical Criminologists. A product of the Manchester Grammar School–Oxford University meritocracy, he has been living in the USA for over ten years.

RICHARD QUINNEY has served on the faculties of several universities in America, most recently at New York University, where he was professor of sociology. Receiving his doctorate from the University of Wisconsin, he has since been the author and editor of several books on law and crime in American society, most notably *The Problem of Crime* (New York: Dodd Mead, 1970); *The Social Reality of Crime* (Boston: Little, Brown, 1970); *Criminal Behaviour Systems* (with Marshall B. Clinard) (New York: Holt, Rinehart & Winston, 1973, 2nd edition), and *Criminal Justice in America* (Boston: Little, Brown, 1974). He lives in Chapel Hill, North Carolina, where he is conducting research for further writing on working-class life and social control in a textile-mill town. He also edits, with others, a community socialist newspaper, *Bread and Roses*, and is continuing his work on legal order and the transition from capitalist to socialist society. He is on the editorial board of the newly-formed journal *Crime and Social Justice*, and also *Theory and Society*.

HERMAN and JULIA SCHWENDINGER are co-authors of *Sociologists of the Chair: a Radical Analysis of the Formative Years of North American Sociology* (1883–1922) (Boston: Basic Books, 1974) and 'Rape Myths: in Legal, Theoretical and Everyday Practice', in *Crime and Social Justice*, the newly-formed journal in radical criminology. They are members of the Union of Radical Criminologists and are presently writing two books on a Marxist theory of delinquency and on women's struggles to defend the victim of the crime of rape. Julia Schwendinger is a project director of the Bay Area Women Against Rape in Berkeley. Herman Schwendinger is an assistant professor of criminology at the University of California, Berkeley, where he has been denied tenure by conventional criminologists because of the radical contents of *The Sociologists of the Chair*.

IAN TAYLOR has taught and researched at the Universities of Durham, Glasgow and Queen's University, Kingston, Ontario. He is currently Lecturer in Criminology at the University of Sheffield. He co-authored *The New Criminology*, and co-edited *Politics and Deviance* (with Laurie Taylor) (the second book of readings from the National Deviancy Conference). He is currently working with Herman Bianchi and Mario Simondi on the publication of the proceedings of the European Group for the Study of Deviance and Social Control.

PAUL WALTON has taught and researched at the Universities of

Bradford and Durham, and is currently Senior Lecturer at the University of Glasgow. He was co-author of *The New Criminology*, and (with Andrew Gamble) of *From Alienation to Surplus Value* (Sheed & Ward, 1972; Penguin, 1974), the winner of the Isaac Deutscher Memorial Award for 1972. He is working on books on Marxism, Weber, phenomenology and industrial deviance.

JOCK YOUNG is the author of *The Drugtakers* (Paladin, 1971), co-author of *The New Criminology*, and co-editor of *Contemporary Social Problems in Britain* (with Roy Bailey) (Saxon House, 1973); *Manufacturing News: Deviance, Social Problems and the Mass Media* (with Stan Cohen) (Constable, 1974) and *Myths of Crime* (with Paul Rock) (Routledge & Kegan Paul, 1975). He has written extensively on drug-use, youth culture, bohemia and the mass media and is currently completing a book entitled *Media as Myth.* He is Principal Lecturer in Sociology at Middlesex Polytechnic at Enfield.

Editors' introduction

The politicization of social philosophy and the human sciences in general over the last decade, in particular, has been subject to considerable comment – most notably, so far as sociology is concerned, by Professor Alvin Gouldner. Few fields of inquiry have been left untouched. We are even witnessing attempts by radicalized natural scientists to unpack the political assumptions underlying the procedures of 'hard' science itself.

But in the area of criminology and deviancy theory, this process of politicization has arguably proceeded farther than in most other, previously 'non-political' areas. At least two reasons can be identified. On the one hand, there is the experience in the Western world of a vast increase in the range of social behaviours deemed appropriate for control *by law*; and, on the other, this experience has forced a reappraisal of the morality of the law being so extended.

Old laws have been reactivated, and new laws created, in order to contain and control (by threat if not actually by apprehension or symbolic prosecution) certain crucially socially-problematic behaviours. In Britain, new laws have been created (in the shape, most outstandingly, of the Industrial Relations Act) to regulate industrial dissent and the rights of workers to organize (and the first victims of associated picketing regulations have been sentenced to prison). Old laws have been resuscitated to enable the nebulous charge of conspiracy to be used against political dissenters; and, in the attempt to control 'squatting' (the possession of unoccupied housing by homeless families) the Forcible Entry Act, 1429, has proven to be a powerful weapon in the hands of local housing authorities. The Housing Finance Act has also created deviants (if not criminals) out of elected local councillors who have refused to implement central government directives to increase the rents in publically-owned housing. And the proposals of the Criminal Law Revision Committee, if implemented, would substantially increase the legal powers of the police to seize and search citizens in everyday police–public interaction. In short, the extension of law has created new criminals, criminals who are no longer so readily identifiable with the stereotypical 'criminals' or 'delinquents' of orthodox 1950s criminology – the disaffiliated or disorganized urban working-class adolescent. The population at risk of criminalization is much more ambiguous and extensive, including not only the criminologist's own students (and the more 'bohemian' criminologist himself), but also the spokesmen and membership of the oppositional social, political and economic movements at large. So, for example, leaders of minority groups as far apart as the migrant grape workers of California and the tenants' associations in public housing in Britain have been increasingly harassed *by law*, and the attempt has been made to define their activities as criminal rather than as political in content.

This shift in the jurisdiction of law has had profound consequences in the teaching, the application, the legitimacy and the meaning of traditional criminology. It has become increasingly difficult to sustain the notion that criminality is a behavioural quality monopolized by a particular and narrow section of the lower class, a behaviour that is removed extraneously from our own everyday experience. The trend in criminology away from a focus on the juvenile 'in need of care, protection or control' towards social theories of rule-creation and rule-breaking, located in a wider, more complex moral and social dynamic, is well illustrated in the attempts by thinkers like Richard Quinney and William Chambliss to create a 'conflict theory' of crime (and law). Examples of their work are included in this volume as an indication of the ways in which the extension of *legal domination* has forced upon criminologists not only a broader subject-matter (a larger population at risk of apprehension), but also a more telling and immediate set of political dilemmas. The extension of law has charged criminologists with a moral responsibility they could often more easily avoid – the *evaluation* of the legal norms (and underlying morality) of a society that criminalizes activities developing out of the contradiction in its political economy. In Britain, the emergence of a critical criminology, moving beyond the confines of the administrative technology of the Home Office and its outposts, occurred slightly later than in America, possibly because of the existence in this country of a radical tradition and a Labour movement that was thought adequate by many for the resolution of the legal, political and economic contradictions of British society. Geoff Pearson's essay in this volume is an attempt to underline, in an historically informed manner, some of the legal, criminal and (notably) personal questions which that radical tradition now appears unable to confront – or, at least, to recognize as a politics in themselves. Jock Young's paper is an attempt to move beyond the kinds of questions that radical deviancy theory erected in reaction to the

'Fabianism' of orthodox, correctional criminology and social work, and to erect the elements of a criminology that was concerned, above all else, to act in defence of working-class interests.

It would be premature to suggest that a new 'critical criminological' paradigm has emerged in the West; and it would be even more absurd to believe that anything of the sort is even quiescent in the Soviet bloc, where (as Connor has so ably shown) the dominant criminologies are only now developing beyond the thesis that crime is a Western 'contamination' (Connor, 1972). The object of this volume, however, is to place on record some of the early attempts that are now being made, by radical thinkers and activists in North America and Europe, to transcend what Tony Platt calls the 'hip concerns' of the sociology of deviance, and to confront the facts of extension of law and the ensuing political dilemmas of the radical criminologist.

The early work in the radical criminological perspective is healthily diverse, and the papers collected here are an attempt at representativeness. Chambliss's paper, in this volume, is a valuable example of the conflict perspective's superiority over the 'functional' paradigms, so dominant in orthodox criminology, in pointing empirically to the criminalization of the lower-class populations of Nigeria and the USA by a corrupt political and economic élite. Quinney's essay, in contrast, is evidence of a logic in his work (and increasingly in that of other radical criminologists) that moves from an existentially-based 'conflict theory' (of the kind that we criticized in *The New Criminology*)[1] to a Marxist model of law-creation and crime. This move to a Marxist economism, in turn, highlights the need to incorporate the aetiological and other insights so derived with the libertarian and civil-rights concerns that inform the Schwendingers' much-quoted (though relatively inaccessible) attempt to formulate the elements of a radical *human-rights* criminology (first published in 1970 in *Issues in Criminology*). Tony Platt's overview of developments in radical criminology in the USA indicates that these concerns, of moving towards a materialist criminology, whilst retaining the diversity of human interests that for so long has been a part of American populist *and* New Left individualism, are at the forefront of the developing 'new' criminology in the USA in much the same way as they are in Britain and in Europe.

However, our intention in reprinting the debate between ourselves and Paul Hirst was to underline the fact that a return to Marx in criminology must inevitably raise the thorny issue of how one engages in the 'reading' of Marx. In an intellectual and political climate where 'Marxism' has so often been equivalent to Stalinism, European deviancy theorists have perhaps been more quizzical about the issues involved in Marxist interpretation than their American counterparts (whose problem has been one of overcoming a monolithic rejection of

Marxism in whatever form). One of the dominant tendencies in contemporary European Marxism (and perhaps *the* dominant tendency amongst Marxists concerned with 'cultural work' – on law, education or the media) is the structuralist Marxism of Louis Althusser (cf. Althusser, 1970, 1971). This reading of Marx denies the authenticity, and specifically the scientificity, of any reading other than its own. Concerned above all with the objective of social revolution (and arguing that this objective is attainable scientifically through correct theoretical practice), the Althusserians would find little time for the issue of *socialist diversity* we have raised in these pages. Marx's work on *man* (at the forefront of his earlier works and sustained in his later work on political economy) is relegated to the status of metaphysical speculation. The papers by Hirst are included because they constitute a developed attack on what Althusserians would see as the idealism (that is, the ontological concerns) of radical deviancy theorists, and because potentially they form the framework for a sophisticated 'criminology' that could be erected in the name of social defence – of State socialist societies. Even the new radical criminologists, with their turn to a materialist analysis of law, would recognize that such a criminology of social defence could be used, illegitimately, to justify a variety of repressive initiatives (e.g. psychiatric hospitalization of dissenters) carried through in the name of the 'socialist' State.

Critical criminology is still in its infancy, and unsurprisingly there are distinct tendencies within its ranks (some of which we discuss in chapter 1). We would, however, insist upon two unifying features in this international development. First, we would assert that the adequacy of the various theoretical offerings in critical criminology is to be assessed *in practice* – that is, in terms of their utility in demasking the moral and ideological veneer of an unequal society, and in terms of its ability to enliven the critical debate about the modes of change, and the post-capitalist alternatives, contemplated by those committed to a radical alternative (whether the agencies be intellectuals, workers or prisoners). In this respect, we would separate off our theoretical tendency from that of critical phenomenology – where the logic of investigation separates man from society, leaving the facts of imprisonment, criminalization and, in general, the forcible segregation of men *from* society unavailable for investigation or critique.

Secondly, we would distinguish our conception of critical criminology from the critical postures adopted by a few isolated criminologists at international and national congresses,[2] and in the literature, in recent years. It was undoubtedly correct of Professor Nagel, for example, to question the morality of the decision by the International Society for Criminology to hold its 1970 Congress in Madrid, and to use that platform to raise issues about omissions in the subject-matter of criminology (Nagel, 1971). But instant exercises of this kind are not equivalent to the project of posing fundamental and consistent challenges to the everyday political assumptions, practices and implications of one of the most influential and State-dominated branches of applied social 'science' – the 'science' of criminology. It is to that endeavour that each of the contributors to this book is committed, and it is with this project in view that this volume of critical essays has been planned and produced.

Notes

1 I. Taylor, P. Walton and J. Young (1973). In part, this collection is intended as an extension of the 'immanent' critique of existing theories of crime and deviance developed in that text. (Cf. in this volume, in particular, chapters 1 and 2.)

2 The orthodox organizations of international criminology (which, by and large, are sponsored by governments and their law-enforcement agencies) have now been challenged by the establishment of the European Group for the Study of Deviance and Social Control (the first conference of which was held in Florence in September 1973). The influence and significance of these organizations will be discussed in the Introduction to H. Bianchi, M. Simondi, and I. Taylor, eds. (1975).

1 Critical criminology in Britain: review and prospects*

Ian Taylor, Paul Walton and Jock Young

The purpose of this chapter is not so much to describe the development and future prospects of critical criminology in Britain, as to argue that the process of transformation of criminology into 'radical deviancy theory' gives rise to a series of theoretical and practical possibilities, and that these possibilities relate to new forms of academic and political practice. The *purposes* for doing 'radical deviancy theory' (or critical criminology) have now clarified to the point where the radical deviancy theorist can no longer remain content with demystifying traditional correctionally-oriented criminology.

1 The revolt against criminology in Britain

Earlier attempts to characterize the 'theoretical' themes in the British sociology of deviance that crystallized out of the formation of the National Deviancy Conference in 1968 have concentrated on what can be called the *formal* features of that sociology (cf. Cohen and Taylor, 1972).

Amongst the most central concerns was the defence of the authenticity of deviance. Here, the concern was to attack the notion that one can explain deviance by reference to some social or personal pathology. Instead, it was argued, deviant action must always be examined in terms of its meaningfulness to the deviant actor. Flowing out of this, in deviancy theory at the time, was the view of society as a series of alternative realities, all with an authenticity and meaningfulness of their own.

Connected with the emphasis on the existence of alternative realities was what then was called the denial of absolutism (Young, 1970). Where the orthodox criminologist has tended to characterize the social order as concensual and monolothic, with a minority of inadequate deviants existing on society's fringes, the deviancy theorist argued for the existence of a diversity of values sited in the plethora of subcultures existing within industrial society. The suggestion was not that these subcultures necessarily had a full-blown contracultural ideology, but rather that there existed a cultural diversity, albeit often of an inarticulate, contradictory and hesitant nature.

A third feature of the embryonic British sociology of deviance was its revolt against correctionalism. Where orthodox criminology, unquestioning in its relationship to the social order (that it was concensual) could see part of its task as the effective management of intervention and reform in the penal system on behalf of existing social arrangements, deviancy theorists came increasingly to see the fact of societal reaction to crime and deviance as problematic, and a crucial matter for examination and critique – a part of the explanation of commitment to deviance. An increasingly critical posture came to be adopted, not only towards the more obvious guardians of the *status quo*, like prison administrators and the judiciary, but also towards the social work and psychiatric professions in their role as agents of social control.

The revolt against correctionalism tied closely into a developing critique of the 'scientificity' that underpinned it – the ideology of positivism. Correctional criminology consistently viewed the deviant as being determined in his deviant activity by forces beyond his control. The 'scientific expert' was seen to have a superior understanding of these forces to that of the layman, or even of the deviant himself, as to the causes of deviant behaviour. In reaction to this particular (criminological) version of positivism, the deviancy theorist came increasingly to stress (and to examine) the exercise of 'free-will' by deviants, and, in particular, to take seriously the 'vocabularies of motive' used by the deviant as an expression of belief that might be related, in a meaningful fashion, to his involvement in deviance (cf. L. Taylor and Walton, 1971; L. Taylor, 1972).

Finally, deviancy theorists rejected, and attempted to bridge, the gap between the narrow (and often simplistically individualist) emphases of orthodox criminology, offering in their place a more extensively sociological explanation of crime-creation, and, in particular, a transactional approach to the social phenomenon of crime. Orthodox criminology, underpinned as it was by a consensual conception of the social order and the unproblematic nature of social reaction, attempted to explain the fact of deviance without significant reference to the society within which it occurs. Deviancy theory, on the other hand, came increasingly to be taken up with the ways in which the power to impose social order was socially differentiated, with the importance of social 'labelling' – and, to some (very halting and undeveloped) extent, with the importance of social power. Centrally, of course, the emphasis in this translation on the work of the neo-Chicagoan school of Howard Becker and others was on the *transactions* between actor and re-actor as important and consequential *social processes*.

These formal agreements amongst deviancy theorists were based more upon antipathies to orthodox criminological formulations than they were upon any clear alternative formulations, and this ambiguity was in large part responsible for the identification by British sociologists of deviance with American labelling theory, and its variants. In retrospect, the alternative positions taken appear to be little more than inversions on orthodox (structural-functional, psychologistic and other) perspectives, and cannot be seen to have transcended the fundamental features of orthodox criminology.[1]

If we were merely to recite the formal features of what Stan Cohen (1971) then dubbed the 'sceptical approach', there would be a danger of underplaying the substantive (that is, the ideological) background to the reaction against orthodox criminology. We would, indeed, be guilty of discussing theories in the abstract without situating them in terms of historical time and social constituency.

Both orthodox criminology, as it manifested itself in the post-war period, and its sceptical adversary relate to interpretations and critiques of the utilitarianism widespread ideologically in the advanced capitalist nations. Criminology on the one hand embraced utilitarianism and on the other inverted it – one theoretical tradition pursued an *objective* analysis which denied any meaning to deviance in that it lacked a utility for the assumed consensual interest of all; the other spurned the analysis of the total society and focused on the *subjective* meanings of deviant action in ever-increasing, microscopic detail. Thus, positivism denied the deviant any consciousness, interpreting his actions from the perspective and ideology of the dominant class, whilst the idealist inversions on positivism granted him a welter of subjectivity, yet imparted to this consciousness no social or ideological significance, in that this consciousness was seen to exist unrelated to the total society, and independently of any historical setting. Both criminology and sceptical deviancy theory tended, therefore, to produce abstractions 'bracketed off' from any historical situation, or the structurally-specific consciousness of the deviant himself.

The alternatives of pure objectivity or pure subjectivity are alternative paradigms of bourgeois thought itself; and, as we shall attempt to show later, the goal of a thoroughly critical criminology must be to transcend the abstract structural or idealist theories which compose the universe of discourse of deviancy theory at the present time. We intend, therefore, to present a brief but *substantive* account of orthodox criminology and deviancy theory, situating both tendencies in their context of the post-war period, with the aim of establishing the social-philosophical fulcrum of both as utilitarianism.

2 Fabian criminology

In a pointed description of the components of Britain's national culture, Perry Anderson (1968, p. 4) has argued that:

> Britain, the most conservative major society in Europe, has a culture in its own image: mediocre and inert. . . . It is a culture of which the Left has been a passive spectator, and at times a deluded accomplice. Twentieth century culture was by and large made against it. Yet the Left has never questioned this 'national' inheritance which is one of the most enduring bonds of its own subordination.

The social-democratic tradition in Britain was a direct production of such an empiricist culture. In the same way as the British bourgeoisie never accomplished a total transformation of an artistocratic society and never recast that society in its own image, so working-class politics in Britain has been endowed with a myopia which could rarely conceive of the total reformation of a class society. Working-class politics has consistently taken the form, from the Chartists to the modern-day Labour Party, of a piecemeal though highly detailed reformism.

The apotheosis of this reformism ideologically was Fabianism, a Fabianism that has been characterized by Nairn (1964, p. 45) as

> a derived Utilitarianism, the timid and dreary species of bourgeois rationalism embraced by the British middle-class during the Industrial Revolution. In it, bourgeois rationalism became socialist rationalism chiefly through the substitution of the State for the magic forces of the *laissez-faire* capitalist market: the former was seen as bringing about 'the greatest happiness of the greatest number' almost as automatically as the latter had been.

The irony of the social-democratic 'opposition' to the laissez-faire philosophy of English utilitarianism was that, instead of attempting to deny the status of utility as the arbiter of social merit, it merely set about the task of rationalizing it. The central contradiction of utilitarianism stems from its emphasis on the importance of reward through merit and effort, and its status as a social philosophy erected in defence of property alongside the continuing inheritance of the means to achieve success in a propertied society. Gouldner (1970, p. 324) puts this well:

> Men who attempt to live by the [meritocratic] value system are demoralized not simply by their *own* lack of means and their own *failures*, but also by witnessing that others may *succeed* even though they lacked the valued qualities.

Fabianism attempts the impossible: it tries to create a truly meritocratic society without transforming the property relationships which work continuously to obstruct such a competitive egalitarianism. So, the British Labour Party's commitments have very largely been to a 'bread-and-butter' politics, spread over with a welfare reformism; and its aspirations have extended little further than the limitation of material poverty, help for the sick, ill and infirm, and, ultimately, the establishment of a healthy meritocracy. This political package is the direct legacy of the Labour Party's origins in Fabianism, buttressed by its religious affiliation to Methodism.

Fabian 'utilitarianism' differed from its bourgeois variant in pointing to the absence of equal opportunity in the wider society. The Fabian project can indeed be seen as the creation of such equal opportunity, via the gradual erosion of the most severe examples of material inequality, in order that a genuinely utilitarian society, based on a universally-appropriate social contract, could be created. The thrust of Labour Party policies in government, and its various manifestoes, is concerned not with a critique of capitalism as a mode of social and industrial organization, but with the inequality of access to participate in such a society (or, alternatively, with the way in which improper control of such a society could enable some to 'get-rich-quick' and others not).

Nowhere is the utilitarian edge to Labour Party thinking so apparent as in its commitment to welfare, *and* in the limits to that commitment. In the period after the Second World War, the Labour government, engaged on behalf of 'the nation as a whole' in what it termed the task of 'social reconstruction', gathered into itself an army of specialist and expert middle-class constituencies – most notably, architects and town planners, academics and teachers, and, most significantly for criminal and civil legislation, the bulk of the British social-worker population. The concern was to win sections of the middle class to the struggle against those personal, social, environmental, educational and even spatial deprivations which helped to disqualify vast sections of the (working-class) population from meaningful participation in the newly-reconstructing society, a society in which the opportunities (to be unequal) would be more equally distributed. If ever the Labour Party had been a defender of class interests as such, this particular role was translated into one of *social* defence, whereby class interests were now seen to involve its incorporation and the imposition on the class of 'universal' (i.e. system) values. The institutional changes to be encouraged were those that would attack deprivation (better industrial relations as a way to fairer distribution of wealth) and those that would encourage the creation of balance and equilibrium in the conduct of social life (mixing of the social classes in newly-planned housing estates). The end-result would be a society based not upon the inequalities of inherited (or other unearnt) wealth, but on merit – success and social mobility would become a matter of personal effort and initiative in a society of equals.

At the back of such policies lie ideological assumptions that can be traced not only to the Fabian translation of utilitarianism, but also to the legacy of Methodism in the early history of the Labour movement. For Methodism (unlike Anglicanism, with its tolerance of inequality and power, a religion that was later to be pilloried by Aneurin Bevan as 'the Conservative Party at prayer') is nothing if not a theology of conformity and unity. Hence, Methodism has often been used as an ideology to castigate and segregate off members of local communities who persist in deviant or militant activities when others have desisted. The role of Methodism during the 1926 General Strike illustrates the ways in which theology can be used to encourage a community to struggle, but also the ways in which it can unite the 'conformists' against, for example, those 'deviant' miners' lodges that refused to surrender so easily. It is the double-edged nature of Methodism as the working-man's Protestant Ethic that helps us to understand the apparently contradictory thrust in the Labour Party's welfare programmes – the commitment to welfare, in the shape, ultimately, of the Welfare State itself; and the commitment to punitiveness towards those 'deviants' identified or construed as unwilling to recognize, or unwilling to participate in, a utilitarian and reconstructing society.

The contradictions are worth emphasis, for it is against such an ideological mix that any serious critique, founded upon a socialist defence of diversity, would have to proceed.

It is possible to argue, contrary to popular impression, that the Labour Party has had more impact on the systems of social control (the prison system, the probation service, the courts, etc.) and on the systems of social welfare than the Conservative Party (for all that the Conservative Party contains so many senior judges and members of the legal profession and for all that that Party is renowned for its perennial debates on the 'crime-wave'). Certainly, it was a Labour government that introduced the militaristic detention centres into Britain in 1948, with the object of administering a 'short, sharp shock' to recalcitrant youth. It was a Labour government in 1966 which appointed and approved the Mountbatten Enquiry into Security in Prisons, an enquiry whose report set back liberal hopes on 'individualization of treatment', in prisons, on parole, and on liberalization of imprisonment generally for years. And, finally, it was a Labour government which, in 1969, five years after the publication of the Party's study group document *Crime – A Challenge to Us All*, legislated, in the Children and Young Persons Act, for a vast increase in the power of social workers to control the disposition of 'troublesome youth' and for the establishment of the benevolent but paternal community homes as substitute family settings for children from 'poor' or 'undesirable' homes.[2]

The influence of the Labour Party in social control is perfectly explicable in terms of its ideological grounding in Fabian and Methodist doctrine. The *primary* concern of Labourism was, and is, to attack deprivation: and it is significant to note the ways in which this insistence has paved the way for alliances to be struck not only with 'sociological' criminologists (in the 1950s, with criminologists like Howard Jones and John Barron Mays, whose works were concerned with the role of 'social' and 'environmental' factors in the creation of criminality, i.e. material inequality), but also with the psychological and social-work professions. The centrality of the family as an agency of socialization (preparing the child for meritorious labour) in large part explains the openness of Labour Party thinkers and policy-makers, on the one hand, to psychiatrists like John Bowlby, who would reduce criminality specifically to a personality disturbance produced by 'maternal deprivation', and, on the other, to more explicitly Freudian and psychoanalytically-oriented casework theorists who would concentrate on the variety of psychic repressions that disable the 'problem' client from 'normal' social participation. The contrast between social-democratic criminology as such and criminology as a whole is best seen in terms of the types of theory *which are omitted*. The aim of Fabianism was to create a meritocratic society and to help (through social-work agencies) those whose home life disabled them from participating in the meritocratic struggle. Thus, social democrats can embrace both opportunity theory on the one hand, and psychoanalytical theory on the other. But, inevitably, as the Labour Party was unsuccessful in ushering in a full-blown meritocratic social structure, the emphasis in the (expanded) social-work profession came increasingly to fall on personality theories. Indeed, given the failure of the Fabian project, theories stressing maladjustment were vitally necessary. But it is important to observe that the initial Fabian emphasis on the environmental causes of crime would lead them to eschew psychological theories stressing the genetic basis of crime, or the conservative theories (of classicism) based on the notion of a widespread *wickedness* (Man's fall from Grace). If environment was the prime factor, and Fabian attempts to change this environment unsuccessful in practice, then the environmental factors of broken home, maternal deprivation or 'bad' area had to assume a primacy in social-democratic criminology.[3]

The numerical ascendancy of the social-work profession during the 1960s (paralleled in Scandinavia with its similar heritage in social democracy, (cf. Stang Dahl, 1971) is explicable in terms of the need to control (and individualize) the emerging social problems of unemployment, racial tension, industrial and social discontent[4] (as well as to contain those members of society designated off in institutions as 'useless'), but its real social *influence* is to be explained in terms of the appropriateness of social-work 'wisdoms' as statements about the disabling deprivations standing in the way of a fair, contractually-based, society.

Labourism, however, cannot conceive of the possibility of meaningful dissent or refusal. The only 'alternative reality allowed is that of power and privilege, and it is from that reality that all Conservative or other opposition must flow. Deviants of any other kind are necessarily either undersocialized (socially, psychiatrically or otherwise) or corrupted (by lack of religion, or by ideologies alien and inappropriate to an equalizing and improving society). Hence, punishment for repentance is *the* social democratic second-line of social defence: it is the proclamation of the general interest against sectarian or individual recalcitrance. Thieves and hooligans harm not only the conduct of a conforming social life, but threaten also the meaningfulness – and hence the existence – of welfare programmes. The collapse of the welfare programmes would, of course, entail the collapse of the Labour Party's social and political ideology as such – it would signal a collapse of the Fabian vision of a society of equals before the Conservative vision of a society dominated by those born to rule, necessarily holding the rest of an unworthy population in check via its system of schooling, individual punishment, social segregation and institutionalization.

Sceptical deviancy theory can be understood, against this background, as a *cri de coeur* on behalf of the victims not only of an inert and conservative judicial system, but also the victims of social-welfare control. Indeed, as both Gouldner (1968) and Young (1970) from slightly different viewpoints have shown, the critical edge of sceptical deviancy theory in the USA (and also in Britain) was very largely directed at the 'mopping-up' agencies – identifying the ways in which social-work treatment, however much it might be described as being in the client's own interest, could often result in spirals of spurious labelling, further deviant commitment and, finally, the irreversible channelling of individuals into careers in prison, in mental hospitals or on skid-row.

Placing the activities of social-welfare agencies in political and ideological context, however, it is easy to see that the everyday decisions of workers in those agencies flow not from an ill-formed understanding of 'deviant' 'maladjustment' but from a clearly formulated, Fabian-conformist, and essentially *liberal* ideology. The key words of social-work training reflect that overarching ideology without ambiguity – the encouragement 'to adjust', 'to encourage good citizenship', 'to mature' – and, indeed, to accept the good offices of the 'helping agencies' themselves.

The logic of the political ideologies surrounding the discussion of crime is now rendered more clear. Orthodox criminology can be seen as an attempt to correct and control the worst excesses of a punitive and repressive Conservative judicial system, via an appeal to the amelioration of the environment or the building of a social-work and helping profession. Sceptical deviancy theory, in its turn, can be viewed as an attempt to highlight some of the excesses of a social-control system that substitutes 'care' for 'punishment' – and tends, in the process, to withdraw those rights (for example, of due process) that Conservatives in the judiciary had paternalistically protected. But sceptical deviancy theory, unlike social democratic criminology before it, has no coherent alternatives (other than those of an abstracted and individualistic idealism) and no organized constituency (like social work or the Labour Party itself). It is exhausted except as a form of moral gesture.

The rise of Fabian criminology is to be related to the post-war development of the Welfare State and the rapid expansion of a non-commercial, middle-class constituency of social workers, teachers, and experts: 'The Welfare State becomes the agency through which the "useless" are made useful or, at least, kept out of the way' (Gouldner, 1970, p. 82). The rewards of the Welfare State for its practising professional persons are apparent, both in Britain and in the USA. Thus (Gouldner, 1970, p. 81):[5]

> The type and level of activity of the Welfare State, and of investment in it often bears little demonstrable connection with the effectiveness of its programs. What frequently determines the adoption of a specific welfare program is not merely the visibility of a critical problem, not only a humane concern for suffering, not only a prudent political preparation for the next election. What is also of particular importance is that the adopted solution entails a public expenditure that will be disbursed, through the purchase of goods or the payment of salaries, among those who are *not* on welfare. It is this that enables the Welfare State to attract and retain a constituency among middle class and professional groups.

3 Anti-utilitarian criminology

For upper middle-class youth growing up in the post-war period of what was (until recently) steady expansion and spiralling affluence, the problem experienced was not so much access to material rewards (which their social and educational background guaranteed), but the meaningfulness of such rewards and standards of utility. The neo-Keynesian vista of a world of material security and unquestionable security became increasingly suspect. Ironically, the doubts and contradictions were most acutely experienced by the children of the non-commercial middle class involved in the creation of the Welfare State apparatus. A new constituency grew out of a rejection of this utilitarianism, a constituency rooted in the non-commercial middle class (Gouldner, 1970, pp. 79–80):

> Since the end of World War II we have seen the beginnings of a new international resistance against a society organised around utilitarian values, a resistance, in short, against industrial, not merely capitalist, values. This is essentially a new wave of an old resistance to utilitarian culture, one that had begun almost at once with its emergence in the eighteenth century and that had crystallised in the Romantic movement of the nineteenth century.
>
> The emergence of new, 'deviant' social types today – the cool cats, the beats, the swingers, the hippies, the acid heads, the drop-outs, and the 'New Left' itself – is one symptom of a renewed resistance to utilitarian values. The emergence of 'Psychedelic culture', if I may summarize various forms with a single term, differs profoundly from the protest movements and 'causes' of the 1930's, however politically radical, for Psychedelic culture rejects the central values to which *all* variants of industrial society are committed. Not only does it reject the commercial form of industrialization, holding money or money-making and status striving in disdain, but, much more fundamentally, it also resists achievement-seeking, routine economic roles whether high or low, inhibition of expression, repression of impulse, and all the other personal and social requisites of a society organized around the optimization of utility. Psychedelic culture rejects the value of a conforming usefulness, counterposing to it, as a standard, that each must 'do his own thing'.
>
> In short, many, particularly amongst the young, are now orienting themselves to expressive rather than utilitarian standards, to expressive rather than instrumental politics, to gratification achieved with the aid of drugs, sex, or new communitarian social forms rather than through work or achievement-striving via individual competition. . . . The continuing development of Psychedelic Culture with its changing forms of deviance suggests that the Welfare State had not developed strategies to control the middle classes and the

relatively well educated. For Psychedelic Culture recruits its members, to a considerable degree, from persons of middle-class origin. The Welfare State, however, still basically conceives its charter as requiring it to cope with the poor, the lower, the working classes.

The work of Richard Flacks in the USA (1967, 1970), Jurgen Habermas in West Germany (1971), and Frank Parkin (1968) and Jock Young in Britain (1973b) have each examined the fundamental ambivalence within the non-commercial middle class towards the values of the dominant culture. The humanistic ideals of this highly educated group involve a deep suspicion of the philistinism demanded in instrumental orientations towards work, and the materialistic criteria used in such a culture to evaluate individual worth. The choice facing the non-commercial middle class, therefore, is between co-optation into the Welfare State and rejection of the prevailing ethos. The alternative – entry into the world of production, of *direct* class relationships – is non-existent, being external to the social limbo to which they have been acclimatized by socialization and preference. The non-commercial middle-class member has either to take up staff (rather than line) management positions (and to accept the values, goals and 'objectivity' that accompany such involvements) or reject 'management' in an absolute sense. In other words, by virtue of his *declassé* position, the non-commercial middle-class youth is tempted to *invert* his values (and is not directly presented with a class option that would involve any attempt to transform his values *via* a transformation of the total society). The scenario for 'a politics of subjectivity' is set; its parameters determined by the group's isolation from the world of productive work and class conflict. A Romantic stance is erected, which involves several distinctive understandings, each of them traceable (in much the same way that the understandings or orthodox criminology are traceable to the ideologies of Fabian managers) in this case to the anti-utilitarian revolt.

Most notably, there is a focus in anti-utilitarian 'criminology' on expressive rather than instrumental forms of deviance. A criminology arises which is rarely interested in crime – in the sense of violation of property relationships (burglary, petty theft, etc.) – but which is more interested (in particular) in 'crimes without victims' of an expressive nature – illicit drug use, bohemian crime in general and 'sexual deviance'.

Secondly, the methodology of anti-utilitarian criminology moves away from a scientific and empirical approach to knowledge towards an intuitive approach to 'meaning' (drawing, variously, on the sociologies or phenomenologies of Husserl, George Mead or Weber). As we shall see later (in our discussion of liberal social science) participant observation and qualitative research gain favour as alternative research techniques.

The primary focus of examination is retrained on the micro-sociology of interaction and away from the wider processes of the social system. Thus, radical 'anti-psychiatry' is concerned with the ways in which double-bind repressions arise in a family context and lead the repressed individual into schizophrenia. The world of work, the world in which the majority of men spend much of the waking hours, is neglected – the deviant is seen as existing in some limbo of leisure, repressed only by the tyranny of family interactions. Exploitation is seen in increasingly personal terms: that of man over woman, 'straights' over 'gays', 'conventionals' over 'hippies'.

The deviant himself is seen to embody expressively an authenticity which allows him to cut through the taken-for-granted world of conventional culture. The long tradition of Romanticism (where those at the edge of society (the lumpenbourgeoisie and the lumpen-proletariat) are seen as existentially superior – the paragons of a more pure and genuine humanity and feeling) is reasserted.

The State itself, so far as it is mentioned, is seen as mismanaging the deviant, intruding into his 'natural' state, and exacerbating and amplifying his deviant characteristics. The message of the anti-utilitarian criminologists to the State is the converse of the Fabian's interventionism – and the message is 'radical non-intervention' (cf. Schur, 1973).

Human action in general is seen as potentially freely-willed. A change in consciousness enables the achievement of individual resolutions that are more substantial than those social revolutions advocated by social critics of the past. The deviant must create an arena of freedom for himself which ignores or avoids the interventions of the wider society (cf. Young, 1973c).

It is our contention in this chapter that a large part of the 'sceptical' deviancy theory of the late 1960s involved, both in its procedures and the appeal it made to its constituency, such an idealistic position. Its potential contribution to a radical critique of society lay in its ambiguous commitment to cultural diversity', but that potential was marred by a failure to evolve a theory of the State and the total society.

Initially, and significantly for our argument, the only innovative theoretical statement that *clearly* distinguished the early work of the National Deviancy Conference from American deviancy theory was the stress on rule-breaking activity as an attempt to assert some form of *control*. This rapidly proved to be a crude, and indeed a false, formulation. It was never clear what was meant precisely by the control concept, and although authenticity might have been thereby restored to the deviant, he was accorded an unreal ability to transcend the exigencies of everyday life. Again, in retrospect, one can see that the control perspective was a crude attempt to utilize Marx's notion of alienation with a view to seeing in deviant behaviour the activity of men struggling against situations of constraint and what later we were to term 'normalized repression'. The research concern was to demonstrate in detail, and for a wide range of deviant 'types', the diverse ways in which men might try to assert their own selves, for example, in defining their cultures of work (Taylor and Walton, 1971) or leisure (Taylor, 1971; Young, 1971a). The control perspective was still only used as a commentary on the powerless, and, used in this way, the ethnographies tended to become a theoretical stop, preventing or obstructing the examination of situations and institutions (like the State itself) which constrained or distorted the exercise of individual or collective control. The use of ethnographic research procedures and the reliance on a single 'control' concept were to prove inadequate for the task of constructing a fully social theory of deviance, and, specifically, of control.

Probably, the development of sceptical deviancy theory, in what was a tenative and uncertain period politically, was informed by a sense of powerlessness we felt ourselves. We were propelled by a dissatisfaction not only with the parochialism, the puritanism and the correctionalism of criminology, but also by a powerlessness as to the possibility of affecting the national culture, the politics of social democracy or, indeed, the politics of the orthodox Left itself. Against this background sceptical deviancy theory can be seen as an attempt to look for alternative, less constrained agencies for change, and as an identification by powerless intellectuals with deviants who appeared more successful in controlling events. In this last respect, sceptical deviancy theory could appropriately be seen as a form of 'moral voyeurism', a *celebration* rather than an analysis of the deviant form with which the deviancy theorist could vicariously identify.

The shift in deviancy theory towards a more radical or critical position was occasioned by a change in the political orientation of both middle-class practitioners and deviants themselves.[6] Thus, in Britain, *Case-Con* organized revolutionary social workers, *Red Rat* psychologists, *The Ass* lawyers, and the National Deviancy Conference sociologists and criminologists. Radical action involved the organization or the defence of groups largely ignored by the orthodox Left – *People Not Psychiatry* with the anxious, the frightened or the 'mentally ill', the *Claimants Union* with the unemployed, *Radical Alternatives to Prison* with prisoners (in association with the prisoners' union *Preservation of the Rights of Prisoners*), and *Up Against the Law* with defendants. The radicalization of the non-commercial middle class in this period also contributed to the transformation of the Women's Liberation Movement and the coming out of the Gay Liberation

Movement; and was paralleled by the politicization of blacks (in the various Black Power movements), prisoners and mental patients.

Now whilst these groups never cohered into a tight intellectual or political formation or into a movement in themselves, they had in common a distrust of rigid ideological conformity (whether to a political, psychoanalytic or legal statement of 'truth'). The emergence of radical deviancy theory can be understood, therefore, as an assertion of the tradition of *radical diversity*. Radical deviancy theory may still tend to reflect on its own procedures in terms of reformulating orthodox criminological models and academic procedures, but it is also consistently underpinned by the same kind of concern for diversity as informed the movements developed by radicalized professionals and clients in the social-welfare and social control systems. It was developed, like them, out of a rejection of the ideologies and personnel controlling those institutions (the Whig intelligentsia in the judiciary, the 'medical doctors' in the mental institution, etc.) as much as it was developed out of a refusal to accept the often very narrow reading of Marxism demanded by movements that were otherwise opposed to these systems of repression. Radical deviancy theory can, then, be understood as part of the attempt to take the tradition of radical diversity into the various academic disciplines, and, also, via its alliances with these other groups, into the oppositional movements created throughout the institutions of social control in the country as a whole. What began, initially, as a Romantic reaction against utilitarian conceptions of the world, was transformed. Realizing the impotence of Romanticism, radical deviancy theorists came increasingly to be involved in organizations committed politically to a struggle against both Conservative and Fabian conceptions of order, in particular with a view to pressing on these organizations the troublesome problems of human diversity. And, at a theoretical level, they returned to the problem of doing theoretical work on the total society (not with a view to understanding the sinews of equilibrium, but with a view to identifying the institutions relevant to radical change).

Radical deviancy theory can now be seen, therefore, as the beginnings of a politics that might link the concerns (with diversity) of sceptical deviancy theorists and the other politicized middle-class constituencies with movements that are capable of realizing such a diversity. And it is apparent that that movement cannot be based on the Labour Party–social-work axis of liberalism, or on 'a politics of subjectivity' (a politics that is raised in a social vacuum). We are faced, theoretically, empirically and practically, with three very distinct approaches to the question of crime – approaches which are also consistent with more general approaches to the problem of social order – and these are the approaches of conservativism, liberalism and radicalism.

4 Radicalism as an emergent paradigm in criminology

In *The New Criminology*, we attempted to elaborate the elements of what we called an 'immanent critique' of existing theories of crime, deviance and social control. In part, this critique was organized around a formal model, which was intended to draw attention to the various analytical stages required in the explanation of rule-creation and/or rule-breaking. It is now our position not only that these processes are *fully social* in nature, but also that they are paramountly conditioned by the facts of *material reality*. Breaking with individual (that is, with genetic, psychological and similar) explanations into social explanations has thrust upon us the political economy as the primary determinant of the social framework. We shall argue later that the processes involved in crime-creation are bound up in the final analysis with the *material* basis of contemporary capitalism and its structures of law.

It is clear that our 'normative theory' was not simply 'useful' in enabling the immanent critique, but also that it formed the elements of a radical politics of crime. Albeit by implication, the insistence in *The New Criminology* was that, insofar as the crime-producing features of contemporary capitalism are bound up with the inequities and divisions in material production and ownership, then it must be possible via social transformations to create social and productive arrangements that would abolish crime. Critically, we would assert that it *is* possible to envisage societies free of any material necessity to criminalize deviance. Other controls on 'anti-social' behaviour (and other definitions of what that might constitute) can be imagined, and, from the point of view of a socialist diversity, would be essential (cf. Young, chapter 2, in this volume). Additionally, there are forms of human diversity which, under capitalism, are labelled and processed as criminal but which should not be subject to control in societies that proclaimed themselves to be socialist. In other words, we were asserting that the 'withering away of the State' – identified in orthodox Left discussions as a feature of thoroughgoing socialist societies – has to feature in the discussion of a socialist criminology.

In this respect, *The New Criminology* was (implicitly) an exercise in radical critique in a way that crucially distinguishes it from conservative and liberal texts in the same area of discussion. It may indeed be helpful to schematize the elements of conservative, liberal and socialist theory paradigmatically here, in order to guide *our* argument, but also to sustain the position advanced by David Harvey (1973) and others: that all contemporary social theoretical debate can be seen to fall into one of such three camps.[7] The emergence of radical and socialist theory in the human sciences has not only served to provide an alternative to conservative and liberal formulations, but has also enabled the identification of existing alternatives as politically conservative or liberal in their initial assumptions, methodological procedures and, most importantly, in the wider ideological and social functions.

Conservative theory

Conservative work in the human sciences is often not so much theory as it is largely a *descriptive* endeavour. That is, conservative social scientists are engaged, by and large, in the further and more detailed characterization of existing social arrangements. The findings of such descriptive work (which, in power-divided societies, is almost by definition description of the activities, behaviour and situation of the powerless) are passed on to powerful agencies and political men – for use as data or arguments in the organization of social control. Underpinning such an unproblematic conception of what social science is about, and such an easy coexistence of researcher and practical man, is a fundamentally conservative – that is, pessimistic and/or paternal – conception of man himself – that he is 'in need of care, protection, or control' by virtue of being a man; by virtue, that is, of the 'obvious' features of 'human nature' as revealed in the conservative's own descriptions of existing social arrangements.

This is not to suggest that conservative theoretical work does not exist in the human sciences. Indeed, much of the best social science is riddled with conservative consensual assumptions. Parsons's monumental theoretical synthesis of diverse thinkers in *The Structure of Social Action* is a classic example of conservative theory; and within that framework deviants and criminals are quite clearly seen as under- or mis-socialized byproducts of an otherwise tightly defined and healthy organic social system.

Common to all conservative work – whether theoretical or descriptive – is the fundamental belief in hierarchy and dominance as the basis of law and order. Indeed, as against liberal conceptions of the wider society (that it is based, in some sense, on a fully equitable, and understood, state of justice), conservative theory makes considerable sense of the ways in which the social order is 'morally bound together'. Conservatives, however, will treat the belief in hierarchy and dominance as a consensus, where radicals will identify in that moral bind the false consciousness which is necessary to legitimate what is in reality an inequitable set of social arrangements.

The development of conservative theory, then, whether in academic circles or beyond, serves an important ideological function of legitimation, where conservative descriptive work is intent on detailing the areas in which such legitimacy might be endangered or in question. Much of the 'police-college' criminology on systems of policing in the USA, for example, adjudicating on the merits of beat *versus* car police in various types of neighbourhood in encouraging a favourable community response to the police, is conservative work of the kind we have in mind. Similar examples can be found in the voluminous literature on techniques of control and behaviour modification in prisons (literature which has recently been expanding further in the aftermath of the prison demonstrations and disturbances in America and in Europe).

Liberal theory

Liberal social science, in contrast, engages much more in *prescription:* that is, it engages in research or reportage on existing social arrangements with a view to making suggestions for institutional reform (e.g. opening up opportunity, as in anomie theory) or cultural change (e.g. in work on 'unrealistic aspirations' among young children or minority ethnic groups). Since this work is engaged in either at the behest of the powerful, or alternatively is intended for their consumption after production, it is work which also serves either purposively or latently to legitimize existing social arrangements (whilst urging reform on their margins). Liberal work, that is, takes for granted in its everyday practice the continued coexistence of social scientists (who are political only in their role as citizens) and political men (who are totally political – and allegedly receiving and sifting the information they do 'in the interest of all'). Liberal social scientific practice takes as given a gap between those who can legitimately act as political men-in-themselves and those who can only advise. Hence, it shores up the conception that those in power under existing social arrangements are in reality engaged in balancing the interests of all, where other groups (including the researchers themselves) are pressing only sectarian claims. Tied into this practical separation of politics from 'science' is the ambiguous set of assumptions about man at the base of liberal work in the human sciences in general.

Man, in the liberal human sciences, emerges as an elusive and contradictory figure. He appears, on the one hand, as the entirely malleable creature of social arrangements (biological givens, psychological traumas or whatever) – and the liberal proceeds to explain man's defaults in terms of these external constraints. On the other hand, the liberal will often criticize the social arrangements themselves, or psychological and social-welfare practice, for their obstructive or distorting effect, implying that man could behave other than he does if circumstances were propitious, if the social arrangements were to allow and encourage him to do so. Some weight is given, that is, to the untapped features of man's potentials, as well as to the observed features of his defaults. Whilst the liberal would rarely argue that such a man could be fully a master of his own fate (or create a society in his own image), he would certainly argue that existing social arrangements do not allow of man's best expression.

Liberal social theory is highly various in form and in content, but very rarely does it aspire to a coherent or systematic account of the workings of the total society. Some liberal theory will leave such macro-sociological questions aside – treating them as unresolved metaphysics (as in some forms of phenomenology which would 'bracket off' society from social theory) or as scientifically unanswerable (as in most forms of social psychology which would separate off individual strain and anxiety from their wider structural context).[8] The bulk of applied criminological research is, of course, of a liberal rather than conservative nature – whether it be concerned with devising prediction equations on the reconviction chances of borstal boys or developing new typologies of institutional régime – since the primary concern of such research is with the improvement of the *existing* social control system in terms of effectiveness and in terms of a welfare commitment. Serving to legitimize existing systems in this way, it tends to avoid confronting the contradictions in such systems (for example, in the concentration of such systems on the lower-status and relatively powerless); but it avoids falling into a simply conservative posture in defence of control and containment.[9]

Radical theory

In just about all respects – in terms of its assumptions about man, in terms of its practical procedures, its conception of the utility of knowledge and in terms of its relationship with other social groups – radical theory is distinct from conservative and liberal theory and practice. A socialist conception of man would insist on the unlimited nature of human potential in a *human* society, and specifically in a society in which man was freed from having to engage only in the essentially animalistic pursuit of material production in order to feed, consume and exist.[10] It is not that man behaves as an animal because of his 'nature' (under capitalism): it is that he is not fundamentally allowed by virtue of the social arrangements of production to do otherwise.

Such a fundamentally different conception of the man under study in the human sciences leads inevitably to a distinctive view of the nature (that is, the purposes, procedures and utilities) of a human science. Most obviously of all, the science (the research work, the theorization and the distribution of the knowledge so gained) is directed at different constituencies to those who receive the data from conservative and liberal social scientists. It is knowledge which is most appropriately directed at those agencies involved in struggles for change and not at those agencies concerned with the conservation or the minor alleviation of existing social arrangements of power. But it also follows from this that the procedures of radical social science must differ very markedly from the procedures specified in the other paradigms. Most importantly, radical social science must neither simply describe nor prescribe (in the passive, liberal sense); it must engage in theory and research as *praxis*. Overused though such a term may be in radical polemic, it retains a core meaning which marks radical theory off not only from the mundane conservative and liberal social theories of the past but also from the essentially descriptive and positivistic phenomenologies currently being offered out as 'critical theory'.[11] The point about theoretical praxis, for us, is that it is concerned to encourge the changes specified by the precepts of its own radical theory, and to develop research procedures relevant to that project. Radical theory cannot rest content with the *description* of existing social arrangements, directed at the establishment of a new intellectual consensus within a radical intelligentsia. It has to develop methodologies for the realization of the societies its own critique would necessitate, for, as David Harvey puts it, 'a revolutionary theory . . . will gain acceptance only if the nature of the social relationships embodied in the theory are actualized in the real world' (Harvey, 1973, p. 125).[12]

Radical theory and practice can become a full-blown form of political practice (where currently it appears largely as a political assertion) if it can find ways of changing the social world whilst investigating it. It is a commonplace, for example, in descriptions of ghettoes, delinquent neighbourhoods and transitional zones that, though general cultures of poverty may exist, and other general problems underlie them (landlordism, rent, local authority indifference, etc.), the resolutions that are posed are largely individual or partial in nature. The ghetto problem is usually seen as a problem of individual mobility or collective rehousing, rather than as a problem of the 'free' (uncontrolled) capitalist market in land and rent. But a research project which played back onto a neighbourhood results which authentically displayed the general problems of that area, revealing to that population the general rather than the private nature of their discontents, could be a unifying political practice, as well as being an authentic form of research.

A comment is in order here about liberal and radical ethics of research. There is an immense literature in liberal social science (social science, that is, that is concerned with the description of existing social relationships) concerning the importance of minimizing what variously is called the 'Hawthorne effect', 'response bias' or 'the imposition of meanings' in fieldwork situations. The danger is that the researcher changes the researched situation in some fundamental (and unknowable) fashion; and, it is argued, so far as is possible, that this is to be avoided, or, that where this is impossible, the researcher should attempt to specify the ways in which he may have altered the situation. Now it is clearly the case that minimizing bias is to be recommended if one is operating in a 'naturalistic mode' – that is, if one's purposes are simply and only to remain faithful in one's description to the phenomenon in question irrespective of the purposes to which such faithfully-developed knowledge may be put by others (e.g. by agents of social control). And it is also a perfectly proper methodological procedure and faith, if it were not for the fact that no social situation ever remains static (the researcher is not only the only social disruptor imaginable), and if it were not for the fact that social research cannot catch a changing situation in a *moment* (in the way, for example, that the cameraman may be able to catch the flux of physical behaviour).

The important point about the liberal intention to avoid disruption of the research situation is that the researcher denies himself the right to change a situation which other social forces in the community (or the group) under study would never deny themselves. Even if he does not intend his work to move beyond description for description's sake, it will certainly be used by others prescriptively (i.e. politically); and where he does intend to use his work prescriptively, he will allow that others may then proceed to act politically on his conclusions (in ways that he himself cannot control) (cf. I. Taylor and Walton, 1970). Prison research is a good example of this. For years, liberal researchers have attempted faithfully to depict the deleterious effect of lumping together in penal establishments, men who may have come from different backgrounds, different 'criminal subcultures' or different age groups. The argument has been that such concentrations unfavourably affect the rehabilitation chances of men with good 'prognoses'. In orthodox interventionist penology, these descriptive researches (cf. Gibbons, 1965; Irwin and Cressey, 1962; Bottoms, 1973) result in the attempt to construct typologies of inmate and typologies of régime, with a view to the prescriptive call for 'individualization of treatment'. The prescriptive work is then carried out in pressure-group commissions and committees with Departments of Corrections or (in Britain) the Home Office. Once there is a crisis in prisons, however, the real force of such prescriptive work is revealed (to be weak indeed). In Britain, the small spate of escapes from British prisons in the early part of 1966 (and the inclusion amongst them of George Blake, the Russian spy) resulted in a report (taking very few weeks to prepare) which regrouped the British prison population not into rehabilitative typologies at all, but into grades defined in terms of 'escape risk' and 'danger to the public'. On the basis of his grade, each British prisoner's chances of parole, his place of 'residence' and his other financial and social privileges are computed. Very few British criminologists, however, have even commented on the distortions introduced into prisons as a result of this report (the Mountbatten inquiry), or drawn lessons from the way in which the typologies constructed descriptively for liberal rehabilitative purposes were so easily translated (by political men) into a grading system primarily operated in the interests of containment, order and social control. Indeed, it is a comment on the resilience of the liberal's faith in the separation of description (research science) from politics that so few criminologists were to side with (or even remark upon) the prison revolts some six years later, revolts that stemmed in no small way from the inflexibility of what came to be called, after the chairman of the inquiry, the 'Mountbatten categories'. Examples of similar splits of 'science' from 'politics' from other areas of criminological concern (sentencing, juvenile institutions, the nature of delinquent areas, etc.) could be multiplied, but the point in each case is that the criminologist's descriptive research findings are very rarely translated prescriptively into political action, and that the influences which make for real political power over criminal and penal politics (the propertied occupational groups and their political parties, the judiciary, prison governments, the police and the media) are underplayed, ignored or taken for granted. To accord these influences any real recognition, of course, would force upon the criminologist the fact of social conflict – such that eventually the criminologist might have to come out from behind his 'scientific' objectivity, declare his position and take sides for or against the facts of a propertied society, and for or against the correction of those labelled (and imprisoned) as criminals in a propertied but inequitable society.

For radical researchers, the point about attempting to remain faithful to the researched population is that he has already taken sides; in the sense that he is concerned to feed back his results, not to the powerful, but to those most immediately and directly affected by the inequalities he is researching. The problem of the 'Hawthorne effect' is really diversionary here, for the radical should recognize that all social situations change markedly and continuously. The point is not that one wants the world to hold still whilst one researches it; it is that one's purposes are to reveal the ways in which the constant flux of social conflict and the taken-for-granted repression of ordinary men in such conflicts can be transcended not in terms of the further accumulation of descriptions of repression, but only in terms of an adequate radical politics. In large part, therefore, the success of the research is to be judged not in terms of static description but in terms of the ability of the researcher to feed back the research work into a form of practice with the population with whom he is working. The difficulties are immense; amongst other things, because the institutional nature of knowledge is such that personnel with professional (research) skills are (by definition) employed in professional practice – socially separated from the 'needs' of the rest of society. One consequence of this is that the timing of professionals may only accidentally coincide with the needs of the group with which they are concerned. This, of course, is obviously true of social work, of teaching, of trades-union organizing, and a host of other 'professionals'. But one important example is that of the media professionals, wielding as they do a massive amount of influence over the 'definition of the situation' in the population at large. Early in 1974, a group of radical film-makers at the National Film School in London who were enraged by the attempt of the Conservative government to blame the 'three-day week' on the miners, chose to film a discussion between a local Conservative MP and representatives of steelworkers in his constituency. Throughout the discussions, the MP asked the steelworkers' representatives to persuade the miners, as fellow trades-unionists, to lift their ban on overtime. The steelworkers resisted this line of argument, and retorted that overtime should not be necessary for men to earn a living wage. The film was shown later to a miners' lodge, the members of which showed surprise at the intensity of support from other groups of workers, expressing regret that the film had not been shown to them when they were involved in discussion in the lodge about the courses of action open to them in pressing their claims.

Another example of the role of the media in supporting a struggle reveals the occasionally accidental nature of such support. For reasons known only to the professional media men themselves, members of the press and the television news-teams in Britain were reluctant to accept the official (Home Office) version of the extent of support for the national one-day strike in prisons on 4 August 1972 (coordinated by PROP, the prisoners' union). Statements issued by Viscount Colville, spokesman for the Home Office at the time, to the effect that few prisoners were engaged in actions and very few prisons were affected, were revealed to be absurd (both to the outside world and the prisoners themselves) when photographs were taken from highly improbable positions (from helicopters, cathedral towers and elsewhere) of mass sit-downs in at least a dozen separate prisons (cf. Fitzgerald and Pooley, 1975).

The problem with this kind of feedback is its very arbitrariness – and the technical problem of rapid media reaction to transitory, or dispersed, events. Filmed material (or indeed written documentary material) is difficult to produce at the point in time when it is needed.

Problems of this kind do not face the conservative or liberal researcher, confronted as he is with a relatively permanent society whose features he either wants merely to describe or tangentially to improve.

But radical theory has to be concerned with praxis, and that specifies that the radical theorist must address his work at appropriate moments to a distinctive set of constituencies. The *choice* of constituencies is, however, not clearly given in the way that it is in conservative and liberal formulations (where it is given, by and large, by considerations of power and vested interest). The choice of constituencies (from a wide range of social groups existing in situations of 'normalized repression') is a matter for the radical theorist's own *purposes*. Orthodox Marxist writing on praxis has insisted on the centrality of the organized working class as the only viable agency of social revolution, and therefore as the only meaningful object of radical or revolutionary engagement and alliance. But, as we argued earlier, this particular insistence, whilst probably correct as a strategic statement (i.e. as a statement about the possible *agencies* for change) says little substantively about the content (for example, the tolerance for diversity) of the alternative socialist formation. Criminal questions are an obvious – but not the only – example of the kinds of questions unaddressed or postponed in orthodox Marxist writing on the 'post-capitalist' society. Problems relating in general to the disposal of those designated as psychiatrically, economically or socially 'useless' (the 'mentally ill', the unemployable, or the 'anti-social' 'elements') are not satisfactorily resolved simply by reference to the necessity for proletarian dictatorship any more than they are happily resolved by a bourgeoisie which also claims to be acting in the interests of all.

It is the task of radical theorists who are concerned about the content (the radical diversity) of alternative forms of society to raise within the movements committed to such alternative forms the troublesome questions of a socialist criminology and penology, as well as questions relating to the administration of an alternative psychiatry and a social welfare that is firmly rooted in its commitment to socialist diversity. And it is their task also to devise and to carry out research identifying the 'diverse' situations in which men are imprisoned, and the 'diverse' ways in which they resist – but, finally, research which aids such resistance to move *from* resistance to liberation.

5 Radical criminology and the necessity for materialism

In the immediate future, empirical radical research is likely to be minimal. The debate amongst radical criminologists is about the appropriate and correct departure points for research (away from liberalism and into praxis), and the chapters in this book are testimony to the lack of consensus amongst radical criminologists at this time. In this section, we shall be dealing with three areas of theoretical work currently commanding some attention amongst radical criminologists. Final statements are not possible in each of these areas – for example, we would not want to have laid down in any conclusive way the elements of a materialist theory of law or of crime. We do want to suggest, however, that there are severe limitations in the two other approaches – the tendency to what we have called 'exposé criminology' and to radical empirical work on the propertied nature of crime in propertied societies. Our argument will be that neither of these two latter approaches is sufficient for a *fully* materialist analysis of crime, an analysis that is adequate to the understanding of the past contours of crime and law, as well as to the present situation and future possibilities.

a The appeal and limitations of exposé criminology

There is a growing temptation in Britain, and in some European countries, to conceive of radical deviancy theory (as against earlier sceptical deviancy theory) fundamentally as an inversion on traditional criminology. The indignation of the radical deviancy theorist is focused on the activities of the powerful, most of which are either not defined as illegal or else are not apprehended in practice. The argument usually is that those rule-breakings which do surface periodically are only a small indication of the full scope of the defaults of the powerful. In Britain recently (1974), this exposé criminology could obviously have been brought to bear on the activities of the North of England architect John Poulson and those of his associates who have been convicted of corruption (mainly involving contracts on local-authority building programmes). For reasons which require examination, there is a spate of cases in Britain involving financial swindles, high-class prostitution, upper-class fraud, bribery and corruption. Against this background, there is the tendency to make these powerful defaults the baseline for a new criminology. This tendency is compounded internationally by the revelations of business malpractices, government burglaries, and civil-rights violations emerging during the course of the Watergate hearings in the USA, and the succession of financial and moral scandals reverberating along the corridors of power in Washington, Bonn, London and Paris.

The problem with this exposé criminology – however useful it may be in demasking the crime-free façade of the ruling class, and in pointing to inequalities in apprehension, definition, and punishment

– is that, ultimately it is based on a mindless, and atheoretical, moral indignation. The guiding theme appears to be one of feigned or real amazement at the double-standards of the ruling groups.

Underlying such work is an essentially moral appeal. The accepted moral values of existing society are shown to have been broken – but on this occasion by members of those groups who proclaim themselves to be society's guardians. At the very moment that governing administrations in Europe and the USA take a political stance on the grounds of 'law and order', they are shown to contain considerable numbers of lawless and disorderly executives within their own ranks. Underlying the pursuit of further examples of ruling-class default, there appears to be the view that a sufficiently detailed exposé will act evangelically as a catalyst for the creation of a genuinely moral society. However, whilst such exposés may puncture the legitimacy of the powerful in the eyes of those other social groups who may previously have accepted such legitimacy, the approach hinges very problematically on the view that the legitimacy of the powerful over the powerless has been and is maintained on the basis of an exclusively moral appeal. The picture of power implied in this form of radical criminology, therefore, is a mix of unstated Durkheimian and Weberian views of authority – that is, that the powerful rule by virtue of moral right, rather than by the realities of ownership and distribution in a society of inequality.

It is obviously true that the ruling group does not establish its rule solely on the basis of a coercive use of material sanctions. Any complex society requires considerably diverse sets of legitimation if it is to be efficient: it has, in short, to convert 'power' into 'authority'. Radical deviancy theory would not deny the importance of indicating that the rule-makers are consistently the major group of rule-breakers in such a society; since it is in this fashion that law can be shown merely to be an ideological façade of 'universal justice' set up to protect the powerful's pursuits of their own particular interests. But, in contrast to exposé criminology, radical deviancy theory has the task of demonstrating analytically that such rule-breaking is institutionalized, regular and widespread amongst the powerful, that it is a given result of the structural position occupied by powerful men – whether they be Cabinet ministers, judges, captains of industry or policemen. The concern is not to suggest that certain powerful individuals are engaged in deviance, or that corruption is on the increase at a particular point in time. Were this the problem, the political answer would be, in the first instance, that the 'bad apples' should be rooted out and subject to the force of law, and, that, secondly, a change of government or government policy should occur with a view to eradicating corruption and re-establishing justice. The focus of radical exposé should not be on the exceptional transgression but the regularized infractions which can only be removed by more fundamental, and radical, change.]

Moral revelations may come as a surprise to some members of the middle classes in advanced industrial societies (and hence, perhaps, the significance of the exposé journalism of the *New York Times* and the *Washington Post*), but elsewhere in such societies (in the ruling groups and amongst the powerless) the realities of inequalities and of double-standard moralities are already clearly experienced. Indeed, a reading of the powerful's own newspapers reveals the regularity with which such double-standards are practised. In a recent court case in Britain, a solicitor aged fifty was ordered to pay debts of over £1 million at a bankruptcy hearing. He was given 4,704 years to get out of debt at the rate of a repayment of £5 a week. Being a middle-class gentleman, 'he promised to increase his rate of repayment when his circumstances changed' (*Guardian*, 18 October 1973). A case of this kind has to be read and understood against the background of a society which will constantly imprison working-class defaulters for debt for amounts of £50 or less.

On occasion, the operation of the double-standard immunizes the powerful rule-breaker from prosecution itself. Recently, for example, a former Recorder of Bristol in England, who had underpaid on income tax by several thousands of pounds, was not indicted, on the grounds that a criminal prosecution might undermine the confidence of the public in the judiciary.

One of the most institutionalized forms of theft in society as a whole, however, is in the area of illegal corporate profit. Frank Pearce has calculated that the value of unreported (and illegal) excess profits made by corporations in the USA during 1957 was in the region of 9 billion dollars (as against the 284 million dollars cost of burglary in the same period); and certainly a close examination of the famous price-fixing conspiracy of 1959 (involving identical bids to the Tennesee Valley Authority from General Electric, Westinghouse and other large American electrical corporations) suggests that *illegal* organization of profit is a regularized and institutionalized, rather than periodic and pathological, form of corporation 'deviance' (cf. Pearce, 1973). British evidence is more elusive, but a reading of official reports by a journalist[13] revealed that, during 1972–3, there were 250 cases in Britain where profits were admitted to be under-declared by £10,000 or more – a theft from the community, that is, of at least £1 million. In the same year there were only 17 prosecutions for false income-tax returns (as against some 80,000 cases settled without prosecution). But there were 12,000 prosecutions over that period by the Department of Health and Social Security for fraudulent claims by its (largely working-class) clients. The amount recovered in these 12,000 cases amounted to less than 15 per cent of the amount recovered by the Inland Revenue in its seventeen income-tax prosecutions. The respective rates of prosecution were 1·3 per cent in the case of the Inland Revenue, and 22·5 per cent in the case of the Department of Health and Social Security.[14] A clearer indication of the systematic nature of double-standard justice in a class society would be difficult to find. But even evidence of this kind is insufficient as exposé, for it is evidence only of the illegal activities of the powerful and their differential treatment at law. A materialist critique of the distribution of wealth in society would also be concerned, of course, with the perfectly legal taking of wealth in a society predicated on capital–labour relationships.

The temptations to exposé criminology are considerable. For just as the liberal sociologist of crime (and the sceptical deviancy theorist) could justify the continuation of further ethnographic work as illustration of the diverse ways in which an anomic society could mould deviant adaptations, so a radical criminology could justify the endless extension of exposé work – without ever having the question of why it might be that a morally bankrupt society can continue.

The omission of any consistent analysis of the structural and cultural basis for law, legitimacy and morality has further serious consequences. The danger is that, faced with those ruling-class infractions which *are* revealed, the radical criminologist will see these infractions merely as 'accidental leakage' or, possibly, as the result of praiseworthy entrepreneurial activity by members of the mass media. A patterned or structural view of ruling-class deviancy is the necessary corrective to this, providing the radical criminologist with a sense of this deviancy as a resolution to material predicaments of ruling-class groups.

The fact that the 1970s have seen an unprecedented number of such cases, and revelations, must be seen as significant in itself. It should lead us away from a monolithic view of authoritative dominance of the ruling group, and towards a position in which we seek to explain the prevalence of divisions within contemporary European and American ruling groups.

The significance of the moral crisis in the powerful groups is well illustrated by historical reference. The practice of double-standard morality has not always created the kind of dissension and disarray that we now witness in the moral authority of society. In 1963, Ferranti Industries, a big British electronics contractor, overcharged the then Conservative government, on a fixed-price contract for the production of Blue-Streak missiles, to such an extent that when, after a certain amount of adverse publicity, it returned the sum of £4½ million to the government, it was still left with an excess profit of 21 per cent on the original agreement. Yet in the same year, when a small group of organized working-class criminals robbed a mail train of over £2½ million, the entire British police force (and Interpol) was alerted; and ultimately sentences of up to 30 years were handed down to the central figures in what became known as 'The Great Train Robbery'. And though this example of 'double standards' was a matter of some public debate, it is significant that it was just one *incident*, and that very largely it was treated as such. In the early 1970s, examples of the double-standard multiply with increasing regularity – and something more than the activities, for example, of a 'biased' judiciary are seen to be responsible. The ruling groups have revealed that they are unable to abide in any regular fashion by their own laws.

At a time when radical economists, politicians and other commentators on the social fabric are forecasting a collapse, or an extremely significant transformation in the economic and institutional structure, it is clear that radical criminology has to place ruling-class crime in the context of that transformation, and it is precisely for this reason that exposé criminology is less than adequate for radical purposes: it is caught within a moral rather than an analytical dimension.

b Crime in propertied societies

Another emergent perspective in radical criminology explicitly or implicitly involves a return to the empirical examination of official statistics and other recorded material, with the aim in view of unpacking the inequitable and class-based nature of crime, imposition of law and police activity (cf. Gordon, 1973; Liazos, 1972; Thio, 1973; Wolfe, 1973; Wright, 1973). Here, the concentration is on the ways in which the legal and penal systems disproportionately (and, by implication, immorally) single out the deprived, the poor, the minority-group member and, in general, the lower class for punishment and control. This form of radical criminology, then, is about what the 'criminal justice system' actually does do, rather than about what (in its own terms) it ought to do (that is, to control and correct the deviant, irrespective of his position of power in the wider society).

Radical deviancy theorists in the past (possibly in over-reaction to positivism) have tended to shy away from the official statistics on crime and its control, and, indeed, have tended to dismiss them as unscientific or simply as measures of highly diverse and complex social interactions.[14] The paradox is that an examination of those statistics reveals the highly patterned, and indeed the class nature, of society and its law *enforcement* (and something of the patterned nature of the crimes committed). In 1971 for example, some 1½ million indictable crimes were reported to the police in Britain (a country of around 54 million inhabitants). This represents an increase of some 1,400 per cent on the number reported in 1901, with an increase in population over the same period of just under 50 per cent. Approximately 96 per cent of these offences were offences against property (the headline crimes of violence against the person and sexual offences being in a very small minority as a proportion of total crime).[15] And in the USA Ramsay Clark has indicated that some seven-eighths of the reported FBI Index Crimes are crimes against property (Clark, 1970, p. 38). Whilst there are significant differences in the rates of increase for different kinds of officially-defined offence (malicious damage being one of the markedly increasing offences in Britain, for example, over the last decade), the important feature of the official statistics is that they demonstrate what should be obvious: namely, in an inequitable society, crime is about property (and that even the various 'offences against the person' are often committed in the pursuit of property). Property crime is better understood as a *normal* and conscious attempt to amass property than it is understood, for example, as the product of *faulty* socialization or inaccurate, and spurious, labelling. Both working-class and upper-class crime (whether reported, apprehended and prosecuted or not) are *real* features of a society involved in a struggle for property, wealth and economic self-aggrandisement. Simply put, a society which is predicated on the unequal right to the accumulation of property *gives rise to* the legal and illegal desire to accumulate property as rapidly as possible.

It is, of course, a fact that only certain kinds of property accumulation are singled out for prosecution and punishment – and that a constant feature of this differential apprehension is that working-class people at large (in all Western societies) have consistently been over-represented in the official statistics. So, for example, in a large national sample of British children born in 1946, 15–20 per cent of the boys from manual (skilled and unskilled) working-class homes had been convicted of at least one offence by the age of 17 (i.e. by 1963), 10 per cent of the boys from 'white-collar' families, and only 5 per cent of those from 'professional and salaried' families (J. W. B. Douglas *et al.*, 1966). Little social-class data is available for America, but it has been shown, for example, that in a society where the class formation has a built-in 'white-skin privilege', there is a vastly disproportionate number of black and third-world persons in the prisons. Nationally in America, whilst third-world persons constitute only 20 per cent of the total population, they make up some 50 per cent of the national prison population. In California, for example, one out of every seven third-world persons is either in prison, or on parole or probation at any one time. In America as a whole, there are more blacks in prison than there are in college.[16]

Research carried out for the President's Commission on Law

Enforcement and the Administration of Justice in 1967 indicated something of the class nature of apprehension and punishment retrospectively, when it discovered that whereas in 1960 men designated occupationally as craftsmen, operatives, service workers or labourers made up some 59 per cent of the general labour force in America, they constituted 87·4 per cent of the prison population.[17]

It is clear, in fact, that the vast bulk of offences for which working-class people are imprisoned or punished in Western societies have to do with the fact that, by virtue of being working class or black, *they are without property*. At the same time, however, as Ramsay Clark, ex-Attorney General of the USA has observed (1970, p. 54):

> Illicit gains from white-collar crime far exceed those from other crimes combined. . . . One corporate price-fixing conspiracy criminally converted more money each year it continued than all the hundreds of burglaries, larcenies, or thefts in the entire nation during those same years. Reported bank embezzlements cost ten times more than bank robberies each year.

And, further, as David Gordon (1973, p. 166) has calculated:

> The economic loss attributable to Index Crimes against property – robbery, burglary, and so on – are one fifth the losses attributable to embezzlement, fraud, and unreported commercial theft.

Liberals critical of 'differential apprehension' have tended to see in these figures evidence for the need for police or legal reform, or (for 'scientific purposes') the extended use of self-report and victim studies in order that a 'true' picture of the crime rate can be developed. The point about the evidence on differential apprehension, however, is that it can also be read as *evidence of differential commitment* at different levels in the social structure to the existing moral order. In so far as crime is significant as a product of economic deprivation, or of a weak position in the power structure, crime is an index of the intensity with which people are committed to the existing social and economic arrangements.

Moreover the statistics, for all the criticisms that have been levelled at them (for example, as evidence of the social organization or phenomenological sensitivity of the middle-level managers of the economic and social-control agencies), can fruitfully be used as evidence of the underlying trends occurring in the wider social structure. For example, criminal statistics over the years can be read, and used, as evidence of the enthusiasm with which the British ruling class is prosecuting individuals and groups under different sets of laws and for different sets of social behaviours. The statistics need currently, and in the future, to be read as evidence of the seriousness with which the British ruling class is prosecuting individuals and groups of workers on strike (the Industrial Relations Act, 1971, the Home Office regulations and House of Lords decisions of 1973 and 1974 on the organization of picketing), politically deviant activity (the reactivated Conspiracy Laws) and even recalcitrant or problematic youth in general (the Children and Young Persons Act, 1969). The Prison Department statistics are important in demonstrating the extent to which prison governors, the Home Office and the Prison Officers' Association are engaged in the repression of an increasingly self-conscious population, there being, for example, a total number of 30,000 offences recorded against inmates in British prisons during the year of demonstrations in 1972, a year in which the average daily population of those prisons was 26,000 men. Statistical material from the Department of Trade and Industry can be used, in the future, as evidence of the determination of managerial sections of the ruling class to regulate a variety of forms of speculation by bankers, brokers and others in the City.

The tendency amongst traditional criminologies has been to use statistics as indicators of the extent of the 'crime problem' (with some residual concern to identify the areas in which social reform should be concentrated), but more recently a more sophisticated approach to statistics has developed. Fundamentally, the concern is to move beyond official statistics on crime to general attitudes towards crime, with a view to identifying the contours of moral attitudes at different levels in the social structure and in different cultures. The ideological thrust underlying these studies – the *Knowledge and Opinion about Law* (or KOL) studies – is one of social defence: the containment of increasingly complex social conflicts via a law constructed and operated in tune with the predominant social attitudes in a population (cf. Kutchinsky, 1972, 1975).[18] The fundamentally liberal conceptions underlying research of this kind are underlined by the fact that the KOL researchers only question their respondents on the 'seriousness' with which they view offences as defined by *existing* law, where clearly there are wide varieties of 'social injuries' – currently outside the scope of existing law – to which members of a class-divided population are submitted in a thoroughly 'criminal' (but legal) fashion (cf. Schwendinger and Schwendinger, in this volume).[19] The point about the expansion of KOL studies – both in Western and Eastern European societies – is that, for all that they are couched in terms of social-psychological exploration – they can only be used (in societies where the law is the law of the propertied) as resolutions to the problems facing the ruling-groups in the regulation of the highly fragile social systems they control.

Returning to the statistics as a resource, the radical criminologist must be sure of his purpose. It is clear that a proper examination of the statistics is helpful in revealing the class-organized practice of criminal and legal systems – in pointing to the disjunction between the imaginary (ideological) social order and the real social order – in the same way that exposé criminology usefully demasks the moral front of the powerful controllers of such an order. But if the radical is to move from revelation to resolution of the social issues, he must be able to put the statistics to analytical and political uses. Again, as in the other areas of dispute with which we have been concerned, there are three distinct approaches to the statistics, each one underpinned by assumptions about man and assumptions about society. A consideration of the traditional criminological assumptions demonstrates how these apparently technical questions of an 'applied social science' are intimately tied into theoretical approaches towards, and ideological perspectives on, the wider society.

Conservative approaches to the criminal statistics derive from the philosophies of classicism.[20] The assumption is that the statistics measure offences against some real social contract, which has otherwise been entered into rationally by free men in a free society. Such a position has few criminological representatives today, though Jack Douglas, particularly in *Crime and Justice in American Society*, comes close to the position of a latter-day Beccaria. But the classicist position commands considerable respect amongst conservative politicians, and particularly amongst the high-ranking members of the judicial system (as well as amongst conservative members of the population at large). The implications of this position are therefore of considerable political importance.

Fundamentally, the classicist model of man would have it that crime is a freely-willed activity occurring when man's passions overreach his reason – that is, when he foregoes his rational awareness that to violate the property of persons of others, is to violate the rights of social contract and to create a situation of war of all against all, a situation in which his own person and property are at risk. In this perspective, crime would be seen as relatively arbitrarily spread through the social structure; and hence the findings of self-report studies and investigations into 'white-collar' crime would come as no surprise to the classicist. The problem for the classicist is the overrepresentation of the working-class in the statistics. An immediate answer given in the nineteenth-century debate over social-contract theory would be that those without property who are at the bottom of the social structure do not have a sufficient stake in society to justify a rational embrace of the social contract. But, in pure classicism, this answer could be satisfactory only for the small lumpenproletariat (divorced very markedly from a propertied society) – and would only partially explain the preponderance of the working class in the criminal statistics. A neo-classicist could take up the problem more effectively, drawing on work of labelling theorists and interactionists, and arguing that the statistics represent the end-result of interactional procedures and communications of policemen, social workers and magistrates, all of whom have false conceptions, 'wrong ideas', about the real or essential nature of deviance. These misconceptions, he could argue, cause them to select out more working-class offenders than, scientifically speaking, they should; and (concomitantly) fewer middle-class offenders than they should.

Hence, to present the conservative with evidence of the kind we presented above (on the class distribution of offences, apprehension and imprisonment) would cause him little concern; he could simply respond with pleas for 'education' and greater 'communication' amongst agencies responsible for the apprehension and social control of those who have broken the social contract, or alternatively with plans and programmes for the extension of the morality of the social contract into the areas (and social classes) indicated by the statistics to be in need of a greater understanding (fewer 'wrong ideas' about) of the social contract and its essentially benevolent functions.

Several problems would, of course, remain unanswered. Notably, the conservative would not be able to explain the origin or the content of the 'false' ideas. He would simply have to assert that they *were* 'false'. We would be left (and asked to be content with) a picture of social control (and the resulting criminal statistics) as the end-result of free-floating ideas, unlodged in any particular (or specifiable) social structure or history. And should we want to know, for example, how to change these ideas we would hardly know where to start.

A variant of conservative ideology – 'realism' – in the interpretation of the statistics centres around the controversy excited by Edwin Sutherland's work in the area of 'white-collar crime'. Sutherland's concern was, in part, to demonstrate that what might appear from one point of view simply as 'sharp business' (to those so involved, and their significant colleagues) would undeniably be seen as criminal elsewhere in the population, and indeed should be acted upon as such (Sutherland, 1949).

The controversy this reasonably uncontentious proposition subsequently excited is some indication of the depth of conservative 'realist' criminology's assumption that crime is an intrinsically working-class phenomenon. Thus, even George Vold (1958, pp. 253–4) was to write that:

> There is an obvious and basic incongruity involved in the proposition that a community's leaders and more responsible elements are also its criminals. Business leaders and corporation executives by and large play an important role in civic and community affairs. They more often than not constitute an

> important source of imaginative leadership for community enterprises of all kinds.

The branding of such individuals as criminal Vold sees as 'illogical', arising out of the 'semantic device of calling all violations of law or regulations "crime".' The argument he uses is that (1959, p. 254):

> In any law it is the fact of community definition, just as significantly as the fact of specific behaviour, that makes any act a crime. The community definition of an individual as a person of high status is therefore of special significance in connection with the concept of white collar crime.

It is inconceivable, therefore, that the same community which grants high status to business leaders will simultaneously label them as criminal. For this reason Paul Tappan, in a much celebrated attack on Sutherland, suggests that the concept of white-collar crime is non-scientific and subjective. For here (1947, pp. 44–5)

> the rebel may enjoy a veritable orgy of delight in damning as criminal most anyone he pleases; one imagines that some experts would thus consign to the criminal classes any successful capitalistic business man. . . . The result may be fine indoctrination or catharsis achieved through blustering broadsides against the existing system. It is not criminology. It is not social science.

A thoroughgoing 'realist' like Tappan would argue that the criminologist who attempts to define what is socially injurious (and to whom) is merely allowing his idiosyncratic value judgments to intrude into the debate. The notion that 'the crime rate is real' is usually posed in terms of the definitions of the law adhered to, in everyday decision-making and practice, by the courts, a practice necessitated by 'public-demand'. And, hence, Tappan argues (1947, p. 47):

> Adjudicated offenders represent the closest approximation to those who have in fact violated the law, carefully selected by the sieving of the due process of law; no other purpose of social control attempts to ascertain the breach of norms with such rigor and precision.

Criminological 'realists' go further and argue that police work is largely a response to citizen complaint, as opposed to being the result of police initiatives or prejudice. Thus: 'The moral standards of the citizenry have more to do with definition of juvenile deviance than do the standards of policemen on patrol' (Black and Reiss, 1972, p. 123).

From this position, the non-implementation of certain statutes and the under-representation, or non-inclusion, of specific 'crimes' in the statistics is seen as an accurate reflection of the public mood and prevailing public will. Talk of the 'dark figure of crime' ignores the fact that few social agencies or individuals actually desire to apprehend what might be the totality of real crime. From the realist position, what is criminal is that behaviour represented by the criminal statistics, for these are seen as indexing those actions which the 'community' (or at least the powerful groups within the community) have deemed it necessary to prosecute.

Illegality in society, therefore, is equivalent to those behaviours reacted against – and the argument is that it ill-behoves the criminologist to interpret, idiosyncratically, the existing legislation. The realists are, of course, right to suggest that alternative interpretations of the criminal statistics to their own have to be based on a clear set of justifications. And it is our argument that a materialist criminology could potentially provide such answers in attempting to link material realities with criminal outcomes.

By and large, 'liberal' and, in particular Fabian social-democratic, interpretations of the meaning and utility of the criminal statistics, involve positivistic, rather than classical, procedures, and the ideologies and world-views which, we have argued, are inextricably associated with such procedures (cf. Taylor, Walton and Young, 1973, chapters 2 and 3). The KOL studies are one example of such work, concerned as they are to specify the existence of a 'variable' (*norm acceptance*) existing invariantly as a medium between law and morality. The fundamental purpose of such studies is to engineer a balance in these relationships in the interests of the continued legitimation of existing social order. But perhaps the most important arena for liberal-social democratic statistical work has been that of the delinquent area and the delinquent subculture. Indeed, from the early 1920s (and the beginnings of the Chicago School) through to the early 1960s, the discipline of criminology has been almost exclusively equivalent to the study of *delinquency* (and has been ideologically dominated by a concern with the prevention of such delinquency). The concern of much of this work has been to specify, by a variety of positivistic techniques, the various *determinants* of involvement in delinquency with a view to intervention at the point of such determination. In this fashion, the social democratic liberal faith had it, one might proceed to 'save the child' from graduation into careers of adult criminality and/or imprisonment.[21] The selection of factors to be investigated (for their *determining* power) has often appeared to be largely an arbitrary matter, or alternatively the selection has been justified in terms of an (alleged) logical progression of queries arising from previous studies. There must be more than a suspicion, however, that the factors chosen have a great deal to do with the underlying theoretical presuppositions of the positivist researcher – and, that, for example, the positivist who believes in the goals of existing society whilst recognizing the unequal distribution of the means to achieve those goals, will formulate his investigations in terms of hypotheses to do with the blockage of opportunity and the relationship of that blockage to delinquent (or illegitimate) outcome.[22]

Irrespective of this problem, however, delinquency researchers have continued to develop more and more sophisticated techniques for analysing what might be called the determining power of variables or factors hypothesized to be productive of delinquent outcome. Bernard Lander's use of 'multivariate statistical analysis' is widely considered to be a highly technically-sophisticated example of delinquency analysis (Lander, 1954). Lander was concerned to examine the relationship (the correlation) of delinquency rates and seven other properties of the Baltimore census tracts (the percentage of homes owner-occupied, overcrowding, non-white population, substandard housing, median rentals, median school years of education and percentage of foreign born). Moving from correlation coefficients between each of these census tract properties and delinquency to a factor analysis of the relationship between the variables, he argued that some of the factors could be seen as *anomic* on the one hand (percentage of houses owner-occupied – negatively related; percentage non-white and the delinquency rate) and others as *socio-economic* on the other (all the other variables – with the exception of the foreign-born, which he separated off). In this fashion, he was able to conclude that (1954, p. 46):

> The factor analysis indicates that, in Baltimore, areas characterised by instability and *anomie* are frequently the same districts which are also characterised by bad housing, low rentals and over-crowding. But the delinquency is *fundamentally* related only to the *anomie* and not to the poor socio-economic conditions of the tract.

In a highly detailed critique of Lander, and also of other 'analytic methods' in delinquency research, Hirschi and Selvin have demonstrated that this conclusion entirely ignores the problem of *causal order*, the fact that correlational evidence is no evidence at all of causal connections, and that there are good methodological grounds for arguing, from Lander's own data, a totally contradictory case to the one that he advances from the interpretation of his data. There may be empirical methods for investigating further the nature of causal order, according to Hirschi and Selvin, but the primary point is that there can be no final break out of this problem without *theoretical* justification (Hirschi and Selvin, 1967, pp. 152–3):

> Both Marx and Durkheim, amongst others, provide theoretical justification for treating socioeconomic conditions as causally prior to anomie. With this causal ordering, the disappearance of the original relation between socioeconomic conditions and delinquency when anomie is held constant, far from ruling out socioeconomic conditions as a cause of delinquency, actually strengthens its causal importance. . . . Socioeconomic conditions lead to anomie and anomie, in turn, to delinquency.

Much the same kinds of objections apply to the work of contemporary phenomenological work on the significance of statistics. It can never be shown whether the official statistics are the causal product, primarily or partially, of 'intersubjective understandings' amongst policemen (for example) (as against being a reflexion of legal changes or political imperatives at a societal level) unless this interpretation is justified theoretically. The problem with most Fabian criminologies is, therefore, not so much a problem of their statistical method alone, as it is a problem of the underlying theoretical presuppositions which inform their statistical practice.

The statistical work on crime and propertied societies by *radical* criminologists, reviewed earlier, tends to rest content with a fundamentally moral purpose, however. And, indeed, the benefits of further radical, *empirical* work on class inequalities in apprehension, imprisonment and punishment are unclear, except for its evangelical edge – unless it is infused with an analytical purpose.

One possible advantage of the criminal statistics from a radical perspective is that they can be used as examination of the extent of compliance in industrial society (in quite the same way, for example, as it is possible to use statistics on strikes as an index of dissensus in direct class relations at the work-place). In particular, the criminal statistics can be read as a measure of the credibility of a propertied society at particular periods in its development – the extent to which the distribution of property is latently accepted or rejected amongst certain sections of the working population. For, clearly, the ability of State law to exercise social control effectively over an unequal society depends in part on the existence of a consensus over the distribution of propertied rewards. A recent survey report (Moorhouse and Chamberlain, 1973) argues that the literature of the 'new working class' in industrial sociology seriously underestimates the nature and extent of oppositional consciousness in the working class. A random sample of 331 council house tenants were asked whether they 'approve[d] or disapprove[d] of homeless families taking over empty houses'. 73 per cent of all respondents approved completely or with reservation, whilst only 22 per cent completely disapproved. The response to a slightly more contentiously-worded question was more divided, but still significant: 'Some people say sit-ins by factory workers are wrong under any circumstances because the factories do not belong to them. What do you think?' 42 per cent of all respondents agreed, but 41 per cent disagreed. Moorhouse and Chamberlain conclude that 'the lower class in Britain have attitudes to property ownership which are opposed, and in some ways constructively opposed, to those which are dominant in society'. The time is clearly ripe for investigation of the extent of consensus or dissensus over crime (and especially particular types of crime, e.g. industrial pilfering, shoplifting) amongst members of the different social classes – given the background changes (of inflation, shortages, mushrooming inequalities) in the wider society. It would be surprising indeed if the degree of dissensus indicated in the BBC audience research survey (BBC, 1961) had not been accentuated by these changes; and certainly the commissioning by the Home Office of a working party into shoplifting and a research project into 'industrial theft' is indication of some concern (to measure and control these expected developments).

Understanding the extent of consensus about property distribution as indication of the resilience or otherwise of the ideology of possessive individualism, however, would in itself be insufficient for radical purposes – insufficient, that is, in pointing to the problems confronting the powerful in the regulation of inequality. Such understandings would have to be placed in the context of structural changes in the wider society – some of which are susceptible to empirical (and statistical) examination. The increase in unemployment in Britain and other Western societies needs to be examined in terms of its impact on crime rates (and law-creation) as does the recruitment by nearly all Western societies (over the last twenty years) of an 'ethnic underclass' (a cheap reserve army of labour from the third world), the increase in the number of women in the work-place and, possibly most significantly, in terms of understanding the changing material basis of social control and 'social welfare', the development in most Western societies of a 'white-collar working class'. Radical criminology should be able to analyse the welfare and social control institutions in the first place as an increasingly significant labour market (given the rapid expansion of the social work profession since the Second World War), as social control agencies which, irrespective of their particular function or ideology, are ultimately accountable for their actions to the powerful ruling groups rather than to their clients, and, finally, and increasingly, as commercial agencies (rather than as agencies financed entirely out of the public purse).[23]

All this is to argue that radical criminology must move beyond the mere collection of further empirical data to the construction of theories which make sense of the (measurable or not-so-easily measurable) changes in the structure of social control, law and crime.

The task is not simply to catalogue inequalities but to create empirically-grounded analyses which point the way out of inequality into a genuinely just and human society. Such an analysis, we shall now proceed to argue, has to be thoroughly materialist in method (and has to transcend the conservative, liberal and radical-empiricist methodologies of description and prescription).

6 Materialist criminology: methodology, crime and law

A people's statute book is its Bible of Freedom (Karl Marx).[24]

Throughout this chapter, we have argued that criminology and deviancy theory can only advance as radical theory and practice. But we have also suggested that the only radical approach which does not degenerate merely into moralizing is a materialist one. There are, therefore, two questions, which we have let pass until now, but which we shall now address. What is a materialist approach? And in what manner is it radical? The answers to these questions are interconnected, for they both turn upon the *purposes* informing the way in which we examine society. *Our* purposes in examining society are quite explicit: since, both in this essay and in *The New Criminology*, we have argued for a criminology which is normatively committed to the abolition of inequalities in wealth and power. And we have strongly argued also that any theoretical position which is not minimally committed to such a view will fall into correctionalism (i.e. individual rehabilitation or tangential social reform). We hope that we were successful in *The New Criminology* in demonstrating that correctionalism (no matter how liberal its aims or formulations) is irretrievably bound up with the identification of deviance with pathology, or that, where it is not, it collapses (like contemporary phenomenological approaches) into a mindless relativism. The task we have set ourselves, and other criminologists, is the attempt to create the kind of society in which the facts of human diversity are not subject to the power to criminalize.

We erected our position in this way not out of any desire to shock or enrage (though we seemed to have had that effect anyway), but because we believed that these are the central questions facing any criminology which sets out to be anything other than an adjunct of the forces of social control, under existing social arrangements. If criminology is to advance as a science, it must be free to question the causes not only of crime, but also of the norms which, in a primary sense, create crime – that is, legal norms. The unquestioning acceptance of a given legal system and given legal norms has been the general tendency in positivist criminology, and the result has been disastrous for criminology's claim to scientificity (cf. Taylor, Walton and Young, 1973, chapters 2 and 3). Ignoring or displacing the propertied nature of crime, criminologists unwilling or unable to confront the facts of inequality in ownership of property have been driven back to individualistic explanations of the differences between criminals and conformists – a task which has proven (not surprisingly) to be unilluminating and inconclusive. Those criminologists who have begun their analysis with an examination of society itself, however, have been led to a normative position which, even in the case of a conservative thinker like Durkheim, leads logically to the demand for a free division of labour untramelled by inequalities of inherited wealth (cf. Taylor, Walton and Young, chapter 4). The analysis of particular forms of crime, or particular types of criminal, outside of their context in history and society has been shown, in our view, to be a meaningless activity; and the analysis of propertied crime without reference to the demands placed by a propertied society on its members especially diversionary. We have ourselves been forced, logically, to turn for such an analysis (and such a criminology) to Marx.

The superiority of Marx's work lies not in his individual genius but rather in his *method.* In part, this method rests on a refusal to separate out thought from society. Thus, for Marx, theoretical reflection is either obfuscation or an exercise in practical reasoning (a fact that ordinary language philosophers and ethnomethodologists, in our own time, conveniently ignore).[25] Marx insists upon two features of any properly social analysis. Firstly, he says that 'to be radical is grasp things at the root. For man the root is Man himself' (1971b, p. 137). Second, he observes (necessarily, given some alternative views) that man is inseparable from society. It follows (if these premises are accepted) that to analyse crime, for example, requires that we examine man's position in *society*. We would claim that the implications of these methodological imperatives have been poorly grasped even in the best of contemporary radical criminology. This shows up notably in the absence of any historical dimension in contemporary work. We are not dealing with a criminology that could possibly be true for all societies, but with a criminology that is specific to societies in a given historical period, and societies of a particular type. In our period, the contours of the advanced societies are heavily shaped by their relationship to the world market; and any criminology which ignores this historically specific feature of its subject-matter cannot be regarded as fully social. Rather, inasmuch as it ignores the historicity of the 'social', it aspires to an ahistorical criminology which it assumes (or asserts) to be valid eternally.

In suggesting that criminologists have to make judgments about the kind of society in which they live, we are arguing simply that criminologists must understand (and analyse) the social forces which shape their 'science'; and that criminologists who refuse to do this, because of the unpleasant political implications involved, are obstructing the development of criminology. Social problems become individual problems in an ahistorical criminology; and the task of criminology is reduced to the examination of 'the causes of crime' largely in terms of individualistic explanations, with the occasional dash of social factors or determinants. Much of modern criminology continues to operate in ignorance or avoidance of the essence of crime – that, above all else, it is a breaching of a legal norm – and that legal norms, like any other social norm, can be outmoded or obsolete. The reconstruction of criminology requires a re-examination of the ways in which such legal norms are constructed, their function, and the extent to which they are appropriate and relevant 'categorical imperatives' at all levels in the social structure and at all points in culture and time.

It is not only the conservative 'realists' like Tappan who refuse to confront the historical specificity of legal norms, but also those more contemporary conflict theorists like Austin Turk, for whom law is in some way autonomous of its wider social context, and an inappropriate question for historical analysis. In *Criminality and Legal Order*, this modern-day 'realist' would have us believe that (1969, p. 51; our emphasis):

> The legality of norms is defined solely by the words and the behaviour of authorities. *How authorities come to be authorities is irrelevant: it is sufficient that a social structure built out of authority relations exists* which is to say that authority and subject status categories are implicit in actual behaviour patterns, whether or not people more or less accurately perceive and symbolize the patterns.

For us, and for other radical criminologists, the questions of how authorities become authorities, *and* the ways in which they translate legitimacy into legality is central; for, unless these questions are understood, we are certainly left (with Turk) with an inevitabilist view of bourgeois society. The shape and nature of an industrial society, we would argue, is not inevitably and indispensibly bourgeois. A precondition for a radical criminology is the separation of the essential from the inessential, the historically-specific from the historically-inevitable. The importance of these distinctions was first outlined by Marx: and one of the few significant advances since in the study of legal norms has been the work of Karl Renner. Renner ends his major work *The Institutions of Private Law and Their Social Function* with a challenge to academics and the legal profession to take seriously what Kahn-Freund calls the 'science of legislation' – what we today would call a materialist criminology. He asks (1949, p. 299):

> Given that, like all else under the sun, norms have their causes, wherein do they lie? Given that they enjoy a real existence, what are their characteristics, what is their mode of existence and how do they change? Given that their origin lies in the conditions of life of the human race, that they are nothing more than a means of preserving human society, what part do they actually play in the existence and development of our generation?
>
> These are the open questions of jurisprudence. The time has come to engage in the solution.

Renner's own particular contribution to 'the science of legislation', to which we shall later return, was in the examination of the changing functions of the legal institution of private property. He had realized, like few others, the full implication of the Marxist method – the need to explain the functions fulfilled by legal institutions at particular points in the economic progress of capitalist society. Renner states of Marx (1949, p. 58):

> No other investigator, whether before him or after him, was more aware of their importance for even the most minute detail of this process. We shall see that no other economic theory gives so much insight into connections between law and economics. Marx's predecessors and successors either refused to recognise the problem or could not do it full justice.

Part of our claim, in extending Renner, is that the nature and content of crime and law *cannot* be grasped without a thorough analysis of its evolution historically; and another part of our claim (with Marx but against Weber) is that such an historical analysis reveals the primacy not of legal thought, but of *material conditions*, as the determinants of normative change in general, and criminal and legal norms in particular.

To assert such a position requires comment, for there is a refusal in the scholarly literature to take seriously Marx's claim to have uncovered the determinants of motion in capitalist society. Orthodox criminology, for example, has either reduced Marx to the position of a crude economic determinist or alternatively has conceived of him as a kind of early functionalist (cf. Taylor, Walton and Young, 1973, chapter 8). It is frequently overlooked, however, that Marx spent many years in detailed study of juridical theory; and that the result was (on his own admission) that he was able to dispel doubts about his own method through a 'critical re-examination of Hegel's philosophy of law'. Doubts about the applicability of Marx's method to the study of legal norms (doubts of the kind raised by Hirst, following Althusser, in this volume) might be dispelled if theorists were to conduct an inquiry (rather than follow an assertion) into the method of Marx's approach. Marx himself states (1971a, p. 20):

> My enquiry led met to the conclusion that neither legal relations nor political forms could be comprehended whether by themselves or on the basis of a so-called general development of the human mind, but that on the contrary they originate in the material conditions of life, the totality of which Hegel, following the example of English and French thinkers of the eighteenth century, embraces with the term 'civil society'; that the anatomy of this civil society, however, has to be sought in political economy.

Marx's method, then, is that one should understand legal relations as originating in the material production of society. He insists that the 'anatomy' or nature of 'society' is to be found in political economy. But this is *not* to suggest that legal or criminal relationships therefore have no place in Marx's method, or that Marxism seeks to reduce legal conflicts into economic conflicts. The position being advanced is one in which legal and criminal relationships are related to, and dependent upon, material transformations in society (Marx, 1971a, p. 20):

> The general conclusion at which I arrived and which once reached became the guiding principle of my studies can be summarised as follows. In the social production of their existence, men inevitably enter into definite relations, which are independent of their will, namely relations of production appropriate to a given stage in the development of their material forces of production. The totality of these relations of production constitutes the economic structure of society, the real foundation, on which arises a legal and political superstructure, and to which correspond definite forms of social consciousness.

Indeed, Marx came to believe that, at certain stages in their development, material transformations in society could lead to conflict with the existing relations of production, or, in legal terms, with property relations of a particular kind. Property relations (legal relations) can become fetters on the development of society – and that, at such times, the law will tend to be challenged. Unless legal transformations occur, then social revolution will occur.

Why should material production be regarded as the main determinant in society? What about culture, for example, and what about individual thought? Marx's responses to such queries turn on the question of his ontological position on man.[26] Before we examine Marx's ontological position however, it will be profitable to examine Marx's use of the architectural metaphor of 'substructure' and 'superstructure'. Renner observes that 'it is obvious that [these metaphors] serve only to illustrate the connection, not to define it in legal terms' (1949, p. 55), that he did not mean to imply that legal relations are merely a reflexion of a crude economic interest, or that legal relations can be grasped, in any simple sense, from a given economic state. For Marx's practical reason for distinguishing between 'economics' and 'law' was merely to assert that, whilst the material foundations of society could be 'scientifically' examined, *social* relationships as such hung upon people's consciousness, a consciousness that is not so amenable to objective study. In any case, the conceptual distinction between the 'economic' and the 'social' is erected by Marx solely for the purpose of highlighting the problems involved in analysing the determinants of social change. In the final analysis, as Marx's work thoroughly and *consistently* demonstrates, this problem is resoluble in terms of his theory of being – his ontological position. Marx refused to recognize the 'economic' as anything other than the result of man's social labours. In other words, there are no 'pure' economic, legal or political categories in Marx's work. There is only the *method* of seeing, and analysing, given problems in terms of ongoing social processes in their social totality. Though he often starts with a given phenomenon in his analysis – for example, with 'commodity production' – he consistently demonstrates how such a phenomenon has to be comprehended as part of a system of *social relationships*, relationships, that is, between people. Marx insists, that is, on anthropologizing what had previously appeared as fixed *things* or *categories*. Marx is (in large part) concerned to render each of his own presuppositions fluid and social. This method of proceeding is necessary, for, as Marx states: 'The *fixed* presuppositions themselves become fluid in the further course of development. But only by holding fast at the beginning is their development possible without confounding everthing' (1973, p. 817).

Legal relations, Marx insists, are but one form of social relations; and he also insists that if a society is not to experience conflict and antagonism then there must be a correspondence between its level of material production and its social relationships. Why should material conditions constrain social relations, and hence law, in this way? For the simple reason that human activity – labour-creation – is the beginning-point of any social process. As Marx puts it 'The process always returns to production to begin anew'. All societies must engage in production to create and recreate their conditions of existence.

Marx's real breakthrough, however, was not merely that he was able to point to the ways in which material constraints should put some limits on social development. He was able to point also to a method – of historical materialism – as the only *method* for analysing such relationships. Historical materialism, the method which lies at the core of both the *Grundrisse* and *Capital* insists on the fact that one cannot proceed to analysis on the basis of general categories (such as 'production'), arguing instead that there are only distinct, historically bound, forms of production, specific to given times and given conditions. Historical materialism sets out to reveal the historical determinations which result in specific sets of social formation. It is precisely the issue of method, of course, which informed Marx's break with Hegel's form of dialectical reasoning. Indeed, in a piece entitled 'The Method of Political Economy', he shows how theorization or reasoning itself must be careful to correspond to actual historical formations (1971a, pp. 207–8):

> Hegel, for example, correctly takes ownership, the simplest legal relation of the subject, as the point of departure of the philosophy of law. No ownership exists, however, before the family or the relations of master and subject are evolved, and these are much more concrete relations. It would, on the other hand, be correct to say that families and entire tribes exist which have as yet only *possessions* and no *property*. The simpler category appears thus as a relation of simple family or tribal communities to property. In societies which have reached a higher stage the category appears as a comparatively simple relation existing in a more advanced community. The concrete substratum underlying the relation of ownership is however always presupposed. One can conceive an individual savage who has possessions; possession in this case, however, is not a legal relation. It is incorrect that in the course of historical development possession gave rise to the family. On the contrary, possession always presupposes this 'more concrete legal category'. One may, nevertheless, conclude that the simple categories represent relations or conditions which may reflect the immature concrete situation without as yet positing the more complex relation or condition which is conceptually expressed in the more concrete category; on the other hand, the same category may be retained as a subordinate relation in more developed concrete circumstances. Money may exist and has existed in historical time before capital, banks, wage-labour, etc. came into being. In this respect it can be said, therefore, that the simpler category expresses relations predominating in a more advanced entity; relations which already existed historically before the entity had developed the aspects expressed in a more concrete category. The procedure of abstract reasoning which advances from the simplest to more complex concepts to that extent corresponds to actual historical development.

Marx stresses that what may appear as commonsense points of departure are in themselves points of arrival – that a concept like 'property', for example, is the sum of many, real historical determinations.[27] Given the interdependence of each of the concepts of analysis, however, and the fact that each has its own unrevealed history, the question of when one stops the analysis must inevitably arise. How, then, does Marx avoid an endless slide into the kind of relativism that characterizes, for example, nineteenth- (and twentieth-) century phenomenological work? He breaks the apparently seamless circle of determinations when he asserts that all categories – like all human action – are both determined and determining. All thought (and hence all categories) presuppose 'society' and societies are differentiated in terms of their modes or systems of material production – and hence modes of thought. As Stuart Hall (1973, p. 32) puts it:

> Formally, production specifies the system of similarities and differences and the points of conjuncture between all the other instances of the mode, including which level is, at any moment, 'in dominance'. This is the *modal* determinancy which production exercises in Marx's overall sense.

In short, historical materialism is a method which reveals the social nature of any concept, the historicity of thought, and the differentiation of historical periods in definite modes of production.

What relevance has such a method to the study of legal norms and crime? It specifies that we should study society as a *process*, and that, in doing so, we should realize that certain modes or systems have definite limits to their development. It is a uniquely radical method, in that it constantly raises the questions of what norms are necessary, when, and under what conditions. Moreover, it enables us to study, for example, the nature of the legal system in terms of its role in relation to a particular mode of production – and to investigate, notably, whether the legal system acts as a fetter on mankind's development, or as a boon. Marx specifically criticizes those who see law as playing the same general role in all societies, refusing in so doing to analyse the particular effects of a given mode of production. He argues as follows (1971a, p. 193):

> Each mode of production produces its specific legal relations, political forms, etc. It is a sign of crudity and lack of comprehension that organically coherent factors are brought into haphazard relation with one another; i.e. into a simple reflex connection. The bourgeois economists have merely in view that production proceeds more smoothly with modern police than e.g. under club-law. They forget, however, that club-law

> too, and that the law of the stronger, only in a different form, still survives even in their 'constitutional State'.
>
> While the social conditions appropriate to a particular stage of production are either still in the course of evolution or already in a state of dissolution, disturbances naturally occur in the process of production, although these may be of varying degree and extent.
>
> To recapitulate: there are categories which are common to all stages of production and are established by reasoning as general categories; the so-called *general conditions* of all and any production, however, are nothing but abstract conceptions which do not define any of the actual historical stages of production.

Althusserian and other critiques to the contrary, Marx is here enjoining us to engage in the study of the specificity of legal relations (and hence of crime), the agencies of social control and all the related apparatuses of the State – precisely because it must be the case that the legal system serves in a crucial way to legitimate and to enforce a particular mode of production. Marx sees such work as indispensable in that 'laws may *perpetuate* a particular mode of production' but also, and more importantly, that 'the influence exercised by laws on the preservation of existing conditions of distribution, and the effect they thereby exert on production has to be examined *separately*' (Marx, 1971b, p. 204, our emphasis). For Marx, then, as for us, it would appear that a central objective of a materialist criminology should be to establish the role of law in affecting production, and, via production, the whole life-style and culture of a given society.

Work of this kind has yet to be undertaken in any full sense, and the absence of work of this kind, underlining the interconnectedness of criminal activity and legal norm-creation with the labour process in a particular society, leaves any radical criminology which ignores the material possibilities in such a society without a realizable programme (whether it be on the abolition of prison, the protection of 'authentic' deviance or whatever).

Marx himself contributed some elements to such a materialist examination of law. For example, his notion of alienation retains, almost exactly, its original juridical meaning – namely, that the right to dispose of the products of labour is not held by the producer of that labour (i.e. the worker) but by an alien force (i.e. capital). Alienation for Marx is rooted, therefore, in a particular mode of production, i.e. capitalism. Under capitalism, property and property rights are transformed from the right to dispose of a thing (material objects) or the right to dispose of the products of serfs (the 'right of disposition' under feudalism) into the right to *control* the labour power of others (rather than simply to *dispose* it). Under feudalism, the lords had the right to part of the product of the serfs' output (in itself one kind of alienation). Under capitalism, the capitalist buys not labour, but *labour power*; that is, the capitalist specifies how, what, when and under what conditions the power of labour is to be exercised (this being *another* kind of alienation). At the same time that serfs are transformed into 'free' wage labourers, the capitalist gains the right to regulate and specify the nature of the contract.

Karl Renner's achievement was to undertake to extend and specify the nature of such a transformation. He states of Marx's work (1949, p. 293):

> He has made it clear to us that property in the capitalist epoch fulfils functions quite different from those which it fulfilled in the era of simple property production, and partly opposed to these. He has made it clear that property has become antisocial, intrinsically opposed to the real interest of society.

Taking up the change in the nature of 'property' under capitalism, Renner proceeds to show how the development of private law favoured non-workers over workers (Renner, 1949, pp. 117–18):

> New functions thus accrue to the legal character 'person' who also has the economic character 'proprietor'. Now he regulates labour, ruling and exploiting. Property, from a mere title to dispose of material objects, becomes a title to power, and as it exercises power in the private interest, it becomes a title to domination.
>
> At the same time, the free person, the labourer with no property, becomes a subject *sui generis*, as history does not repeat itself. Among all those who have the power and are destined to be his master, he may choose the master who appeals to him, but as a class the subjects are chained to the class of the masters.
>
> We see that property at this stage of simple commodity production endows the worker with the detention of his means of production, making man the master of matter. How property changes its function without a corresponding change in the law. It gives the legal detention of the means of production to the individuals who do not perform any labour, making them thus the masters of labour. Property automatically takes over the function of regulating power and labour, and it becomes a private title to domination. The law endows this non-worker with the legal detention of the means of production, but in any society only the worker can actually hold them, as he must have them in his hands in order to work with them. Thus the law, by means of a complementary institution, the contract of service, takes actual detention away from the owner. The worker may

> mind the machine, but he must pay the price of submitting himself to exploitation. A permanent state of war between legal and actual detention is thus established.

As both Renner and Kahn-Freund note, 'property' which is not ownership of material or tangible goods comes to play an increasingly important role as capitalism develops. England had a legal system which was more suited to this transformation from feudalism than most. The influence of Romanist law on the Continent meant that it contained, as a matter of principle, the element of eternity, whereas English law was able very readily to introduce a 'time element' into the property concept. On the Continent, an 'estate' which is limited for a fixed period of lease or life of a person is not strictly property. In England, landed property for 'time' has been possible since late feudalism. This does not mean that capitalism and/or law are fundamentally different on the Continent but rather that the greater flexibility of English law in general, and the English property concept in particular, contributed towards a more rapid shift from feudal to capitalist relations; and, as Marx elsewhere reminds us, 'all economics is the economics of time'. The work of Renner in the area of private law, developing out of the concept of alienation, is indication of the direction in which a materially-based examination of law, property relations and crime could profitably and extensively proceed.

A thoroughly materialist criminology would, then, have to encroach upon 'academic' divisions and proceed to build a proper 'sociology' of law and crime alongside a social explanation of their roles in particular societies with particular modes of production. A crucial task would, of course, be to explain the structural and the class differences existing within and between capitalist societies, in contributing further to our understanding of the antagonisms which result, as Marx understood, from the lack of correspondence between the development of material production and the development of social and legal relations. Marx comments on the unequal development of material production and art, for example, in the following manner (1971a, p. 215, our emphases):

> The concept of progress is on the whole not to be understood in the usual abstract form. Modern art, etc. This disproportion is not as important and difficult to grasp as within concrete social relations, e.g. in education. Relations of the United States to Europe. However, the *really difficult point* to be discussed here is how the relations of production as *legal relations* take part in this uneven development. For example the relation of *Roman civil law* (this applies in smaller measure to *criminal* and *constitutional law*) to modern production.

Thus Marx was clear that differences between Romanist law and English law and differences between criminal and constitutional law would have to be examined to account for differences between nations. For him, this was fundamental in explaining 'unequal development,' that is, differences between nations with approximately the same material potential.[28]

It is precisely on the question of 'unequal development' of material production and legal relations that the sociology of law, as presently constituted, has failed to pronounce. This is not surprising, for the nature of crime and law in propertied societies cannot be grasped without a thorough analysis of 'property' as such.[29] The project, then, must be to build a materialist criminology which flows out of a materialist analysis of law in propertied, capitalist societies.

Under late capitalism in contemporary Britain, the increasingly social nature of production (i.e. the interdependence of one sector of the production process on another, and one group of society on another) is increasingly subject to regulation by the legal system (particularly out of a fear of industrial disruption). Smaller numbers of increasingly propertyless workers work with increasingly large amounts of capital equipment. The law insists increasingly upon the 'right' of capital to exercise its discipline over the workforce; and, indeed, one section of the population comes to impose a massively controlling instrument like the Industrial Relations Act upon the working population. In Britain, one central task for a materialist criminology would be to explain the social forces which made for the Industrial Relations Act, how it should be that an act designed to restrict the power of labour to organize became so necessary to one section of the ruling group and how it was also that other sectors of the State were committed to its repeal. Renner himself hints (rather prophetically) at the answer (1949, p. 117):

> If ever labour remembers its personal freedom in fields where it is manifest even to the most stupid brain that work is a function of the social body (e.g. in the railway industry or in the provision trade), if labour makes use of this freedom by strike, then the bourgeoisie makes labour a military institution or replaces free labour by a labour organisation on military lines, achieving a direct socialisation of labour.

Any such act is designed to 'socialize' labour, to get it to 'agree' to continue production. Much contemporary labour legislation is in the process not only of socializing labour, but also in criminalizing those (e.g. pickets) who refuse to be so socialized. The task of a materialist criminology would be to explain the evolution of such acts, such legal norms, in Britain and other late capitalist societies.

All other legislative activity (whether it be in the area of juvenile justice and 'welfare', in the organization of prisons, in the extension of laws over the rights and the behaviours of the homeless, the unemployed, or the 'ill'), is equally amenable to the same kind of materialist questioning. It is precisely these kinds of questions, however, we would argue, that are ignored in existing sociologies of law (resting content as they do with homilies on the relationship of 'consensual' law and social morality, or the relationship of law and organizational and merely bureaucratic interests). And yet the most perplexing question for existing sociologies of law is the question of why legislative change should occur at all (the pressure for change being seen to be explained sufficiently by reference to the (unexplored) existence of a social interest and its needs). No answers are forthcoming in these approaches to the question of why new laws (like those regulating the organization of juvenile justice) should relatively recently be necessary, and what it is about the period in which such laws are created that is conducive initially to their creation.

Materialist criminology must set about the task of seeking to explain the continuance, the innovation or the abolition of legal and social norms in terms of the interests they support, the functions they serve to particular material arrangements or production in propertied societies, realizing that the legal norms in question are inextricably connected with the developing contradictions in such societies. At a time when the law (especially industrial law – but also 'law and order' in general) becomes a subject for constant dissension in major political debate, it is clear that the powerful social forces in our society (ultimately, those of capital and labour) are coming into conflict – and that the *legal* expression of these conflicts has no power in itself. The mystification of social conflict in legal expressions is no new phenomenon, and it was Marx himself defending himself against a charge of conspiracy in the Cologne Trials of 1849, in a speech which won over the jury, who made the case which should win over radicals to the understanding of law, and the creation of a materialist criminology:[30]

> Society is not based on law, that is a legal fiction, rather law must be based on society; it must be the expression of society's common interests and needs, as they arise from the various material methods of production, against the arbitrariness of the single individual. The *Code Napoléon*, which I have in my hand, did not produce modern bourgeois society. Bourgeois society, as it arose in the eighteenth century and developed in the nineteenth, merely finds its legal expression in the Code. As soon as it no longer corresponds to social relationships, it is worth no more than the paper it is written on. You cannot make old laws the foundation of a new social development any more than

these old laws created the old social conditions. . . . Any attempted assertion of these old laws created the old social conditions. . . . Any attempted assertion of the eternal validity of laws clashes with present needs, it prevents commerce and industry, and paves the way for social crises that break out with political revolutions.

Notes

* This chapter is an expanded version of a paper given to the First Conference of the European Group for the Study of Deviance and Social Control at Impruneta, Florence, Italy, in September 1973. The authors would like to thank Bert Moorhouse for permission to quote from his survey report, and also Peter Archard, Sean Damer, Stuart Hall and Frank Pearce for comments which, in one way and another, were helpful in the development of this paper.

1 For further discussion of the limited nature of the alternative models developed by 'sceptical deviancy theory', see chapter 2 below.

2 For examinations of the increasing influence of social-work lobbies on juvenile legislation, see Platt (1969) and Lemert (1970) on the USA, Stang Dahl (1971) on Norway, and Bottoms (1971) on England and Wales.

3 The parallels here between the failure and transformation of Fabianism and the metamorphosis of the Kennedy-Johnson Mobilization for Youth programme in America in the 1960s are not accidental. Mobilization for Youth initially involved a commitment to the social-democratic 'opportunity-structure' theory developed by Richard Cloward and Lloyd Ohlin (1960). Over time, the project came up against a variety of vested interests which resolutely opposed the creation of new opportunities for deprived youth; and the resort of the project leadership, in such circumstances, was to move over to theories of personality maladjustment (which had the important quality of being inoffensive to middle-class conceptions of the causes of delinquency). For an exposition and critique of the Mobilization for Youth project, see Frances Fox Piven's 'Federal Intervention in the Cities: The New Urban Programs as a Political Strategy', in Smigel (1971, pp. 591–608).

4 The individualizing of social problems ('public issues') into private problems in social work was first highlighted by C. Wright Mills (1943), but the analysis is extended by Geoff Pearson in the chapter on 'Misfit Sociology' in this volume.

5 For a trenchant analysis of such a process, see James A. Jones's

'Federal Efforts to Solve Social Problems', in Smigel (1971, pp. 547–90).

6 The politicization of the non-commercial middle class is a subject-matter in itself, and we shall not attempt a full discussion here. Obviously relevant matters, however, include the increasing difficulties faced by the non-commercial middle class in earning a living wage in a period of inflation (a fact reflected in the vast expansion in white-collar trades-union membership); the influence of the anti-utilitarian youth culture in providing, for example, young social workers with ideologies antagonistic to casework and psychoanalysis; the paradoxical situation in which non-commercial middle-class social workers might find other members of their own culture on their caseload (a situation unconducive to deviant labelling), and the general political background (of law and order) in which the emergence of 'social problems' (and the extension of caseloads) was more clearly related to the extension of social control than to the expansion of psychoses.

7 Harvey's conception of the three theoretical paradigms in the human sciences differs a little from that advanced here, identifying the three perspectives as (a) '*status-quo* theory', (b) 'counter-revolutionary theory' and (c) 'revolutionary theory' (Harvey, 1973, pp. 150–1). For him, *status-quo* theory ascribes 'a universal truth status to the propositions it contains (and is) capable of yielding prescriptive policies which can result only in the perpetuation of the *status quo*' (p. 150). It is, therefore, a compilation of what we have called conservative *and* liberal theory (the claim to universality, *and* the concern for prescription). Counter-revolutionary theory, says Harvey, 'obscures, be-clouds and generally obfuscates (either by design or by accident) our ability to comprehend that reality' (p. 150). This would appear to be a statement about the *functions* again, of both conservative and liberal theories in the human sciences, differing from our conception only in tending to assign a conspiratorial status to some theoretical endeavours. Whilst recognizing that some work can be so grounded (e.g. work in counter-insurgency, or indeed some of the work in prison- and police-planning), we would prefer to speak of conservative and liberal work as such, in order to emphasize the latent (unapparent) political content and consequences of much apparently non-political work. In the meantime, we would recognize that there is a considerable overlap between Harvey's conception of 'revolutionary theory' in the human sciences and our own conception of 'radical theory', although, perhaps rather preciously, we would avoid some of the more scientistic concepts in which his revolutionary theory is couched.

8 For a critique of the lack of structure and a sense of society in contemporary social psychology, see Resler and Walton (1974).

9 The essentially liberal nature of orthodox criminology as a whole should not blind us, however, to the growth of very specifically conservative pieces of 'control' research in applied penology – and, in particular, to the development (with official governmental approval) of techniques of behaviour modification (including brain surgery) for use on 'violent prisoners' and sexual deviants in America, Brazil, Britain and Western

Germany. According to Aryeh Neier, Executive Director of the American Civil Liberties Union, the US Bureau of Prisons is currently constructing a $13 million behaviour-modification centre in Butner, North Carolina. Cf. for further details, Neier and Mares (1974). In research of this kind (little of which is openly documented), all vestiges of the liberal vision are, indeed, lobotomized.

10 The ontological position we are adopting here is entirely consistent with our insistence on materialism as method, for it is a part of that position that man's human potential is only realizable under certain material conditions and via certain material arrangements for labour in particular. In this respect, we keep man alive as reality where the new structural Marxists, following Althusser, have already had man dead and buried as metaphysic (cf. Walton and Gamble, 1972, chapter 5). We might add here that this ontological position is also thoroughly historical – that it stands or falls by test of history, and is not undercut simply by the contemporary assertion of other competing ontological positions. For all the current attempts to construct a new philosophy of universal truth, we would argue that no set of knowledge (including that provided by Marxism) can claim to be valid eternally, and that the way in which we arrive at our position, and the way that others arrive at theirs, must be assessed in terms of contemporary and historical possibilities.

11 A good example of the claims of phenomenology to be *critical* (in terms of its being reflexive on its *own* practices, as against those of the wider society) is the review of *The New Criminology* by Michael Phillipson (1973). Incestuous though it may be to use this example, his statement seems to us to catch the obscurantism and idealism of the new phenomenology most succinctly.

12 It is, of course, possible to argue that the task of 'unifying' neighbourhoods (or any other social group or institution) requires no such prior research practice; and that the radical interventionist requires nothing more than a set of plausible stories and/or conjectures about the neighbourhood as his organizing weaponry – or, alternatively, that the generalities of received rhetoric will suffice for the task at hand. Objections of this kind imply that it is possible to know in advance (by commonsense intuition or by a good grasp of correct politics) the *specific* features of neighbourhood problems. Such objections emanate from an inauthentic form of radical politics which refuses to recognize the diversity and complexity of human situations, and which assumes an omniscience about man in all such situations (an omniscience which asserts only that the correct politics are insufficiently disseminated throughout society). But it is also important to remark of this form of radical research practice that it can radicalize the researcher; that it forces the researcher to confront the realities of the situation as he finds it (rather than reading it narrowly in terms of, liberal or conservative, academic wisdoms, or the constraints of academic disciplinary boundaries). Such research can contribute to the abolition of the division of 'intellectual' labour (that is, between intellectuals and others by playing back the results on to the researched population, challenging

the notion that social consciousness is the preserve of the 'literate' population. Again Harvey puts this well: 'A social movement becomes an academic movement and an academic movement becomes a social movement when all elements in the population recognise the need to reconcile analysis and action' (1973, p. 149).

13 Adam Raphael, in the *Guardian*, 17 December 1973.

14 For a critique of the phenomenological interpretations of 'statistics' in general, cf. Hindess (1973). The salient article in this tradition on the *criminal* statistics as indices of 'rate-production' is Kitsuse and Cicourel (1963).

15 For more detailed discussion of these constancies, see McClintock and Avison (1968), especially chapter 2, 'Trends in Crime'.

16 Cf. American Friends Service Committee (1971).

17 Statistics taken from Task Force Report on Corrections, President's Commission on Law Enforcement and the Administration of Justice (1967, p. 3).

18 Kutchinsky's voluminous work in this area undoubtedly stems from his interest in the relationship of legal and structural realities and moral or social outcome as a problem in social psychology. He is interested in the question of 'norm acceptance' as 'an intervening variable between law and behaviour' (Kutchinsky, 1972, p. 14). The fact remains that in his general work on KOL, and in his more specific work on the relationship between liberalization of laws on pornography and the prevalence of certain sexual offences, Kutchinsky refuses to move beyond a politically liberal 'prescriptive' posture (Kutchinsky 1971). Hence, where his work on law as constructed and developed can only be used to shore up the legitimacy of existing social arrangements at large, his work on 'sexual legislation' can only be used to reduce certain sex crimes *at the expense of* shoring up existing (commercial and exploitative) arrangements organizing sexual interaction. There is no alternative vision of a society in which sexuality might be recognized *openly* and *freely* (non-exploitatively) as a matter of human need and expression.

19 It is also, of course, the case that there is evidence of considerable dissensus amongst members of different social classes in advanced societies as to the *relative* seriousness of different *offence* behaviours. Research carried out by the BBC in 1961, for example, demonstrated a considerable punitiveness towards offences involving motor vehicles amongst working-class respondents (to a much greater extent than amongst other respondents), and indicated also a greater tolerance towards interpersonal violence amongst the working-class, except in the case of 'sexual crimes' (cf. BBC, 1961). These findings were substantially confirmed by a survey carried out for the *Daily Mail* newspaper in 1967. KOL researchers have not really confronted the question of dissensus in a population, since to do so would throw up the problems of *social interests* and law in a clear way, threatening the monolithic and consensual model of social order which underpins their concern for 'social defence'.

20 Cf. Taylor, Walton and Young (1973, chapter 1), for a lengthier

discussion of classicism in criminology.

21 The centrality of the 'saving of children' ideology in the formation of American social welfare is fully discussed in Platt (1969).

22 Certainly, one of the features of positivistic research is the infrequency with which its initial hypotheses are ever finally negated: there are always good grounds for suggesting that the hypothesis, whilst not sustained, might well have been upheld in other research situations. This is very notably the case in positivistic researches into the effectiveness of juvenile 'correctional programmes'; cf. the critique of the self-fulfilling prophecies built into this research, by Glaser (1965).

23 A significant and under-researched development in what might be called 'the political economy of social control' is the increasing industrialization of prisons. Whilst it would probably be spurious to argue that prison administrations will ever be able to finance their own operations out of the profits from prison labour, it is clear that the ongoing industrialization of 'corrections' will offset some of the costs of the prison-building programmes. It is certainly not without significance that the British Prison Department was able, in 1972, to report, for the first time, an overall profit (of £513,511) from the prison industry programme; and that the marketing of prison-produced goods was undertaken with a serious commercialism under the new brand name of *Prindus*. Similar developments have occurred in Scandinavia, and are touched upon in Mathieson (1974).

24 Karl Marx: 'The Proceedings of the Sixth Rhenish Parliament', *Rheinische Zeitung*, 10–14 July 1842, reprinted in McLellan, ed. (1971).

25 A new statement of this position, continuing to confuse these issues, is Coulter (1974).

26 For a fuller statement of this ontological position, see Walton and Gamble (1972, chapter 2).

27 Parts of the following derive from a recent unpublished paper by Stuart Hall (1973).

28 For a further development of this argument, see Walton (1974).

29 Such an analysis of property is clearly crucial in deciphering what is meant by 'crimes against property' in a propertied society, and in understanding what is being attempted when agencies of social control (like the police) apprehend offenders for such crimes. In an unpublished paper, Rosenberg has argued that when police intervene in strikes they do so not in defence of property *per se* (little property damage occurring during the course of strikes), but in defence of the management's *right to property* (Rosenberg, 1972). If such a perspective on property law and the police is adopted, the liberal vision of law as an arbitrating instrument between conflicting interests looks weak. One has to proceed to an examination of the class codes contained in the sinews of law itself, and the consequently class-organized nature of police and social-control activity.

30 Marx: 'Speech in his Defence', reprinted in McLellan (1973, pp. 215–16).

2 Working-class criminology
Jock Young

> Those who have wished to emphasize the sober constitutional ancestry of the working-class movement have sometimes minimized its more robust and rowdy features. All that we can do is to bear the warning in mind. We need more studies of the social attitudes of criminals, of soldiers, and sailors, of tavern life; and we should look at the evidence, not with a moralizing eye ('Christ's poor were not always pretty'), but with an eye for Brechtian values – the fatalism, the irony in the face of Establishment homilies, the tenacity of self-preservation. And we must also remember the 'underground' of the ballad-singer and the fair-ground . . . for in these ways the 'inarticulate' conserved certain values – a spontaneity and capacity for enjoyment and mutual loyalties – despite the inhibiting pressures of magistrates, mill-owners and Methodists (E. P. Thompson, 1968, pp. 63–4).

Attacking a theoretical position to which one is opposed often tends towards the erection of an alternative position which is merely an inversion of one's opponent's. To avoid this failure, it is necessary to extract the kernel of an opponent's argument in order to *transcend* it, encompassing all his data but moving to a superior position. At the outset, it is essential to be clear about one's own fundamental tenets (for example, one's conception of human nature, social order and epistemology). To attack the 'false ideas' of another without being clear about one's own ideas, merely leads into the construction of theories which are mirror-images of the false ideas being attacked.

The central contention of this chapter is that the 'new deviancy theory', originated largely by American sociologists around The Society for the Study of Social Problems in the early 1960s, and developed by the National Deviancy Conference in Britain, fell precisely into this trap. So it was that the attack on the type of positivist criminology, which we characterized in chapter 1 as Fabian, resulted not in an escape from the utilitarian theatre of discourse but merely in a crass inversion of it.

The history of the new deviancy theory is a story of a well-meaning opposition to conservative thinking – leading from a laissez-faire liberalism to a full-blown Romanticism.[1] In its liberal phase, the deviant was seen to be propelled from involvement in a nearly-ubiquitous and innocuous deviancy into an essential and committed membership of hardened criminal subcultures by the clumsy mismanagement of the powerful. In its romantic sequel, the deviant – whether nestling warmly in the tenderloin of the city or making inarticulate but penetrating attacks on the bourgeois order – became a hero for the sociologist of deviancy.[2] The movement led from 'zookeeping' of the deviant to a 'moral voyeurism', wherein the 'propinquity of the wicked' sustained our careful dislike of the 'virtuous'.[3]

Let us first examine the basic premises of the correctionalist criminology against which the new deviancy theory reacted, concentrating on two aspects: the specific characteristics of such theories, and their ideological implications.[4]

1 *Consensual view of social order*

Correctional criminology's conception of society postulated an overwhelming agreement over definitions of the conventional and the deviant – the vast majority of individuals acting within this consensus, and a small minority being unambiguously deviant. Thus, we are presented with a 'taken-for-granted' world where social reaction against a particular individual or group was obvious. One does not ask why the burglar or the marihuana smoker should be prosecuted – any reasonable man is seen to be opposed to these activities. The workings of the State and its relationship to law and the judiciary, therefore, are left unexamined. Thus, the *reaction* (against deviance) is declared unproblematic.

2 Homo duplex *conception of human nature*

The deviant individual is seen as a pathological product of undersocialization into the consensus. In its classic form, deviancy is seen as the formless force of the *id* bursting through a hernia in the *superego*. In this way, alternative takes on reality are negated – for meaning has been wrenched from the deviant actor, and he is cast into the realm of the asocial. Thus, the deviant *act* is rendered meaningless.

3 *Determined nature of the deviant act*

The deviant individual is pathological and hence his activities are not those of choice, for no 'normal' individual would ever contemplate them. He is ineluctably propelled into his deviancy. Thus, no normal person would choose to be deviant and the deviant's actions cannot be of his own making.

4 *Primacy of primary socialization*

Deviancy is determined by factors operating in the far past of the individual. There is a split between 'real time' and 'actual time'. Real time has causal significance and is located in the traumas or deprivations of the past which are repeatedly enacted in the future. Actual time is relevant only to the extent that the individual encounters 'precipitating circumstances' which bring out the underlying 'real-time' predispositions. Thus, if we can explain deviant behaviour in terms of events that happened ten years ago we are doing well; if we can explain in the first five years of the actor's life we are doing excellently; but if we can do so in terms of the individual's autonomic nervous system or chromosome structure, that is science! Thus, present circumstances are granted only tangential relevance, and explanation is individualized in the past history of the solitary actor.

5 *Reductionism*

Individual choice and action within the social world is reduced to fixed, psychological, physiological and/or genetic propensities. Deviancy becomes an outcome of these 'essences', and has no meaning outside of an atomized psyche or bodily structure. This is the ultimate break with the present predicament of the actor.

6 *Scientism*

The necessity for the scientific analysis of the causal factors propelling the deviant allows the expert to speak *ex cathedra*, giving credence to the interpretations of the actor himself only as one of many factors under consideration. This gives scientific respectability to the analysis and assumes the insulated neutrality of the expert from the deviant. Thus, scientific credibility is added to the break that is made with the present predicament.

7 *The therapeutic impact of social reaction*

The expert is seen as having no moral or financial axes to grind; he makes recommendations which manipulate or negate the regressive forces that exist within the deviant actor with a therapeutic purpose and a therapeutic impact. The lay conservative, being more punitively oriented, is presented as one who may potentially exacerbate precipitating factors, which in turn may worsen the deviancy. In contrast, 'scientifically prescribed' social reaction is seen to arise out of neutral assessment, bearing no relationship to the deleterious influence of conservative (or other) ideologies. In this fashion, 'enlightened' or 'rehabilitative' social reaction can be presented as dispassionate and innovative and the expert is dissociated from the ongoing constellation of social reactive forces which maintain the deviant in a stigmatized position.

8 *The divorce of deviant from victim*

The deviant is seen as propelled by his essential propensities into the contemporary world – his victim being the first accidental social atom into which he collides. The suggestion here is that there is little that the deviant might rationally desire of his victim – so that any idea of conflict between deviant and victim is defused.

The ideological significance of these premises in correctionalist criminology is that they achieve a four-fold fracture of reality: first, the actor is severed from his present predicament; second, that predicament is wrenched from the total society (including the 'social reaction' of contemporary society); third, the deviant act itself is separated out from any consciousness of it by the deviant actor; and, finally, the deviant is divorced from his victim.

The central task of the new deviancy theory was to reunite the deviant actor with the contemporary world.[5] The consensual view of the world in correctionalist criminology was replaced by a pluralist view of social action and values. Deviancy was seen as a problematic product of a series of transactions between definer and defined, each in his own social world. Social order was seen, in an extremely pluralistic fashion, as a collection of normative ghettoes, each jostling with each other for elbow-room and for status. One of these groups, however, somehow has more power than others – it is able to impose its own values and conceptions of behaviour on others. Power is stumbled upon, but the reasons for its existence, and for its frequent forays into the plural world (whether in the form of 'the bureaucracy' or Commissioner Anslinger) are not explored, or dissected. Divisions in civil society are found, but their social basis left unexamined. Instead, the call is for a 'culture of civility', wherein the mores of diversity will be respected by all groups.[6] Tolerance will reduce the present war of group against group into a situation of diversity and coexistence – San Francisco and Amsterdam being cited as pointers to a civilized urban future.

The pathological conception of deviancy is overturned: in a pluralistic society, all people are potentially deviant (cf. Douglas,

1971a, chapter 4), all people experience deviant 'impulses', it being the intolerance of power which translates such *normal* action into action which is stigmatized and labelled (cf. Becker, 1963, p. 26). Deviance is not inherent in an action: it is a quality bestowed upon it. So, normal variation in behaviour is transformed by *mismanagement* into behaviour which is seen to be dangerous to the individual and to the wider society.[7] Social reaction against 'the deviant' exacerbates the problems; before that, deviancy is either just the manifestation of the capricious whim of the actor or alternatively an inadequate but rational attempt at problem-solving.[8] Deviancy attempts to solve social problems; social reaction maintains and increases them. There is a fundamental irrationality about State control, for not only does its control activity frequently lead either to 'deviancy amplification' or to the ossification of the actor in his deviant status and position,[9] but also (given that deviant behaviour is ubiquitous throughout the social structure) the State's selection of scapegoats is arbitrary and based, by and large, on the 'false concepts' of policemen, social workers and courts. These false conceptions generate a stereotype of the criminal as lower class – a stereotypical construction which occurs because of the relative powerlessness of the lower class, rather than the fact of greater involvement in criminality as such (cf. Chapman, 1968). Furthermore, these social processes tend to generate the positivist aetiologies under attack, such as the 'broken home' hypothesis, aetiologies which are self-fulfilling in the sense that control agencies select miscreants for apprehension with precisely such criteria to the fore.[10] Criminal statistics, therefore, are seen as fabrications which, at best, can merely give us a head-count of those who have been labelled[11] or, at worst, serve to confirm state mystifications (mystifications which conceal the fact that there is no generalized standard which could meaningfully generate any such figures).[12]

In the new deviancy theory, the present circumstance and the secondary socialization of the deviant take the place of primary socialization and the constellation of determining factors as the focus of investigation. The actor's past is seen largely to be irrelevant – his physical body virtually vanishes, and his self-concept achieves a high degree of continuity with his subcultural environment. For, in the new deviancy theory, the deviant is, above all, a rational, conscious actor, free of the determinants of past events and physical or psychic disturbance, and existing in a homogeneous and normatively-consistent subculture. The concepts of undersocialization and social disorganization as causes of deviancy are replaced by an emphasis on the differential socialization of individuals – dependent on their proximity to one particular normative social organization within the plurality of organizations that make up the total society.

In the new deviancy theory, man's possibilities are open-ended – man does not possess any *essential* features predisposing him towards deviance. The notion of *essence* is associated with an incorrect method of categorization applied by official society in the process of social reaction, notions which sometimes are taken up and acted upon by the actors themselves.[13] Human action is teleological and irreducible to bodily or subconscious processes. Because this is so, the principle method of access to the knowledge necessary for explaining the existence or the content of specific subcultures is experiential and intuitive. The conceptualization of the social universe held to by the actors in question is seen to be of absolutely central importance in explaining their action. 'Insider' information becomes paramount, and the 'outsider' (*qua* sociologist) attempts to return from the particular normative ghetto he has been exploring with a precise image of insider's definitions, untarnished by the outsider-sociologist's own 'middle-class' preconceptions. Conceptual relativism becomes the order of the day, and the sociologist is seen merely to be readjusting 'the hierarchy of credibility' (used to define valid social information) away from its domination by the powerful.[14]

In its attack on the utilitarianism of Fabian criminology (which was discussed in chapter 1) the new deviancy theory tends to embrace a *romantic* conception of the social universe.[15] That is, the image of a naturally good man – whose goodness would be expressed more extensively were it not for the interference of 'civilized' society – is proposed. Thus, true human expression and authenticity is most likely to be found at the margins of the social world. Elsewhere, official society (whether in the form of the nuclear family, the education system or the social-control agencies) tends to transform the natural round of innocuous diversity (and its beneficent consequences) into a state of intractability and brutalization. On the basis of such a romantic image of man, the new deviancy theorists tend to address their attacks against the utilitarian mismanagement of deviancy, the transformation of the 'useless' into the 'useful' and the incarceration of the intransigent.

Utilitarian crime is of little interest to the new deviancy theory. Indeed, it is engaged in an astonishing accomplishment – the development of a criminology that does not deal with property crime, and a criminology whose subjects live in a world not of work, but of leisure. Expressive deviancy is the centre of attention: marihuana-use rather than burglary, prostitution rather than homicide, 'psychopathy' and 'schizophrenia' rather than 'hysteria' or 'neurosis'. The emphasis is on 'crimes without victims' and the contention, overall, is that a big proportion of crime control involves undue and unnecessary interference in the liberty of the individual.[16] The spectre of John Stuart Mill is here: there is even a suggestion that the non-interventionist catechism be extended to many 'utilitarian' crimes (for example, some forms of juvenile deliquency, on the grounds that they are innocuous prior to reaction) and to homicide, rape and child-molesting (on the grounds that these crimes can involve precipitation by the victim, and hence contain complicity by the victim in the offending activity).

The theory and practice of voyeurism

However much there is that is progressive in the idealism of the new deviancy theory (for example, in its attacks on manifestly repressive and mystifying potential of criminological positivism)[17] too many problems remained unsolved. In particular, although there were many texts to delight the connoisseur of deviancy, there were few guidebooks to provide pointers to practical struggle. Paradoxically, of course, correctionalist criminology was guilty of no such omission. In its constant endeavour to achieve a staffing position in the management of society and in the disposal of the 'useless', correctionalist criminology has developed a consistently practical concern, and a policy-orientation of considerable sophistication and scope. Indeed, in many criminological texts, the final arbiter of the 'truth' or 'validity' of a theory is its practical utility. The new deviancy theorists have nevertheless been stridently non-interventionist. In the earlier phase, the theorist's attitude to his subject-matter was rather like that of a wild-life conservationist. His message to the State was 'hands off!', reaction and intervention against deviants being seen as unnecessary and exacerbating of the situation. Associated with this avoidance of intervention was what Gouldner (1968, pp. 121–2) was later to lampoon as the 'Theory and Practice of Cool', a poise of studied neutrality, involving a careful and strictly limited support of their subjects:

> Like the zookeeper, he wishes to protect his collection; he does not want spectators to throw rocks at the animals behind the bars. But neither is he eager to tear down the bars and let the animals go. The attitude of these zookeepers of deviance is to create a comfortable and humane Indian Reservation, a protected social space, within which these colourful specimens may be exhibited unmolested and unchanged.

Later, with the rise of more militant and aggressive deviant groups, the tune changed somewhat. For *carefully*, and *theoretically*, the new deviancy theorists delighted in a voyeuristic way in the activities of the new-style deviant. In particular, they relished the overt attack mounted by the new deviants on the 'straight world' – the world of the utilitarian middle-class. Whether the deviant in question was a marihuana smoker, a gay, a football hooligan, a sexual deviant, a blackmailer, vandal, greaser or industrial saboteur, the sign was that somebody had sensed that 'society' was 'wrong' and that, moreover, that somebody had the guts to do something about it.[18] A greater contradiction was presented for this later version of the new deviancy theory – for now the message of the deviancy theorist to official society was 'hands off, you'll only make matters worse' but *at the same time* the implicit ideology was 'believe and hope that the new deviant constituencies do represent a genuine threat to the social order'. If an activity was anti-State in any conceivable sense, this was sufficient for it to be celebrated or approved. The project of the new deviancy theory was to show how the reaction of the State to such threats was nevertheless irrational, amplifying deviance whilst at the same time contradicting in the process of reaction its own democratic codes and rule-book.

The problems with this position were two-fold. First, the new deviancy theory was still trapped theoretically – within the confines of an inverted utilitarianism. Second, there was *no* clear conception of practice – power had really been discovered, but there was no desire to dirty one's hands in actual struggles (and certainly no programmes or policies spelt out for those who might so desire).

There two problems were an almost unavoidable feature of an essentially idealist politics: an idealism, that is, which was firmly convinced of the possibility of social change brought on by a demystification of the 'theories' (i.e. the ideologies) of the enlightened middle class, and sustained by the co-operation of diverse and expressive strands within the *marginal* middle and working classes. It was a radical idealism desperately seeking a social base in the wider society. This is not to deny the importance of such marginal groups (as, for example, the new bohemia)[19] – but it is to assert (as these groups were later themselves to discover) that radical ideas by themselves are abortive unless linked to a wider analysis of the total society, and unless tied into a wider struggle in a class society. It should be said that although the organized Left could have contributed a great deal at this point, and raised the level of debate and practice considerably, the response made from that direction was theoretically and practically impoverished. The prevalent attitudes to deviant behaviour on the organized Left fitted largely into two categories, which we can summarize as: the 'After the Revolution' perspective, when, presumably, the activities of deviants would either vanish, or alternatively better 'therapeutic' facilities would be instituted; and the 'Leave 'em alone' perspective, where deviants (like, for example, the homosexual or the marihuana smoker) are seen as irrelevant to the struggle for socialism, and, therefore, to be tolerated. Both of these were strange responses – in the first perspective, an unwillingness (on the part of

Marxists) to be involved in discussions as to the real possibilities for a genuine social diversity, and, in the second, an espousal of an essentially liberal and moralistic view of 'tolerance', as a kind of free-floating sentiment to be mobilized irrespective of social context. The tenacity of a utilitarian perspective and culture is clear: the Left is exposed largely to an economistic position, which is atheoretical and grossly limited in its conception of the nature of socialist culture.[20] The Party increasingly focuses, as a result, on bread-and-butter issues and increasingly adopts an *ouvrierist* stance, which uncritically accepts existing working-class attitudes to crime and deviancy (and, hence, to questions of human diversity).

The problems facing the new deviancy theory

In this section, our concern is to examine the empirical problems which confronted the new deviancy theorists, problems which were a direct product of the limited conception of human nature and social order with which they had chosen to work. The object here is to show that although the new deviancy theory was successful in reuniting the fractured man of criminological positivism, in reuniting actor, action and society, it succeeded at the expense of erecting a rational Frankenstein constructed out of the inverted conceptual debris of its positivist opponents.

1 *The problem of consensus*

However much the new deviancy theorist talked of diversity and dissensus in society, the ineluctable reality of a considerable consensus over certain matters could not be wished away. This was particularly noticeable, moreover, in the widespread and uniform social reaction against various forms of deviancy (and, especially, against *crimes* against the person and certain crimes against property).

The positivists had declared there to be a consensus to which all normal men adhered. Deviancy was irrational or meaningless: a product of a pathology that was either individual or social or both. The new deviancy theorists, in contrast, tended to see the social world in pluralistic terms and deviant action itself as problem-solving behaviour. The problem for the new deviancy theory, indeed, was not the extent of crime and deviancy, but the relative lack of it. Given the lack of any clear rationale for consensus in the new deviancy theorist's view of the social world, the problem was that conformity *per se* was irrational. More particularly, in turning to a typical industrial society like Britain, where some 7 per cent of the population own 84 per cent of the wealth, a society not only of palpable material inequality, but also an associated repression of minority groups, and sexual repression, why was there even a shred of consensus, and why did actors not pursue their reasonable interests with even greater vigour and commitment than the reported delinquent of orthodox criminology? Again, why should it be that people are so falsely conscious as to react against crimes which do not directly damage their interests (as, for example, some forms of professional crime and the crimes without victims)? And, moreover, why do people not react more 'rationally' against activities (whether illegal or not) – like the activities of corporations and the powerful in general – which manifestly do disturb their interests?[21]

2 *The problem of statistics*

However dubious the positivist's acceptance of the criminal statistics at face value, the wholesale rejection of the statistics by the new deviancy theorist was equally cavalier. It would be a strange industrial sociologist, for example, who would reject the strike figures on the grounds that they were evidence only of labelling and social reaction – even though he would still be cautious in his interpretations of their significance at a particular time. The rejection of the statistics absurdly disqualifies the new deviancy theorist from contributing to the topical, and politically consequential debate as to the significance of the crime-rate, whether it is rising and in what way. And the new deviancy theorist is unable either to investigate – on his own admission – questions of comparison over time and across cultures. The new deviancy theorist excludes himself in this important way from the hot questions of crime, the arena of immediate political debate and any kind of intervention in the escalation of control that follows from statistical increases in crime.

Moreover, the new deviancy theorist is left without a conceptual armoury in the discussion of 'unofficial crime-rates'. To argue that the law is a weapon constructed by the powerful in its own interests (that it solves problems confronted by the powerful), hardly enables explanation of the widespread law-breaking currently exposed, and normally institutionalized, in the activities of powerful corporations and political men – law-breaking which, according to Gordon (1971), Pearce (1973) and even Ramsay Clark (1970), is carried out on a scale that makes Al Capone and the Great Train Robbers look like novices. The rule-makers comprise the most ardent of rule-breakers; and, for the new deviancy theorist sensitized to the inequality of the wider society, the problem is that there is far too much rule-breaking amongst the powerful for his simple conception of law to make sense. On the one hand, then, the new deviancy theory is unable to cope with the relatively infrequent and unextensive amount of working-class deviancy in a divided society; and, on the other, it cannot explain the prevalence and persistence of the criminality of the powerful.

3 *The problem of social disorganization*

The new deviancy theorists accused those who operated with notions of social disorganization of belittling, or denying the authenticity, of alternative forms of social organization developed in pursuit of other than dominant goals. However important this accusation may have been in pointing to the plurality of social organizations in a divided society, the fact remains that certain ecological areas *are* disorganized; and that this disorganization relates both to the external and internal forces acting on such areas (for example, on skid-row, or in 'hippie' communities). And it is absurd to deny that phenomena like marital breakdown are irrelevant, at the micro-level of interaction, in the aetiology of deviant behaviour. To accord a subcultural solution authenticity is not equivalent to endowing it with health.

4 *The problem of irrationality*

Why should men act in certain ways that, according to the tenets of the new deviancy theory, were patently irrational? Why, for example, should men behave in ways which suggested determination of precisely the kind described by the positivists (in terms of childhood experience, in predictable fashion, as if determined by the facts of bodily reality)? Why should some behaviour appear random, meaningless and unrelated to specifiable human motivation? Why do some people describe themselves as being sick and determined? Why should some people opt for manifestly untenable solutions to their problems, solutions that were clearly against their own interests? Why should men behave as if afraid of freedom (limiting their own solutions and possibilities in a variety of ways)? Why should the powerful, also, act in such a way as to increase and exacerbate the problems *they* faced (for example, in their attempts to control others)? Why, indeed, do individuals appear to resist the presumably liberative ideas and strategies thrown up by the new deviancy theorists and by other social and political movements at large?

Specifically, it would be instructive to know why Howard Becker and Irving Horowitz's much-vaunted 'culture of civility' (a culture of mutual tolerance, and a social contract of genuine liberality) should not exist except (briefly) in a small area and in a period of high prosperity. Why, indeed, is the reader they produced on *Culture and Civility* prefaced by a eulogy to the tolerance existing in San Francisco at the time, but then followed by a series of essays detailing the defensive formation of Red Guards by the young Chinese, the repeated racism of the police in its attacks on the black community, the frightening destruction of the hippie colony and the continuing immiseration of the ghetto?

5 *The problem of psychic disturbance*

Where the new deviancy theorist portrays his deviant as an open-minded, calm, rational actor, we are beholden to explain the social realities of guilt as a universal form of human experience, the ongoing reverence for authority (which often intensifies to the point of rendering anti-authoritative action impossible), the existence of internal contradictions in individual desires, values and needs, and (for the deviancy theorist as well as for the deviant) the prevalence of situations in which one knows 'what ought to be done' but feels unable to carry through the necessary solutions.

6 *The problem of bodily discomfort*

The tendency in the new deviancy theory was to ignore the fact that the human actors under discussion possessed a human body. Thus, there was violation of evidence confirming the experience of bodily anxiety produced at the 'invitational edge' of criminality – the activity of the autonomic nervous system that does occur as one's hands move towards the 'goodies'. Additionally, little or no discussion was given the existence of hysteria and other psychologically-induced illnesses or psychosomatic complaints.

7 *The problem of objectivity*

Attributing rationality to deviant decisions, asserting the differential tenability of various human acts, and denying the reality of consensus implies the existence not of a totally relative world, but of an elusive though complex standard (a standard that is not recognized or portrayed in law or in dominant social norms). In other words, there is some standard somewhere, whereby one is able to talk of appropriate and, most importantly, of inappropriate responses to problem-situations. The spectre of normality and pathology, once exorcized, re-emerges. Only by holding to some standard of normality is it possible, indeed, to talk of lapses in rationality on the part of an individual, a group or even on the part of a total society. But this standard need not be simply a description of what human nature and social order are, under existing social arrangements, but, crucially, can be statements about what they *might* be – statements, that is, about their potentiality. To talk in terms of objectivity, moreover, demands that one relates the notion of deviance to conformity within a total system. The alternatives are either to adopt the positivist's identification of deviance as a departure from the existing arrangements of interest and power, and to use these arrangements as a standard of objectivity and rationality, *or* to analyse society in terms of a conflict between classes, the falsely conscious nature of much working-class behaviour, and the illusory nature of appeals to a consensus.

The parameters of normality

> What inducement has the proletariat not to steal? It is all very pretty and very agreeable to the ear of the bourgeois to hear the 'sacredness of property' asserted; but for him who has none, the sacredness of property dies out of itself. Money is the god of this world. The bourgeois takes the proletarian's money from him and so makes a practical atheist of him (Engels, 1969, p. 145).

As we have indicated earlier, a central problem facing the new deviancy theorists was the irrational irresistance of individuals to crime, the psychic and bodily weightings towards conformity, and the apparently senseless commitment of the subordinate to consensual values. In a society where the producers of wealth remain relatively impoverished – where real poverty is widespread and where the worker in 'decent' employment still finds it difficult to budget – this conformity is all the more difficult to explain. Yet crime is not so obvious a decision as Engels might have us believe. The continuing respect for property in grossly inequitable societies underlines two interrelated questions: in the immediate situation, why is there *not* a widespread and rational pursuit of criminal careers, and why in the long-term is there not the obvious pursuit of socialism? Why is property respected and why is the working-class involved in supporting political ideas which manifestly fail to meet or are opposed to their interests? The 'problem of order' and the tenacity of 'order' generates the same kinds of questions within deviancy theory and within socialist theory. A British libertarian socialist magazine poses the question most pointedly:[22]

> Let us consider for a moment – and not through rose-tinted spectacles – the average British middle-aged working class voter today. He is probably hierarchy-conscious, xenophobic, racially-prejudiced, pro-monarchy, pro-capital punishment, pro-law and order, anti-demonstrator, anti-longhaired students and anti-drop-out.

Attempts to explain this travesty of consciousness, the *Solidarity* article continues, have typically taken three forms:

1 *Betrayal of left-wing leaders*

No doubt such betrayals have occurred, but *why* are repeated betrayals tolerated, and *why* are left-wing leaders so timid? Is it really simply that such leaders would exchange a bottle of brandy and a handshake with Princess Anne for the realization of a new society, the actualization of a dream?

2 *The mass media*

The argument here is the media have successfully instilled in the population an all-pervasive respect for property and an abhorrence of criminality. No doubt the media *does* attempt to spread such messages, but, again, *why* should the distorted media messages find such an eager audience? Why are the televisions left on, the newspapers read so avidly? Why do the ideas slot so easily into the heads of the viewing population? Ideas must have some meaning, some response for their audience and life situation, or else other – more radical – ideas would find their audience more readily.[23] At this juncture, *Solidarity*, like many other libertarian socialist groups, plumps for a third alternative.

3 *Long-standing conditioning: distorted character structure set up in infancy through sexual repression*

In this perspective, fascism in Germany, working-class quiescence, respect for property and prudery are all seen to be functions of rigid and repressive parents, and hence child-rearing itself is seen as a product and a producer of an authoritarian system. Or, as Wilhelm Reich (1946, pp. 25–6) put it:

> Suppression of the natural sexuality of the child, particularly of its genital sexuality, makes the child apprehensive, shy, obedient, afraid of authority, 'good' and 'adjusted' in the authoritarian sense; it paralyzes the rebellious forces because any rebellion is laden with anxiety, it produces by inhibiting sexual curiosity and sexual thinking in the child a general inhibition of thinking and of critical faculties. In brief, the goal of sexual repression is that of producing an individual who is adjusted to the authoritarian order and who will submit to it in spite of all misery and degradation. . . . The result is fear of freedom, and a conservative, reactionary mentality. Sexual repression aids political reaction, not only through this process which makes the mass individual passive and unpolitical, but also by creating in his structure an interest in actively supporting the authoritarian order.

Earlier, we noted how the attack on positivism from the new deviancy theory resulted merely in its inversion (into idealism) and how left-wing explanations of criminality often simply replicated bourgeois accounts. If we reverse the problematic from 'why do people deviate?' to 'why do people conform?' – as in Reich – we obtain a similar result. All of the three 'socialist' explanations for the widespread respect for property and the consensus are mirror-images, only, of conventional explanations of criminality.

The *corrupt leadership* theory is the precise counterpart of the notion of 'bad company' and the corruptor–corruptee relationship in conventional criminological explanation; the understanding here being that no deviant would act in the way that he did unless he were sick, under the influence or corrupted. The same understanding is extended, in left-wing accounts, to the activities of the left-wing leader, and to his effect on those whom allegedly he represents.

The *baleful image of the mass media* theory is idealist, in that it assumes that people are in some way motivated by ideas, *irrespective* of their material circumstances. Any ideas can be 'caught' from the media, provided that they are marketed with sufficient intensity and duration. The parallels with differential association theory in orthodox criminology as an account of the learning of norms and values are apparent.

The *authoritarian character armour* theory of Reich, of course, is an exact replica of theories of undersocialization in both psychological and sociological positivism.

All three theories – whether phrased in left-wing or right-wing rhetoric, and whether developed for the purposes of control or liberation – tend to ignore the material situation of the individual and his present social predicament. All three of them rely on the idea of a passive, non-reflective individual who is prey, without significant defences, to external or internal 'malignant' influences. No doubt each of them contains a kernel of truth but to accord them primacy, as explanations of working-class passivity, over explanations located in the real social and material situation of working-class members is unjustified, and is disastrous for understanding both working-class politics and working-class crime. To understand the material situation of the working-class criminal, it is necessary to examine the ideological underpinning of social-control activity (in the widest possible sense). The project here is to understand how the precepts of bourgeois ideology (a) contain within them a sufficient though distorted degree of truth as to be rationally, if mistakenly, believed, (b) act upon and provide some measure of reassurance for the very real problems of justice and order confronting the working-class, (c) are presented with a high degree of unanimity and with a denial of any existing alternative so as to don a 'natural' appearance, and

(d) are maintained by means of an entirely real and contemporary social-control apparatus that does operate with a view to controlling and checking the deviation of, in particular, threatening working-class behaviours.

These four features of bourgeois ideology will be examined in greater detail.

1 Distorted truth

Engels (1969, pp. 144–5) wrote:

> There is . . . no cause for surprise if the workers, treated as brutes, actually become such; or if they can maintain their consciousness of manhood only by cherishing the most glowing hatred, the most unbroken inward rebellion against the bourgeoisie in power. They are men so long only as they burn with wrath against the reigning class. They becomes brutes the moment they bend in patience under the yoke, and merely strive to make life endurable while abandoning the effort to break the yoke.

For Engels, the working man faced with economic deprivation had four alternatives. He could, firstly, become so brutalized as to be, in effect, a determined creature, 'as much a thing without volition as water' (1969, p. 159), giving way to the disorganizing social forces that beset him. Or, secondly, he could accept the prevalent mores of capitalist society, and enter into a war of all against all (1969, p. 161):[24]

> In this country, social war is under full headway, everyone stands for himself against all comers, and whether or not he shall injure all the others who are his declared foes, depends upon a cynical calculation as to what is most advantageous for himself.

Thirdly, the working man could steal the property of the rich (1969, p. 240):

> It was not clear to his mind why he, who did more for society than the rich idler, should be the one to suffer under these conditions. Want conquered his inherited respect for the sacredness of property, and he stole. . . . Theft was the most primitive form of protest.

And, finally, of course, Engels argued, the working man could struggle for socialism.

However crude this 'typology' and however much Engels confused these options elsewhere, the classification of options, coined in 1845, has obvious advantages over the welter of schema developed from 1938 onwards as criminological typologies, typologies which have become the bugbear and the source of mystification for generations of students in criminology and deviance. Crime can be a product of the thoroughgoing brutalization of social forces impinging upon the actor, it can involve the voluntarism of competitive individualism, or it can be an individualized and primitive form of consciousness, easily broken by the 'social reaction' of the ruling class.

In the first instance, the positivist's conception of criminality as 'determined' is correct – though the explanation of this (as a matter of human nature or essential criminality) is not. The determination of criminality is more a matter of human (mis)fortune. In the second case, the criminal, like the rate-buster on the factory floor, is acting divisively; he is acting against the interests of the work-group and the class as a whole. In the third, a measure of consciousness is involved which presages the developed form of rationality of the final instance: the collective struggle for socialism. If we confuse these categories, we are unable to be discriminate in our attitudes to crime[25] – i.e., we either condemn it out of hand or we romanticize it. Either way, we accept legal categories at face value and neglect to study criminal phenomena from the perspective of class interests and socialist principles. For the working class does have a real stake in a genuine social order, however much it may be that conservative 'law and order' campaigns are a sham behind which particular interests advance themselves, and proclaim themselves to be acting in the interests of all. It is a simple fact that the majority of working-class crime is *intra-* and not *inter-*class in its choice of target, area of activity and distribution. Working-class people suffer from crime, confront daily the experience of material desperation, undergo the ravages of disorganization and competitive individualism. The ideology that plays on this – bourgeois ideology – contains an element of truth, and touches on the genuine interests of the class – albeit in a distorted fashion.

2 Moral indignation

Members of the working class also have a considerable stake in the notion (and the achievement) of social justice; they want a fair return for their labour, and are antagonistic towards those who obtain easy money parasitically upon the work of others. Bourgeois ideology plays upon this genuine fear, arguing that all will be rewarded according to their utility and merit, and that those who cheat at these rules will be punished. In this way, ideology aspires to acceptance as a universal interest, although in reality it conceals the rampant particular interests of the ruling class as displayed in both their legal *and* illegal aspects. The thoroughly meritocratic society of social utilitarianism is impossible in the context of existing property relationships, and thus the exhortation in bourgeois ideology towards free competition with the inducement of success for those who do is both an illusion and a mystification. The moral indignation of the powerless against those who succeed in material self-aggrandisement, in such circumstances, flows out of an entirely correct sense of malaise, an accurate reading of real possibilities for self in such a society. It is, however, a moral indignation that is directed at the visible criminals in the media, rather than the invisible criminals within bourgeois society's 'institutions of privacy'.[26] The criminal is an enormously useful scapegoat – to be put to use as a target for the sense of injustice of the powerless – and he is realistically a target in the sense that he often does act against class interests, yet unrealistically so in that his 'villainy' pales once set against that of the powers that be.

There is, however, a rather more profound sense in which moral indignation is played upon by ideology. Cattier's biography of Reich contains the following insight (Cattier, cited in *Solidarity*, 1969, p. 22):

> It would be wrong to believe that working people fail to revolt because they lack information about the mechanisms of economic exploitation. In fact revolutionary propaganda which seeks to explain to the masses the social injustice and irrationality of the economic system falls on deaf ears. Those who get up at 5 in the morning to work in a factory, and have on top of it to spend 2 hours of every day on underground or suburban trains have to adapt to these conditions by eliminating from their mind anything that might put such conditions in question again . . . revolutionary ideas slither off the character armour of the masses because such ideas are appealing to everything that people have had to smother within themselves in order to put up with their own brutalization.

To make sense of hardship, men must attempt to believe in an ultimate justice, however much their daily experience constantly belies it. Without embracing Reichian notions of 'character armour', and also without exaggerating the availability of revolutionary alternatives, we must be aware of the power of resistance to rational social action. This does not demand, as we shall see, a focus on childhood socialization, but it is certainly a crucial element in the social reaction against deviant behaviour and 'unconventional' ideas.[27]

Ideological displacement

Ideology is not, then, merely a set of false notions slotted into men's heads irrespective of their own real needs and desires. Ideology involves some degree of attention to men's felt needs and the world-views with which they attempt to live in the world. This is seen even more clearly in the case of what we may call 'ideological displacement'.

Donald Cressey, in his famous book on the Mafia, *Theft of the Nation*, notes how a tight-knit group of criminal families with a clearly differentiated hierarchy of function, exerts a pervasive and parasitic influence throughout the American economy. These families are thieving the wealth of the nation – every time an American eats a hamburger, buys milk, real estate or whatever, a certain percentage accrues to the Mafia. What is more, they do not even pay taxes! Now whereas the existence of such an all-pervasive and hierarchially organized group of families is doubtful (and Albini argues powerfully that it does not, cf. Albini, 1971), organized crime in America is a reality. It is more diffused and localized, however, than the 'octopus with tentacles reaching to all parts of the country' as in Mickey Spillane or the romantic villainy of *The Godfather*, and ideological fantasies of the internal enemy repeatedly evoked by the Kennedy–Johnson administration. This is not to suggest that organized crime does not harm working-class interests, but it is to argue that it does so much less than the illegal (and, of course, the legal) activities of corporations in America (cf. Pearce, 1973). The extraordinary point is that the picture of the Mafia portrayed in Cressey, and also (importantly) in the media, is a direct parallel of the structure of family control over the 'legitimate' American economy. It is as if the reality of bourgeois domination was taken up and projected as a social image on to a conveniently caricatured and alien outgroup. Similar processes occurred, of course, in pre-war Germany, where if one erased the word Jew in 'Left' Nazi propaganda and replaced it with 'bourgeoisie', one would be left with something looking remarkably like a crude Marxist tract. As Peter Sedgwick notes in his analysis of fascism in Germany (1970, p. 33):

> What has to be determined is the function of anti-Semitism and anti-Slavism in the belief-system of the National Socialist movement as a whole. For, despite the programmatic timidity and opportunism of all wings of Nazism, from Hitler to the so-called 'Left Nazis' like the Strassers, the 'Socialism' of 'National Socialism' has to be taken very seriously. All the militancy and sacrifice, all the hatred of privilege and corruption, all the determination to make a better and cleaner world, which among revolutionary Socialists is attached to a

> class perspective upon society, was present among the Nazi pioneers, only linked to a racial vision. Demagogy and conscious deception were practised constantly and consciously, but within the limits of a terrible sincerity. *Pessima corruptio optimi*: the worst vices come through the corruption of the noblest instincts – and the worst cruelties through the deflection of class-militancy upon a non-class target . . . no movement without some kind of ideological parallel to Marxism could have hoped to master a society like Germany in which the contours of class-division were so deeply graven.

3 The natural appearance of ideology

Lukács, in *History and Class Consciousness* (1971, p. 262) points to the vital role of ideology in the functioning of a social system, noting that although 'the coercive measures taken by society in individual cases are often hard and brutally materialistic . . . the strength of every society is in the last resort a spiritual issue'. The State is seen as a 'natural' entity outside of man's own creation (1971, p. 257):

> That is to say, the organs of authority harmonize to such an extent with the [economic] laws governing men's lives, or seem so overwhelmingly superior that men experience them as natural forces, as the necessary environment for their existence. As a result they submit to them *freely* [which is not to say that they *approve* of them].

Thus, the criminal in his isolated violation of laws still feels guilty and, moreover, even in periods of revolution, when this 'natural' environment is disturbed the 'instincts' of the average man are so deeply violated 'that he regards it as a catastrophic threat to *life as such*, it appears to him to be a blind force of nature like a flood or an earthquake' (Lukács, 1971, p. 258).

Especially in Anglo-Saxon countries, where revolutionary alternatives are minuscule and radical rhetoric largely absent, the consensus appears as a monolith. Proponents of diversity forget that this consensus throughout society corresponds to the uniformity of the mode of production dominating the social order. Far from being 'problematic', it is all too palpable – it is, as Lukács describes it, a fact of nature.

4 The soft machine

The control system in such societies works not through beatings or paddy wagons (though these are always present as an ultimate arsenal, at the terminus of social control), nor indeed by beliefs and ideologies marketed as natural and uncontestable, but by a judicial distribution of rewards tied into a thousand pinpricks of punishment in the workplace that is society. These pinpricks act on the personality structure set up in childhood. The family itself is the product of such personality constructions, and is in turn geared to producing more children to undergo such character-training. Thus, a certain personality set is maintained throughout life in aspic. Both the individual, and the working-class culture of which he is a member, are dominated by memories of the costs to be paid for deviation and dissent. Such a culture contains and relays knowledge of the inhumanity of unemployment, the gross stigma of prison (and its *real* social consequences – in terms of job chances *and* personal isolation), and is acquainted with the poverty and despair of the lumpenproletariat. At the same time, it has knowledge of the contemporary and continuing mechanisms of the soft machine of control: the perks of conformity, the incessant minutiae of punishment for rebellion in the job situation. Cudgels and baton charges are unnecessary in the maintenance of this aspect of control. *The real locus of social control is in the work situation.*[28] In this respect, it should be noted that the degree of freedom experienced by particular segments of the population (i.e. in being immunized from the 'social reaction' of the powerful) contains its own rationality. The deviation of those without real social power is tolerated. It is a thousand times easier to become a radical academic than a militant shop steward: the first course of action leads to Penguin Books Ltd and the second to the blacklist. The irony of socialist ideology gaining headway amongst the intelligentsia is the lack of any power in the intellectual groups; but, of course, tolerance even for 'academic socialism' is withdrawn when the economic climate changes and radical ideas find ready ears.

The hard edge of the soft machine is directed largely at those beyond the systems and rewards of the work-place – towards the 'disorganized', 'unproductive' or idle. The criminal statistics, in this sense, are indicative of the dispersal of power deemed necessary to create a control situation. It would be absurd to punish all offenders; the object is to create a symbolic group who are psychically and materially degraded in order to define a hard parameter to the workings of the soft machine of control.

The effectiveness of the soft machine is most clearly seen in the context of the post-war period of prosperity, moving ahead, until recently, apparently without hindrance. The extent of conformity amongst privileged sections of the working class in a period when those sections remembered the experience of unemployment, and could compare it to the relatively beneficent present, is hardly surprising and certainly not irrational. Similarly, the response of the

German working class to fascism, however disagreeable, was not a product of madness nor merely the consequence of the compilation of authoritarian personalities. Sedgwick puts this well (1970, p. 33):

> Marxism, the most dedicated and developed social theory that human civilisation has attained, has nothing to contribute towards our understanding of Nazism's politics of race murder. The very use of expressions like 'barbarism' and 'medieval' by Marxists at this point testifies to the replacement of analysis by horror. It is little wonder that so many on the Left have resorted to psychological explanation as the first available alternative to the Marxist vacuum. . . . The 'Frankfurt School' of FreudoMarxists has extracted a variety of psychoanalyses from the mass unconscious: thus, mass society expresses either the submissiveness engendered by an authoritarian pattern of family upbringing (Adorno, Reich) or alternatively the confusion produced when these patterns get relaxed and replaced by permissiveness (Marcuse). Apart from their contradictory nature, these are answers to a false question, namely: 'Why did the Germans follow Hitler?' But on looking at the various phases and sources of mass support for Nazism, it becomes hard to believe that one requires any special psychological factors, other than those which explain, e.g. why the masses supported Churchill or Wilson. Nazi society was not a 'mass society' of atomized, hypnotized individuals: underneath the totalitarian armour, it was a typical advanced industrial society displaying all the sectors of varying and colliding class consciousness. It doesn't need Freud to tell us why people cheer a politician who stops unemployment, or why they fight savagely when their homes are bombed.

This is not to deny the physiological and psychological components of conformity, and neither is to say that individual biographies are irrelevant. Rather, it is to argue that the autonomic nervous system and the conformist, quiescent personality are not simply products of childhood conditioning, but that they are maintained *in stasio* by the continuing system of 'opportunity', social control and ideological domination. To say that there is continuity in personality structures over time is to say no more than that the social situation has remained largely unchanged.

Show me a man whose social situation is changed markedly, and you will see a change in personality; show me a class which has successfully clarified its situation in an act of praxis and then you will have massive changes in personality. Show me a man who has been typed as of lower intelligence and placed in a job deemed suitable for his level, and you will observe a constant (and) low level of intelligence being maintained. Or a man brutalized into psychopathy, further brutalized by prison, and returned to his initial and stultifying milieu – there is the constant psychopath. It is at the desperate end of the social spectrum where the overwhelming milieu precipitates men into highly determined roles wherein the tyranny of the organism is best displayed, and where the psychologist or the biologist comes into his own. But this is a product of historical time and place – it is *not* a part of 'human nature'; of 'man's essence' in the way that psychologists might have us believe. The correlations of psychological positivists, between the organic and the social, may indeed hold water in a period where the possession of certain organic attributes (for example, the XYY chromosome) is related to the moral careers made available for those with organic afflictions: such correlations *describe* the power-invested processes so established; they do little to undermine the idea that such processes are necessary and inevitable.[29]

Social and psychic conflict

Western man exists constantly in a state of contradiction. On the one hand, he is dominated by a conservative ideology which is monolithic and largely unopposed, legitimized by its very continuity and sustained by a social-control apparatus directed at the containment of those who may deviate. And, as we have argued, this ideology also draws strength from the fact that it plays on real needs, and justifiable fears. On the other hand, the individual's knowledge of reality contradicts the ideology – he is anxious that the world is not what it purports to be, he is troubled by the injustice of the system, and he is racked by alienation in the work-place. These contradictions are expressed in a *consensus* (about fundamentals, on which we are all agreed) and a diversity of values and opinions about the attainment, the expression or the experience of these fundamentals. On a psychological level, this contradiction can lead to intra-psychic conflict[30] of a sort which leads to moral indignation, to conservatism, to negativistic violence and destruction, to a guilt and neurosis, and, at times, when the opportunities arise, to vast changes in attitudes (changes, incidentally, which become inexplicable in an empiricist sociology). But neither psychic tension nor contradictions in attitude occur in a vacuum: it is the task of a critical criminology to situate them historically and to study the ways in which such tensions and contradictions can be resolved and removed.

Demands

A radical criminology, like radicalism in general, has to develop a programme of demands. Amongst these demands must be a concern for the following:

1 *Power and class*

> The scholar or scientist's way of becoming partially blind is, inadvertently perhaps, to structure fields of enquiry in such a way as to obscure obvious connections or take the connections for granted and leave the matter at that. The great task of disconnection – it was arduous and time consuming – fell to the positive school of criminology. Among their most notable accomplishments, the criminological positivists succeeded in what would seem the impossible. They separated the study of crime from the workings and the theory of the state (Matza, 1969, pp. 143–4).

In *Becoming Deviant*, Matza describes the fifty-year 'task of disconnection' in positivist criminology in detail, and we shall not repeat the story. From the late 1960s, however, criminologists have become increasingly aware of the fact of power. Yet at no time have they wanted to be involved in power. They have pointed increasingly to the fact of class inequalities in apprehension and 'labelling', but have stopped short of working out policies in terms of working-class interests. Thus, Edwin Schur writes (1969, p. 337):

> All available evidence indicates that crime in America will not be effectively reduced until we make basic changes in the structure and quality of American life. Respect for law and order will not be restored until respect for the nature of our society is restored. Our confrontation with crime cannot be successful if we persist in viewing it as a battle with some alien force. Since American's crime problems are largely of our own creation, we have it well within our power to modify them and bring them within reasonable control.

The use of the royal 'we' is preposterous here. It is unclear to this writer how *we* have created crime, and news to all of us, indeed, that *we* have the power to bring it under control.

The task facing socialist criminologists is to replace paradigms of this kind, with their continual reference to hypothetical publics and national problems, with paradigms developed around the interests of the class. Such a paradigm will reveal what demands are in fact revisionist, what demands we can pose as interim measures, and what strategic confrontations make sense politically. We will need to examine the relationship of organized Left parties and the class in terms of deviant behaviour, in the process attempting to substitute a conception of socialist diversity for the pluralism of the idealist tradition. Methodologically, we shall have to reject the bland formulation of 'participant observation', with its insistence on retaining a subculture or social situation unchanged. The only scenario where such a programme would ever have made sense would have been in a mortuary. In order to understand a subculture in the fullest possible sense, it is essential to understand its potentialities – that is, how it can *change*. The researcher, therefore, must be involved in the subculture – not afraid to argue, not refraining from exercising influence, and not resistant to change in himself.

2 *Statistics*

The criminal statistics represent the end-result of the deployment of social-control agencies by the powerful. The policeman on the beat, the courts, the social workers are all geared into this process in the sense that their areas of discretion are usually within the parameters their bureaucratic controllers permit. It is only in atypical situations that the idiosyncratic values and ideologies of particular social-control agencies assume *paramount* importance. To see each sector as conflicting over fundamentals is misleading, and is a product of the kind of pluralism which cannot distinguish differences of emphasis from differences in objective position. The statistics provide us with a blurred but useful picture of the degree of respect for property and the extent of social disorganization and conflict in the society in question. The categories represented in the statistics, however, must be interpreted with extreme caution, for given their legal basis they do not capture the meanings of crime for the actor, nor indeed the aetiological context of the act. For example, we are not so much concerned with the amount of property stolen as we are with the targets of property theft (and hence the motives informing such crimes). The criminal statistics are subject to the same good use, and the same problems of interpretation, as the strike statistics; but they form the basis for a socialist analysis of the development of contradictions and conflict in a propertied society.

3 *Freedom*

> What state, what time and under what conditions? It depends. I work not with abstractions, only with realities (Leon Trotsky, 1973b, p. 28, on asked whether the press would be free under socialism).

The idealist tradition in criminology (which we discussed earlier as 'anti-utilitarian' criminology) refused consistently to be involved itself with power. Indeed, it went close to arguing that power corrupts (or 'amplifies') the very deviants the powerful wish to control or to 'purify'. So, idealist criminologists were led into an unconditional support for freedom. Marihuana-smoking, heroin-use, prostitution and gambling were activities which individuals freely chose – and they should have the right to pursue these activities unimpeded. But the meanings of such activities and their objective significance varies with time and place. There is nothing implicit in the heroin molecule which is either progressive or reactionary, but heroin addiction, for example, in the black ghettoes is without doubt an insidious expression of exploitation, and an agency for passivity and defeat. To call for absolute freedom in a population driven to the edge of desperation is to invite the exercise of the laws of the laissez-faire market and the continuing rule of the powerful. Who is to say that the Black October group, who made it a part of their programme to eliminate heroin-pushers in the black slums of the USA, were not acting progressively?

The tendency to see heroism in the adaptive deviancy of those suffering most from the vagaries of capitalism is closely related to this appeal for freedom. As Joe Warrington argued bitterly in his critique of Laing's approach to schizophrenia (1973, p. 15):

> But expressing X $\neq$ understanding Y. Some people do learn valuable things from abnormal experiences; some even escape from the coils of the system but many, probably most, are wrecked. . . . The gut thing about schizophrenia is dreadful, dreadful unhappiness. Encouragement to wallowing in some vapid 'special status' is like encouraging a compulsive gambler in his solitary romanticization of the betting shop when one has no betting problems oneself. I regard this kind of weird, surrogate vampirism of another's terrible experience as being gravely immoral.

The development of social responsibility in the criminologist demands that he discriminate, that he does not merely collect exotica, that he separates out desperation from solution, and that he relates the deviant solution to its effects on others (situating it historically in terms of a class struggle). This requires a radical paradigm change in the study of deviancy. It does not rule out interim demands but it insists that such demands be part of an overall strategy. Thus, it does not lecture social workers and mental nurses that their function is *necessarily* as an instrument of social control, nor does it deny intermediate solutions, tentative graspings for survival on the part of the deviant. To do this would be utopian – it would be to suggest that men are necessarily either fully conscious revolutionaries or alternatively altogether reactionary. Rather it suggests that it is only through struggle, however limited at first, that consciousness is realized.

4 *Neo-correctionalism*

The idealists argued that social control was impossible in terms of the elimination of deviancy. They maintained that the requirement was a radical programme of decriminalization. Such a programme neglects to acknowledge that the process of decriminalization has important and ineradicable control functions within capitalist society, and that decriminalization, where it has occurred, is a product more of bureaucratic stategies evolved to deal with an overloading of inmates or social work cases than it is a genuine attempt to create a society free of the necessity to criminalize. Appeals to the powerful, however idealistically phrased, tend to be taken up in terms of the powerful's own interests, in order to serve ruling-class interests rather than those of the oppressed.[31]

It is unrealistic to suggest that the problem of crimes like mugging is merely the problem of miscategorization and concomitant moral panics. If we choose to embrace this liberal position, we leave the political arena open to conservative campaigns for law and order – for, however exaggerated and distorted the arguments conservatives may marshal, the reality of crime in the streets *can be* the reality of human suffering and personal disaster. We have to argue, therefore, strategically, for the exercise of social control, but also to argue that such control must be exercised within the working-class community and not by external policing agencies. The control of crime on the streets, like the control of rate-busting on the factory floor, can only be achieved *effectively* by the community immediately involved. Working-class organizations have eventually to combat the war of all against all that is the *modus vivendi* of civil society. Further, it is only in the process of struggle for control that the community can evolve out of its frequently disorganized and disintegrated state. The radical criminologist's task is to aid and inform such struggles and projects. His task is not to help the courts to work, nor to design better prisons. The problems of social control are problems for those who want to control *existing* social arrangements.

Radical criminological strategy is not to argue for legality and the rule of law but it is to show up the law, in its true colour, as the instrument of a ruling class, and *tactically* to demonstrate that the State will break its own laws, that its legitimacy is a sham, and that the rule-makers are also the greatest of rule-breakers. The law may be used where there are advantages in so doing, without succumbing to the notion that the law can universally be so useful. For it is precisely the nature of law to conceal particular interests behind universalistic ideology and rhetoric. The task is not to romanticize illegality: it is, as Lukács suggests, to judge deviant action in terms of its relationship to the struggle, ignoring the classifications of legality and illegality created by the powerful in *their* struggle against the powerless.

5 *Socialist diversity*

The ultimate goal in such a struggle must be a socialist culture which is diverse and expressive – that is, a culture which takes up the progressive components in pluralism, whilst rejecting those activities which are directly the product of the brutalizations of existing society (however diverse, expressive or idiosyncratic their manifestation). This involves a fight on two fronts: first, against the existing class society; and, secondly, against those tendencies within the socialist movement and the working class which would gravitate towards a strictly economistic interpretation of the socialist revolution. We argued earlier that capitalism is successful in creating a rubric of personal repression to which individuals do adapt: and hence it is clear that great resistance will occur against the achievement of a diverse and expressive society. There will, indeed, be a 'fear of freedom'. Just as it now a truism to say that Women's Liberation, Gay Liberation and the new bohemia need to evolve out of a 'politics of subjectivity' into a fully socialist analysis, so it is also correct that the organized Left needs its own healthy transfusion from these movements.

Conclusion

Whereas the positivist ascribed deviant behaviour to a series of determining forces which excluded human choice and reason, the idealist vacillated towards a theory which portrayed deviancy as a product of reason bereft of time and place, a pure form impeded only by the clumsy administration of the State. Both stances ignored the material rubric and biographical frameworks within which human choice occurs and is moulded.[32] We have seen how the material circumstances of the criminal and his subjective assessment of the situation are affected by the stick and carrot of social control, and obfuscated by the domination of a highly persuasive ideology. We have argued that the biographical characteristics that lead to psychic conflicts and resistance are ossified by the ongoing institutions of the social-control apparatus, and by the lack of any real moral or material alternatives. Choice occurs within a cage, whose bars are obscured and glimpsed with certainty only at the terminal points of the social-control process. It is the role of the radical criminologist to demystify control, and to join with those movements which seek to provide tangible alternatives and areas of choice.

Crime and deviancy from a socialist perspective are terms which encompass an uneven array of activities and behaviours – at times, behaviours which are quite inimical to socialism; at other times, rebellions against property and repression which are as justifiable in their consequences as they are primitive in this conception. Forms of illegality exist within the working class which are adaptive, collective in their accomplishment and progressive in their function (objects 'fall off the back of lorries', factory property metamorphosizes as bric-à-brac within the home). Forms of deviancy occur as attempts to create unhampered and livable space, the tyranny of the work-place and conventional sexuality being left momentarily behind. Marihuana and booze, pub-life and gay-bars, black music and white rhythm-and-blues – a tenderloin of the city where a sense of 'the possible' breaks through the facticity of what is. But just as one must discriminate actively between crimes which are cultural adaptations of the people, and crimes which derive from the brutalization of criminal and community alike, so we must clearly distinguish the contradictory nature of many of these adaptive manifestations. Deviant sexuality, for instance, will contain both positive and negative moments: the breakthrough from repression is distorted and beguiled by the reality from which it sprang. The intellectual task of a socialist criminology is to provide a materialist analysis of deviancy, and strategy which will link such theory to a real social practice. The goal is a socialism of diversity, the problems enormous but the goal even more so.

Notes

1 For a discussion of the place of romantic thought in deviancy theory, see Young (1972c).
2 For a description of the 'control perspective' as an organizing theme in the early work of the National Deviancy Conference, see chapter 1.
3 The discerning reader will note how the moral voyeurism of the enlightened middle-class sociologist was an inversion of the state of moral indignation which Albert Cohen (1965) succinctly defined by asking 'what effect does the propinquity of the wicked have on the peace of mind of the virtuous'.
4 In chapter 3 of *The Drugtakers* (Young, 1971a), I examine in detail the characteristics of such theories and their use as a conflict weapon. Suffice it to say that there are tendencies towards the kind of relativism which is criticized here. The ideological implications of correctional theory are to be developed in the introduction to *Myths of Crime* (Rock and Young, eds, 1975) and are touched on in Young (1973a).
5 This characterization of the new deviancy theory is presented in a highly articulated, ideal-typical fashion. It is, obviously, true that individual writers will often present a superior position on a few of these theoretical themes. The task is not, however, to pause over the limited features of difference within a general tradition, but to focus on a coherent theory which embodies this tradition. The difficulty here is that theoretical products are very rarely presented as a total theory. Protestations as to the limited nature of one's project, accompanied by a rapid change of emphasis, are not thereby rendered defensible, however (cf. Becker, 1974). One exception to this is Jack Douglas (1971a), who allows us to glimpse a vision of where such theoretical relativism might lead, if a way to break the relativism is not found in time.
6 The best examples of such a social contract are Becker and Horowitz (1971), in the essay on 'Culture and Civility', Becker (1968) in his comments on the solution to campus drug problems (campus authorities are to ignore them in order to avoid public scandal, in exchange for which the student should play it cool) and Jack Douglas (1971b) in *Crime and Justice in American Society*.

7 For a criticism of the mismanagement thesis, see Gouldner (1968). An excellent example of the thesis in action, in the drugs field, is Duster (1970), which I criticized in detail elsewhere (Young, 1972d). One of Gouldner's contentions – that reason for the critique of mismanagement was the desire for research-funding from federal agencies – is, however, misconceived. Labelling theory was mounted in opposition to all official social-control agencies – it was only as the theory was taken up and ideologically transformed that the position castigated by Gouldner ensued. This transformation was accompanied by a rejection of the Romanticism of labelling theory (where official intervention led to the corruption and degeneration of the 'natural deviant') to a positivism and an absorption into Fabian criminology which saw in stigmatization and social reaction merely another factor to be reckoned with in the *management* of deviancy. A concrete example of this is the government White Paper, *Children in Trouble*, Cmnd. 3601 (London: HMSO, 1968).

8 Idealism opposes two 'aetiologies' to positivism: capriciousness (as in Becker, 1963) or rational problem-solving (as in Lemert, 1972, especially chapter 3). Either way, the actor is detached from his structural position (and hence his problems) and apparently decides, in a social vacuum, the course of action which would best suit his needs.

9 This is the reverse of the positivistic 'correctional' approach which sees as its prime task the elimination of crime. For the idealists, the elimination of crime was seen as impossible, and indeed social reaction merely buttressed and amplified crime or deviant behaviour.

10 See Cicourel (1968) for a discussion of the self-fulfilling nature of the 'broken-home' hypothesis.

11 See Kitsuse and Cicourel (1963) for an attack on positivistic uses of the criminal statistics from a phenomenological perspective (tied into the social-reaction approach).

12 See Jack Douglas (1971a, chapter 4) for a thorough advocacy of this position.

13 See Everett Hughes's discussion of the notion of master status, as the identity which men may be ascribed and simultaneously embrace (Hughes, 1958). The idea is developed in Becker (1963), Duster (1970) and Douglas (1971a).

14 For the idea of the 'hierarchy of credibility', see Becker (1967).

15 The relationship between labelling theory and Romanticism is discussed by Gouldner (1968) and Young (1974a).

16 For the development of the debate over 'crimes without victims', see Schur (1965; 1969), Duster (1970) and Douglas (1971b).

17 To attack the new deviancy theory is not to deny the very real advances such a theoretical tradition achieved. E.g., interactionist work on the mentally subnormal and the physically handicapped has produced devastating yet neglected arguments against the genetic determinist theories, which currently appear to be experiencing a revival.

18 For essays illustrating this approach, see the two volumes emanating from the work of the National Deviancy Conference: Cohen (1971) and Taylor and Taylor (1973).

19 For a critique of the idealism of the hippie movement, alongside an appraisal of its potential importance, see Young (1973b).
20 And in stark contrast to the work of earlier Marxist thinkers, see Trotsky (1973a).
21 See Pearce (1973) for a discussion of the comparative cost of burglary, organized crime, tax evasion and illegal profit.
22 See *Solidarity*, pamphlet no. 33 (1969).
23 For an analysis of the reasons for the appeal of the mass media, see Young (1974b).
24 This is, of course, similar to the 'competitive individualism' ('institutionalized de-institutionalization') which Durkheim (for entirely different political purposes) attacked. See Young (1974b).
25 However confused Engels sometimes was in his use of these 'categories', he frequently distinguished between crimes which are the product of a total determinism and those which involve an element of voluntarism (extending as far as the point of a primitive class-consciousness). It is important to note that when Hirst (in chapter 8) cites Engels in his argument he quotes from the well-known passage (1844, p. 159), wherein crime appears in its totally determined form. This is not the only aetiology of crime identified by Engels.
26 An important contribution to our understanding of the ways in which the powerful immunize themselves from view (of the public in general, as well as from social control) is Stinchcombe's (1963) discussion of the development of public and private areas of space and living.
27 For a discussion of the concept of moral indignation in this light, illustrating the ways in which the mass media play on such deeply-felt needs, see Young (1974c).
28 The importance of the work of Richard Cloward and his associates, from *Delinquency and Opportunity* (Cloward and Ohlin, 1960) to *Regulating The Poor* (Piven and Cloward, 1972) is that they accord work (and opportunity) such a central place in their discussion of social control and social order, and the ways in which the State uses opportunity (together with welfare and relief) to maintain such 'order.'
29 For examination of contradictions in attitudes and sudden changes in attitudes in the course of action, see Blackburn (1969).
30 The work of Albert Cohen, particularly in his development of the notions of 'reaction-formation' (1955) and 'moral indignation' (1965), is, in part, an attempt to relate social and psychic conflicts.
31 See the discussion by Cohen (1974a) of the politics of depenalization, and in particular the point that reductions in the prison population are more likely in the context of economizing on the cost of maintaining 'high-security' prisons than they are as a result of any genuinely liberal attempts to eliminate prisons.
32 Gordon (1973) takes up an option which we might call 'Left rationalism' – where crime is seen as an obvious *economic* choice, given the disparities of wealth in the USA. It should be clear that the present analysis focuses on the problems of the seeming *irrationality* of crime and conformism.

3 Prospects for a radical criminology in the USA*

Tony Platt

Introduction

In the USA, we are presently witnessing and practising a radical criminology which has been developing in its latest form since the early 1960s and has begun to challenge the hegemonic domination of the field by liberal scholars. The roots of this radicalism are to be found in political struggles – the civil-rights movement, the anti-war movement, the student movement, third-world liberation struggles inside as well as outside the USA and anti-imperialist movements – and in the writings of participants in these struggles – George Jackson, Angela Davis, Eldridge Cleaver, Tom Hayden, Sam Melville, Bobby Seale, Huey Newton, Malcolm X and Ruchell Magee, to name a few.[1]

Radical scholarship in criminology by university-trained intellectuals is much less developed, due generally to the prevailing bourgeois ideology in the social sciences and the absence of a Marxist tradition,[2] and more specifically to the social-control orientation of applied criminology. The political events of the 1960s had a profound impact on some intellectuals and, in the last few years, a number of sociologists and criminologists have begun to develop a more radical analysis.[3]

The development of a radical criminology in the USA requires in part a full understanding of conventional criminology and its underlying ideology. This chapter attempts to identify and analyse the domain assumptions in criminology, as well as to sketch out the prospects for the development of a radical criminology.

Liberalism and criminology

The prevailing ideology which dominates research and theory in criminology is liberalism. Although there is a tradition of more conservative thinking (typified by the work of Ernest Hooton, Edward Banfield and Ralph Schwitzgebel), it is liberals who dominate the field – writing the most influential literature, serving as government consultants, staffing local and national commissions, working in think-tanks, and acting as brokers for large agencies and foundations. Liberal theory is by no means monolithic or consistent – there is considerable disagreement, for example, amongst conflict theorists (like Turk and Skolnick), labelling theorists (like Becker, Lemert and Scheff) and more traditional positivists (like Wolfgang, Cohen, Ohlin and Miller). At the same time, however, liberal theorists share many of the same domain assumptions and are unified by their common ideological functions.

State definition of crime

Most criminologists assume a State definition of crime, taking as their initial reference-point the legal code as the subject-matter of investigation and analysis.[4] Criminology has been and continues to be predominantly concerned with the background, reform and control of legally defined and prosecuted 'criminals'. The 'rehabilitative ideal' has so dominated American criminology that, comparatively speaking, the officially constituted agencies of the criminal law have not been subjected to serious criticism and research.[5] The positivist heritage in criminology, as David Matza has observed, serves to direct attention to the 'abnormal' aspects of criminal behaviour and to the construction of the methods of social control.[6]

Criminology as an academic discipline has typically reflected and reinforced the values of the State: in the late nineteenth century, it provided the brains trust and technical skills for major changes in legal and penal institutions; in the early part of this century, it helped to develop and legitimize bureaucratic professionalism and centralized forms of administration; and more recently, following widespread political conflict and rebellion in the 1960s, it proposed ways of refining and rationalizing the criminal justice system. In accepting the State and legal definition of crime, the scope of analysis has been constrained to exclude behaviour which is not legally defined as 'crime' (for example, imperialism, exploitation, racism and sexism) as well as behaviour which is not typically prosecuted (for example, tax-evasion, price-fixing, consumer fraud, government corruption, police homicides, etc.). The most serious crimes against the people, as the American Friends Service Committee noted, have been neglected:[7]

> Actions that clearly ought to be labelled 'criminal', because they bring the greatest harm to the greatest number, are in fact

accomplished officially by agencies of government. The overwhelming number of murders in this century has been committed by governments in wartime. Hundreds of unlawful killings by police go unprosecuted each year. The largest forceful acquisitions of property in the United States has been the theft of lands guaranteed by treaty to Indian tribes, thefts sponsored by the government. The largest number of dislocations, tantamount to kidnapping – the evacuation and internment of Japanese–Americans during World War II – was carried out by the government with the approval of the courts. Civil rights demonstrators, struggling to exercise their constitutional rights, have been repeatedly beaten and harrassed by police and sherriffs. And in the Vietnam war America has violated its Constitution and international law.

Reformism

A second component of liberalism is reformism: reform of criminals, reform of the criminal justice system, and even reform of society has always been a central goal of criminology. What distinguishes liberal reformism from more fundamental anti-capitalist criticisms of American society is the belief that it is possible to create a well-regulated, stable and humanitarian system of criminal justice under the present economic and political arrangements. Whilst it is true that criminologists have subjected social-control institutions (police, courts, prisons, etc.) to a variety of criticisms – including inefficiency, mismanagement, corruption and brutality – their reform proposals are invariably formulated within the framework of corporate capitalism and designed to shape new adjustments to existing political and economic conditions.[8]

Liberal reformism in criminology supports the extension of Welfare State capitalism and gradualist programmes of amelioration, whilst rejecting radical and violent forms of social and political change. This is often accompanied by a reliance on technocratic solutions to social problems and a belief that progress will occur through enlightening managers and policy-makers rather than by organizing the oppressed.[9] This kind of reformism has helped to create probation and parole, the juvenile court system, reformatories and half-way houses, the indeterminate sentence, adjustment and diagnostic centres, public defenders, youth service bureaus and many other 'reforms' which have served to strengthen the power of the State over the poor, third-world communities, and youth. As the American Friends Service Committee has observed, 'the legacy of a century of reform effort is an increasingly repressive penal system and overcrowded courts dispensing assembly-line justice'.[10]

Pragmatism and cynicism

A third quality of liberalism in criminology is a rejection of macroscopic theory and historical analysis, in favour of an emphasis on behaviourism, pragmatism and social engineering. The pragmatic perspective, as Stanley Cohen has observed in a critique of British criminology, is typically anti-theoretical and relativistic, seeing some good in all approaches and adopting an indiscriminate eclecticism.[11] This has led to a narrowing of scientific interest, to provincialism and parochialism, and even to a certain amount of anti-intellectualism in much criminological research.

Finally, liberalism in criminology is often characterized by an underlying cynicism and a lack of passion. The technocratic tradition in criminology, typified by the *Journal of Criminal Law, Criminology and Police Science*, characteristically encourages narrowly conceived, microscopic studies which fail to raise general moral and political questions about the nature of society. Even the more socially sensitive interactionist theorists are prone to a preoccupation with trivia and politically irresponsible hipsterism.[12] The criminological literature is for the most part dry, without passion, and replete with technical jargon. Criminologists are not reaching the general public with vital and exciting ideas, preferring instead to maintain an incestuous and closed discipline amongst professionals and academics. The most imaginative criminology has been written by 'criminals' – Brendan Behan, Claude Brown, Eldridge Cleaver, Angela Davis, George Jackson and Sam Melville, to name a few.

While liberal theorists are often critical of the established order, the lack of a historical and dialectical perspective inevitably sets the stage for nihilism or a wishy-washy relativism. In a recent paper on the future of the criminal justice system, Sheldon Messinger predicts the inevitable development of new strategies of coercion, intrusion and centralization. '*The* problem', he says, 'will be to keep control over the possibly monstrous system we [*sic*] are creating, a system that will be able to track and influence our activities at almost all times and places.'[13] Messinger's cynicism derives from his failure to analyse the historical and material conditions underlying State policies, to specify who benefits from repression, and to evaluate the possibility of mass movements developing to challenge the 'monstrous system'.[14]

Other liberal critics catalogue various inadequacies and injustices in the present system, but stop short of condemning capitalism or fall back to apologetic relativism. 'A virtue of our democratic [*sic*] system', writes Marvin Wolfgang in a recent paper, 'is its inefficiency and flexibility. Thus, although many criminal offenders may [*sic*] have been hurt themselves as victims of politico-corporate crime, they can be healed; and although the corporate system has been damaged, it is not destroyed.'[15] And in a recent critique of 'law and order', Jerome Skolnick points out that whilst conditions are bad, they could be worse: 'Even for those experiencing oppression the USA is not nearly so legally repressive as a nation might be.'[16]

The cynicism implicit in liberal ideology is closely tied to élitism and paternalism. Liberals do not envision ordinary working people as the motive force in history, but rather see enlightened experts fighting a losing battle against an 'ignorant public' and corrupt government. Skolnick, for example, concludes in his critique of 'law and order' that 'the public demands simple and straightforward solutions based on criminal sanctions both without comprehending the price such solutions entail and the complexity of the roots of crime'.[17] For Skolnick, the criminologists who helped to build and legitimize the present criminal justice system should now turn their attention to enlightening an ignorant, infantile and backward public!

The liberal emphasis on pragmatism, short-range solutions and ameliorism reveals an attitude of cynicism and defeatism concerning human potentiality and the possibility of far-ranging changes in society. This focus serves to exclude or underestimate the possibility of a radically different society in which co-operation replaces competition, where human values take precedence over property values, where exploitation, racism and sexism are eliminated, and where basic human needs are fulfilled. Liberal cynicism served to reinforce the malevolent view that radical change is utopian and visionary, thereby helping to impede the development of revolutionary social and political movements.

The structure of liberalism

The dominance of liberalism in criminology is not an accident or fashion but rather reflects fundamental relationships between the State, social institutions and the intellectual community. Of the many complex reasons for the prevalence of liberal ideology, the following structural conditions play a significant role:

Scholar–technician tradition

As Howard Zinn has pointed out, 'there is an underside to every age about which history does not often speak, because history is written from the records left by the privileged. We learn about politics from the political leaders, about economics from the entrepreneurs, about slavery from the plantation owners, about the thinking of an age from its intellectual elite.'[18] Similarly, we learn about the criminal justice system from judges, prison wardens, the police and government consultants. This is especially true of the earlier development of American criminology, when research and study were for the most part monopolized by persons intimately concerned with the regulation of crime. This scholar–technician tradition helped to produce a great deal of managerially-oriented research and 'official' history, that is a history written by the managers of and spokesmen for the criminal justice agencies. The emphasis in liberal analysis on pragmatism, professionalism and technocratic solutions is partly explained by this scholar–technician relationship.

Agency-determined research

The source and conditions of contemporary research-finding are a significant indicator of liberal analysis. Much criminological research is 'agency-determined' and subordinated to institutional interests, whereby the formulation of research problems, the scope of enquiry and the conditions of funding are determined by the 'agency' rather than by scholars.[19] The Ford Foundation has poured millions of dollars into carefully specified action-research in various criminal justice centres throughout the country. President Johnson's Crime Commission and several 'riot' commissions provided work and pre-determined problems for hundreds of lawyers and social scientists.[20] Another example of agency-determined research is the Law Enforcement Assistance Administration in the Department of Justice, created by the Safe Streets Act, 1968, with a budget of $63 million, which was estimated to be funding 'acceptable' research and programmes with an estimated budget of $1·75 billion in 1973.[21]

The rise of the 'multiversity' in recent years as a broker between scholars and funding agencies has served to strengthen and institutionalize relationships, in which scholars are encouraged to formulate research programmes which are of interest and politically acceptable to established agencies.[22] The research marketplace, dominated by large foundations and the government, is thus structured in such a way that research grants, prestige, facilities and other fringe benefits are more easily achieved by scholars who are willing to work on behalf of the State and its official institutions.

There are at least three major ethical dangers in agency-determined research, as Herbert Blumer has pointed out. First, it imposes restrictions on the freedom of scientific enquiry by predetermining the problems to be studied and by inhibiting academics from examining distasteful or controversial issues outside a particular range of possibilities. Second, notes Blumer, it is 'prone to treat lightly the interests and claims of people who are the objects of study or whose lives are to be changed by applying the results of the study. The interests and needs of the agency on whose behalf the research is to be undertaken have priority in governing the research enterprise.' And, third, agency-determined research tends to have a corrupting influence on scholars through the lure of research grants, travel, prestige and other benefits.[23] Accordingly, much of what passes as scholarly research in criminology tends to avoid issues which may lead to structural criticisms of American society and instead caters to facilitating the efficient and smooth operation of established systems.

Academic complicity

Whilst it is true that criminological research has been dominated by professional and funding interests, it should also be recognized that academics have generally been willing, even enthusiastic, victims of this kind of relationship. The image of social scientists as value-free technical experts ready for hire is one which social scientists have themselves helped to build. There are many criminologists who are not only willing to do 'agency-determined' research, but also share the agency's perspective on the problem to be studied.[24] The 'diluted liberalism', to use C. Wright Mills's apt term, of most research on juvenile delinquency, for example, results from the fact that researchers are typically prepared to accept prevailing (i.e. State) definitions of crime, to work within the premises of the criminal law, and to concur at least implicitly with those who make and enforce laws as to the nature and distribution of the 'criminal' population.

Compared with the role played by economists, political scientists and anthropologists in the formulation of domestic and foreign policies, criminologists have traditionally had minimum influence on national policy-making. This is quickly changing, however, as foundations and government agencies are now turning to criminologists for their expert help in developing new forms of social control following the political rebellions of the 1960s.[25] The willingness of academics to lend themselves to these kinds of demands arises from their occupational marginality and insecurity, as well as from their limited and specialized view of the world. The marginality of criminology as an academic discipline makes it vulnerable to 'agency-determined' research and co-optation by funding agencies. Furthermore, the training of most criminologists, with its emphasis on technical virtuosity and narrow specialization, serves to insulate them from broader considerations about the ethical and political consequences of their work.

Dirty workers

Finally, it should be remembered that many agencies within the criminal justice system (especially the police and prisons) are politically sensitive communities which resist intrusions from academic outsiders unless the proposed research is likely to serve their best interests. Research which undermines established policy is generally viewed as insensitive or subversive, aside from the fact that it serves to justify and harden administrators' suspicions of 'intellectuals'.[26] Most workers in the criminal justice system are linked to a professional system that relegates them to the lowest status in occupational and political hierarchies but also makes them vulnerable to public and political scandals. They are society's 'dirty workers', according to Lee Rainwater, who are 'increasingly caught between the silent middle class, which wants them to do the dirty work and keep quiet about it, and the objects of that dirty work, who refuse to continue to take it lying down'.[27] They are doomed to annual investigations, blue-ribbon commissions, ephemeral research studies, and endless volumes of propaganda and muck-raking. They live with the inevitability of professional mediocrity, poor salaries, uncomfortable living conditions, ungrateful 'clients', and tenuous links with established institutions. It is understandable that they should protect their fragile domain from intrusive research which is not supportive of their policies.

Prospects for a radical criminology

Breaking the chains of the past

> History offers no answer per se, it only offers a way of encouraging people to use their own minds to make their own history (William Appleman Williams, 1961).

The building of a radical perspective requires a self-critical analysis of criminology's development during the last 100 years as well as discovering continuities in earlier radical traditions in the USA. There are efforts currently under way to analyse the liberal underpinnings of criminology and its role in helping to manufacture and legitimize a repressive criminal justice system. *The New Criminology*, written by three English sociologists, is the first systematic critique of criminological theory.[28] David Gordon has written a more specialized critique on economic theory and crime,[29] Alexander Liazos and Alvin Gouldner on sociological theory and crime[30] and Richard Quinney on liberalism and criminology.[31]

Whilst it is important to break the chains of past historical errors, it is also important to rediscover our radical roots and, as Howard Zinn has suggested, to learn from concrete historical experiences where people's struggles were successful as well as failures, and men and women acted as heroes as well as culprits or fools.[32] The nationalism of the 1940s and repression of the 1950s have cut us off from a vigorous and important radical American history, a history which includes vigorous struggles against the criminal justice system and eloquent debates about the definition and meaning of 'criminality'. In addition to populist, nationalist and anarchist literature, there is also a large body of socialist criminological thought, neglected by criminologists but available in a variety of non-academic sources.[33] A radical criminology must come to terms with its historical roots.

The real criminals

A radical criminology requires a redefinition of subject-matter, concerns and commitments. In the past, we have been constrained by a legal definition of crime which restricts us to studying and ultimately controlling only legally-defined 'criminals'. We need a definition of crime which reflects the reality of a legal system based on power and privilege; to accept the legal definition of crime is to accept the fiction of neutral law.

As the Schwendingers propose in chapter 4, a radical perspective defines crime as a violation of politically-defined human rights: the truly egalitarian rights to decent food and shelter, to human dignity and self-determination, rather than the so-called right to compete for an unequal share of wealth and power.[34] A socialist, human-rights definition of crime frees us to examine imperialism, racism, capitalism, sexism and other systems of exploitation which contribute to human misery and deprive people of their human potentiality. The State and legal apparatus, rather than directing our investigations, should be a central focus of investigation as a criminogenic institution, involved in corruption, deception and crimes of genocide (Watergate, Indochina, etc.). Under the legal definition of crime, the solutions are primarily aimed at controlling the victims of exploitation (poor, third world, youth, women) who, as a consequence of their oppression, are channelled through the criminal justice system. Under a radical, human-rights definition, the solution to 'crime' lies in the revolutionary transformation of society and the elimination of economic and political systems of exploitation.

A radical criminology requires that we combat narrow specialization. Intellectual enquiry should not be carved up into artificial domains like pieces of private property. Antonio Gramsci, the Italian communist leader, said somewhere in his *Prison Notebooks* that all the essential questions of sociology are nothing other than questions of political science, i.e. who controls and benefits from the established order, how is power and wealth distributed, how can change occur, etc. Similarly, in criminology we are addressing major questions about how a society defines and controls exploitation. This is not to suggest that criminologists should only study system crimes like racism and imperialism; we also need to be concerned with the victims of system crimes and their managers (police, courts, prisons, etc.). A dialectical analysis requires an understanding of relationships between the two levels; to study one without the other can lead to either utopian or pragmatic solutions.

Radical theory

The poverty of radical theory is due to the repression of Marxist scholarship in universities and the liberal emphasis on pragmatism and social engineering. This is most apparent in the area of historiography. In an analysis of a recent book of essays on nineteenth-century urban history, Norman Birnbaum notes that 'the United States, insofar as major aspects of its past are concerned, remains an unknown country'.[35] Our ignorance of urban history is perhaps only surpassed by our ignorance of the origins and development of the criminal justice system and its relationship to economic and political conditions. The field of criminology is long overdue for serious historical scholarship. The history of the police is unwritten, with the exception of 'house' histories and a few microscopic case studies; the history of the criminal courts has been systematically neglected; we know very little about the modern prison system, its variations over time, its relationship to other institutions, or its impact on the lives of prisoners; finally, we know even less about the nature and range of 'criminal' behaviour in the USA before the twentieth century, even though European scholars have demonstrated the importance of such studies.[36] Radical criminologists recognize this deficiency and we are beginning to develop a historical analysis in our writings and courses, stressing a class and material perspective, so that we can break free from the myths which distort our views of the past and limit our vision of the future.[37]

The need for radical theory is not limited to historiography. We also need an analysis of the relationship between the criminal justice system and other sectors of the State apparatus, federal policy and strategy, of the organization and ideology of the criminal justice system labour force, of the illegal marketplace, of the political functions of the correctional system, and of efforts to organize mass movements in support of political prisoners and community control of the police. A variety of such studies are available, though they have not as yet been systematized or integrated into a consistent framework.[38]

Practice

Marxist philosophy holds that the most important problem does not lie in understanding the laws of the objective world and thus

> being able to explain it, but in applying the knowledge of these laws actively to change the world (Mao Tse-tung, *On Practice*).

A radical commitment to practice consists of 'practical critical activity' and participation in ongoing political struggles. Outside the academy, there has been a long tradition of radical practice against the State apparatus, from the labour and Wobbly struggles around the turn of the century, through the programmes of the socialist and communist parties, to civil rights, anti-war, student anti-imperialist and third-world struggles during the last twenty years. Criminologists' commitment to practice, on the other hand, has invariably been in the service of the State or liberal reformism.

In recent years, however, radical criminologists have begun to participate in political struggles by organizing educational conferences, supporting defendants in political trials, participating in campus protests, and helping to develop programmes such as community control of the police. This is a difficult task because criminologists, like intellectuals generally in advanced capitalist societies, suffer from élitism and arrogance as a result of our socialization, specialized training and privilege which insulates us from working people. Our practice must necessarily involve, therefore, breaking down this insulation and class distinction between mental and manual work. As the Chinese put it, it is not enough to 'look at the flowers while on horseback' or even 'dismounting to look at the flowers'. Shared struggle and solidarity must replace guilt and benevolence.

We should begin with our own workplace and with what we know best – the university. This can be done by challenging the fragmentation and exploitation of our own labour, by organizing for new social relations between professors, students and workers within the university, and by developing radical curricula. At the School of Criminology in Berkeley, we have developed courses on racism and crime, sexism and crime, the crimes of colonialism, Nixon's crime policies, crime control and the rise of the corporate liberal State, and socialist legal institutions in China and Cuba, as well as experimented with new forms of teaching such as collective projects, field-work, team-teaching and individualized grading. Recently, the Union of Radical Criminologists was formed and adopted the following statement of principles (Newsletter no. 1, Summer 1973):

> In this time of domestic and international repression, the activities of the police, the courts, the prison system, and other institutions of 'social control' have become an increasingly pervasive and significant factor of life in the United States. At the same time, the conventional approach to these institutions in the academic fields of criminology and sociology has served to both mystify their repressive function and to rationalize their

resistance to change. Criminology, in particular, has functioned in the United States and elsewhere as an integral part of the apparatus of state repression.

In response to this situation, a Union of Radical Criminologists has been formed in Berkeley, Califoria. The Union is designed to promote radical alternatives to the overwhelmingly racist and sexist ideology and practice that dominate criminology today. The Union welcomes any contribution that exposes the fundamental political and economic causes of crime and delinquency; that constructs definitions of crime which are in the interests of oppressed peoples and exploited classes; that critically analyse the legal and extra-legal strategies of coercion employed by the State and its supportive institutions; and that generally contributes to the development of a people's criminology.

Civic organizations, academics, state workers as well as various collectives have become interested in changing the theories and practices of criminology. Some of these individuals and groups are generating important radical insights and programs which should be widely disseminated. On that premise, the Union of Radical Criminologists will engage in collecting and distributing these ideas, materials, and other information for research, education, and political action.

Problems and dangers

Academic repression

If there is no struggle, there is no progress (Frederick Douglass)

The development of an authentically radical criminology inevitably risks repression. This will be no surprise to anybody except those who have illusions about academic freedom. In the USA there has never been a tradition of Marxist or otherwise radical scholarship within the university. Token radicals are occasionally hired to give an impression of benevolent tolerance or to appease student demands. But most radical scholars are excluded from university jobs and those who become radicalized in the course of their careers risk being fired or denied promotion to tenure.

This is not a new phenomenon, though in times of political turmoil academic repression becomes more explicit and crude. At a recent conference of socialist sociologists on the west coast, every participant told horror stories about the casualties of repression in his or her particular university. The victimization of radical intellectuals is not an individual problem but rather reflects on the political function of universities in capitalist societies. In Berkeley, the Regents and administration are presently planning to eliminate or drastically sanitize the School of Criminology because a minority of the faculty and a majority of the students have become radical critics of criminology and the criminal justice system. Rather than being surprised by academic repression, we need to develop strategies for exposing its purposes and supporting its victims.

Communication

> The leading of a mass of people to think coherently and in a unitary way about present-day reality is a 'philosophical' fact of much greater importance and originality than the discovery by a philosophical 'genius' of a new truth which remains the inheritance of small groups in intellectuals (Antonio Gramsci, 1970).

The development of a radical criminology requires a forum for critical writing, discussion and systematic analysis. An increasing amount of radical criminological writing has appeared in widely scattered publications during the last few years. At present, no single journal exists which can express the ideas underlying this distinct body of radical writing in a systematic and uncensored fashion. The highest priority, therefore, must be given to the creation of a radical journal, comparable to *Telos* in philosophy, the *Insurgent Sociologist*, and the *Review of Radical Political Economics*. Without such a forum, our capacity for sophisticated theory will be retarded and we will be vulnerable to critiques from established liberal journals. Hopefully, the Union of Radical Criminologists' *Crime and Social Justice*, will remedy this problem.

Liberal co-optation

> The viewpoint of critical criminology as it stands today probably cannot be said to be true or false. Rather, it is a bet on what empirical research and theoretical development in the field will reveal in the future – and in many ways I think the bet is not a bad one (Gresham Sykes, 1973).

> The extent to which these new approaches (radical and critical criminology) have or will invade current pedagogy and the malleable minds of young scholars is not yet clear. . . . But we may be witnessing an intellectual change of considerable consequence, and we must mark its development with careful analysis (Marvin Wolfgang, 1973).

With the rise of a radical criminology during the last few years, established criminologists have launched a counter-attack, using tactics of derision or co-optation. This suggests that radical criminology is developing legitimacy and challenging the hegemony of liberal theorists. We should welcome debates which allow us to publicize and discuss our perspective but at the same time we must avoid co-optation and concentrate on extending and systematizing an authentically radical criminology.

During 1973, Marvin Wolfgang, Albert Cohen and Gresham Sykes all wrote critiques of radical criminology.[39] Their essays indicate strategies of co-optation in at least three important ways. First, there is an attempt to define for us the content and parameters of a radical perspective before it has been fully developed. Miller reduces issues to schematic distinctions between left- and right-wing ideologies, including liberal concepts like 'decriminalization' and 'labelling' on the left, and blurring liberal and conservative strategies on the right. Sykes confuses labelling and conflict theorists with a Marxist perspective, whilst Wolfgang distinguishes between 'new criminology', 'critical criminology', and 'radical criminology'. It is interesting that these writers have already developed a typology and charts of our perspective before we have developed a systematic analysis. But we should not be distracted from our work by their attempts at parody.

Secondly, these writers have already begun to define what is acceptable and legitimate in radical criminology. As a sympathetic antagonist, Cohen warns us to avoid mystification and to examine our own ideological biases. Sykes points out that we have a tendency to 'degenerate into glib cynicism', to 'often use a model of social stratification that is either overly simplified or ambiguous', and to be absolutist. Skolnick says that we are on the right track but we go too far.[40] And Wolfgang finds a 'civility of language and a general grammar of rational discourse in the new criminology' in England that he finds 'missing in the radical sociology and criminology' in the USA. The English version, according to Wolfgang, is 'more logically adequate, more bound to reason, less polemically political'. As for radical criminology in the USA, 'there appears to be no linkage with the proletariat, and often the writings seem ahistorical as well as anti-scientific and anti-rational'. Our liberal critics have not only become instant experts on a correct class analysis, but they are also trying to divide us against each other.

Finally, these critics have incorporated into their own work a veneer and rhetoric of radicalism, whilst rejecting radical categories of analysis and radical practice. Walter Miller, for example, selects the best dishes from the left–right cafeteria:[41]

> The left provides the cutting edge of innovation, the capacity to isolate and identify those aspects of existing systems which are least adaptive, and the imagination and vision to devise new

> modes and new instrumentalities for accommodating emergent conditions. The right has the capacity to sense those elements of the established order that have strength, value, or continuing usefulness, to serve as a brake on over-rapid alteration of existing modes of adaptation, and to use what is valid in the past as a guide to the future. Through the dynamic clash between the two forces, new and valid adaptations may emerge.

Similarly, Sykes regards 'critical criminology' as not a 'bad bet', so long as it is consistent with 'the need to control crime'. And Wolfgang concludes that he is 'prepared to abandon neither the criminal offender nor the criminal components of the system but shall continue to use malleability of both as a cause for revision, reform and reconstruction.' In their counter-attack, our liberal critics have adopted a superficial radical rhetoric and accused us of bad manners, arrogance and crudeness. We should not get side-tracked into a debate on etiquette, for it is through our theory and practice, not manners, that our efforts will be judged. At the same time, we should continue to demonstrate to our constituencies how we differ from the 'defenders of order' on the fundamental issues of dialectical materialism, liberation movements and the struggle against capitalism and other forms of criminal exploitation.

Notes

* Paper originally prepared for conference organized by European Group for the Study of Deviance and Social Control, Florence, Italy, 13–16 September 1973.

1 See, for example, *The Autobiography of Malcolm X*, Eldridge Cleaver's *Soul on Ice*, Bobby Seale's *Seize The Time*, George Jackson's *Soledad Brother*, Tom Hayden's *Trial*, Sam Melville's *Letters from Attica*, Angela Davis's *If they Come in the Morning* and Huey Newton's *Revolutionary Suicide*.

2 See, for example, Cockburn and Blackburn (1969).

3 See, for example, Richard Quinney, *Critique of Legal Order: Crime Control in Capitalist Society*, (New York: Little, Brown, 1974); Quinney (1974); Charles E. Reasons (ed.), *The Criminologist: Crime and the Criminal*, California: Goodyear, 1974; Alan Wolfe (1973); Elliott Currie, 'Beyond criminology', *Issues in Criminology*, 9, 1, 1974, pp. 133–42; Herman and Julia Schwendinger, 'Defenders of order or guardians of human rights?', *Issues in Criminology*, 5, 2, 1970, pp. 123–57; Dorie Klein, 'The etiology of female crime: a review of the literature', *Issues in Criminology*, 8, 2, 1973, pp. 3–30; Alexander Liazos (1972, pp. 103–20); Robert Lefcourt (ed.), *Law against the People: Essays to Demystify Law, Order and the Courts*, New York: Vintage, 1971; and David Gordon (1971, pp. 51–75).

4 See the article by Herman and Julia Schwendinger, *loc. cit.*

5 Francis A. Allen (1964, pp. 125–7).

6 David Matza, (1964, chapter 1).

7 American Friends Service Committee (1971a, pp. 10–11).

8 See, generally, Alvin W. Gouldner (1968, pp. 103–11).

9 Irving Louis Horowitz, ed. (1967, p. 353).

10 American Friends Service Committee, *op. cit.*, p. 9.

11 See, generally, Stanley Cohen, in Rock and McIntosh (1974a).

12 See, for example, Gouldner, *loc. cit.*, and Barry Krisberg's book-review of Laud Humphreys's *Tearoom Trade* (Krisberg, 1972).

13 Sheldon Messinger (1973, p. 11).

14 For a more extensive critique of liberal cynicism, see Liazos (1972).

15 Marvin Wolfgang (1973, p. 21).
16 Jerome Skolnick (1972, p. 17).
17 Ibid., p. 18.
18 Howard Zinn (1970, p. 102).
19 Herbert Blumer (1967, pp. 153–7).
20 On the role of social scientists in riot commissions, see Anthony Platt and Jerome Skolnick (1971, pp. 3–54).
21 Joseph C. Goulden (1970, pp. 520–33).
22 See, for example, Clark Kerr (1961).
23 Blumer (1967, p. 165).
24 For an analogous critique of the complicity of intellectuals in American foreign policy, see Noam Chomsky (1967).
25 See, for example, Lee Webb (1971), and Mike Klare (1971, pp. 1–20, 66–73).
26 Controversial studies of official criminal justice agencies run the risk of hampering further academic investigations, as was apparently the case with Jerome Skolnick's (1966) study of a California police department, *Justice Without Trial.*
27 Lee Rainwater (1967, p. 2).
28 Ian Taylor, Paul Walton and Jock Young (1973).
29 See Gordon (1973).
30 See Liazos (1972) and Gouldner (1968).
31 See Quinney, *op. cit.*
32 Zinn (1970, p. 47).
33 See, for example, Bruce Rappaport and Peter Garabedian, 'American socialism and criminological thought', unpublished paper presented at the 1973 meetings of the Pacific Sociological Conference in Scottsdale, Arizona. For original examples of socialist writings on crime, see Eugene Debs, *Walls and Bars*, Chicago: Charles H. Kerr, 1973; Bill Haywood, *The Autobiography of Big Bill Haywood*, New York: International, 1969, pp. 327–38; and Kate Richards O'Hare, *In Prison*, New York: Alfred A. Knopf, 1923.
34 H. and J. Schwendinger, *op. cit.*
35 Stephan Thernstrom and Richard Sennett (1969, p. 422).
36 See, for example, George Rudé (1964), E. P. Thompson (1968, especially pp. 59–83); and Eric J. Hobsbawm (1959).
37 See, for example, Anthony Platt (1974); Herman and Julia Schwendinger (1974); Jon Snodgrass, 'The American criminological tradition: portraits of the men and ideology in a discipline', unpublished doctoral dissertation, 1972; Gregg L. Barak, 'In defense of the poor: the emergence of the public defender system in the United States (1900–1920)', unpublished doctoral dissertation, University of California, Berkeley, 1974; Elliot Currie (1973); and Ronald L. Boostrom, 'The personalization of evil: the emergence of American criminology, 1865–1910', unpublished doctoral dissertation, University of California, Berkeley, 1974.
38 In addition to studies previously cited, see also American Friends Service Committee (1971b); Erik Wright (1973); Susan Griffin (1971, pp. 26–35), and Anthony Platt and Lynn Cooper (1974).

39 Marvin Wolfgang (1973); Albert Cohen (1973); Walter Miller (1973, pp. 141–62); and Gresham Sykes (1973).
40 Skolnick (1972).
41 Miller (1973, p. 154).

4 Defenders of order or guardians of human rights?*

Herman and Julia Schwendinger

Crime, most modern sociologists agree, is behaviour which is defined by the legal codes and sanctioned by the institutions of criminal justice. It is generally agreed, moreover, that the legal definitions of crime and the criminal are ultimate standards for deciding whether a scholarly work should be considered criminological.[1] Because of this, the contention that imperialist war and racism are crimes is not only considered an unjustifiable imposition of values, but also an incompetent use of the notion of crime. In order to challenge this prevailing judgment, it is necessary to critically review some of the complex issues involved in a thirty-year-old controversy about the definition of crime.

1 The thirty-year-old controversy

Towards the end of the great depression, sociologists became involved in a controversy about legal definitions of crime and criminals. At least two developments stimulated the issue raised at the time: the rapid growth of a corporate liberal, sociological empiricism and the socially critical interest in white-collar crime. The former gave rise to what was primarily a scientific, methodological critique of the traditional legal definition. The second generated a substantive and ethical criticism. The positivist, reformist and traditionalist aspects of this controversy will be selectively reviewed, as they were represented by three of the chief participants: Thorstein Sellin (1938), Edwin Sutherland (1945) and Paul Tappan (1947).

a Positivism and the definition of crime

In the controversy, American sociologists and lawyers argued furiously about definitions which would distinguish crimes from other types of behaviour and criminals from other types of persons. It was observed that, traditionally, criminologists used definitions provided by the *criminal law* and, as a result, the domain of criminology was restricted to the study of behaviour encompassed by that law. However, one sociologist, Thorstein Sellin, declared in 1937 that if the criminologist is interested in developing a science of criminal behaviour, he must rid himself of the shackles forged by criminal law. Criminologists, Sellin added, should not permit non-scientists (e.g. lawyers or legislators) to fix the terms and boundaries of the scientific study of crime. Scientists have their own unique goals which include the achievement of causal theories of criminal behaviour. In evaluating the usefulness of legal definitions for scientific purposes, Sellin noted that such definitions merely denote 'external similarities' rather than 'natural properties' of criminal behaviour. The legal definitions, therefore, do not arise from the 'intrinsic nature' of the subject-matter at hand. They are, in Sellin's view, inappropriate as *scientific* definitions of crime (1938, pp. 20–21).

How can scientific definitions be developed? In an effort to answer this, Sellin pointed out that scientists are interested in universal relationships. Since 'conduct norms' represent such relationships (they 'are found wherever groups are found'), studies of conduct norms 'afford a sounder basis for the development of scientific categories than a study of crime as defined by the criminal law'. 'Such a study', Sellin added, 'would involve the isolation and classification of norms into *universal categories*, transcending political and other boundaries, a necessity imposed by the logic of science.' Conduct norms transcend any concrete group or institution such as the State, in Sellin's opinion, because 'they are not the creation of any normative group; they are not confined within political boundaries; they are not necessarily embodied in the law' (1938, p. 30).

Sellin's argument, it should be noted, was organized around the assumption that scientific definitions are determined by the goals and methods of the scientist *qua* scientist. The limits of Sellin's critique, consequently, focused primarily on the achievement of *scientific* explanations. Moreover, his scientific *standards* for constructing definitions of crime, including his preference for universal, and obviously formal categories and generalizations, are apparently devoid of any moral content: they coldly reflect allegedly intrinsic 'natural properties' of human behaviour and the 'necessity imposed by the logic of science'. Sellin's approach to the definition of crime is therefore ostensibly *value-free*.

b A reformist definition in which the State still reigns supreme

For many years European and American sociologists incorporated specific references to the ethical properties of criminal behaviour in their definitions of crime. Willem A. Bonger (1936, p. 5), for example, referred to crime as 'a serious anti-social act to which the state reacts consciously by inflicting pain'. Other terms such as 'social injury' were also used for this purpose (in the sense that crime involved socially injurious behaviour). In some cases these ethical defining criteria provided an implicit warrant for defining unethical practices as crimes, even though these practices might not have been covered by the criminal law. Because these ethical-defining criteria have implications for social policy, we shall regard statements embodying their usage as *reformist* definitions.

In 1945 another sociologist, Edwin Sutherland, added fuel to the controversy over the legal definition of crime. His research (1940, 1941) into unethical practices among businessmen and corporation managers produced evidence that, even though very injurious to the public, these practices were considered violations of the civil rather than criminal law. (Consequently, penalties for petty thieves resulted in imprisonment while businessmen who defrauded the public of large sums of money were given insignificant fines.) Sutherland asserted that some of these unethical business practices, while unlawful, were being classified as civil violations because legislators were subservient to powerful interest groups who wanted to avoid the social stigma and penal sanctions imposed under criminal law.

Other consequences followed official subservience. Since criminologists were traditionally limited to behaviour prescribed and proscribed by the criminal law, it followed that they were not assured of finding direct legal precedents[2] for the study of the unethical practices by groups powerful enough to fashion the law to their own advantage no matter *how socially injurious their practices might be.* In order to rectify this arbitrary restriction, Sutherland justifiably brushed aside the criteria used by legal scholars to differentiate between criminal and civil violations. He suggested (1945) that social scientists define crime on the basis of the more abstract notions of 'social injury' and 'legal sanctions'. The legal sanctions he had in mind were not restricted to criminal law but were to include those in civil law. And although legal scholars traditionally contended that civil violations were viewed as injuries to individual persons, Sutherland's definition of 'white-collar' *crime* obviously designated some civil violations as crimes because they were *social* injuries rather than private wrongs. Sutherland's use of the terms 'social injury' and 'legal sanctions' for defining crime was understandably not wholly endorsed by legal scholars.

Sutherland's argument, it should be noted, made no reference to scientific goals and standards. Unlike Sellin's ostensibly value-free approach, moreover, Sutherland's solution to the problem assumed that there exist *moral* criteria of social injury which can be used to formulate definitions of crime. However, when Sutherland insisted that the abstract notion of 'sanctions' be interpreted to mean legal sanctions, his conception of the relevant laws conjoined both criminal and civil laws. The domain of criminological enquiry, therefore, was extended beyond the limits of criminal law.

On the other hand, this domain still continued to reside within the limits of whatever was deemed socially injurious and sanctionable by the *State*. Although Sutherland never delineated his criteria of social injury in any organized manner, it can be inferred from comparisons between his different definitional statements that these criteria cannot exceed those legitimated by agents[3] of the State. In a definition, therefore, Sutherland (1949, p. 31) stated, 'The essential characteristic of crime is that it is behaviour which is prohibited by *the State* as an injury to *the State* and against which *the State* may react, at least as a last resort, by punishment.' (Our emphasis.)

c The traditionalist approach to the definition of crime

In 1947 Paul Tappan indignantly exclaimed that the criminal law contained the only justifiable definition of crime. Those who wanted to abandon this definition were saying, in his opinion: 'Off with the old criminology, on with the new orientation' (1947, p. 96). Since these laws also referred to procedural rules, Tappan added that a person could not be considered criminal until he was adjudicated and found guilty of a crime by the State. Were the new trends allowed to triumph, he foresaw potential hazards in that 'the rebel may enjoy a veritable orgy of delight in damning as criminal most anyone he pleases; one imagines that some experts would thus consign to the criminal classes any successful capitalistic businessman'. Such an approach to the definition of crime, Tappan explained, 'is not criminology. It is not social science'. Sutherland's approach, therefore, received methodological denunciation because the terms 'unfair', 'discrimination', 'injury to society', and so on, employed by the white-collar criminologist cannot, taken alone, differentiate criminal and non-criminal. Until redefined to mean certain actions they are merely epithets (1947, p. 99).

Tappan criticized Sellin's and Sutherland's universal concepts for the absence of criteria defining such terms as 'injurious'. Furthermore, he felt these concepts served to delude the sociologist into assuming that 'there is an absoluteness and permanence in this undefined category, lacking in the law'. 'It is unwise', Tappan added, 'for the social scientist ever to forget that all standards of social normation are relative, impermanent, variable. And they do not, certainly the law does not, arise out of mere fortuity or artifice.' As a consequence, he condemned Sellin's and Sutherland's 'vague omnibus concepts defining crime' as 'a blight upon either a legal system or a system of sociology that strives to be objective' (1947, p. 99). Indeed, he suspected subversive motives and attacked the critics of the legal definition for attempting to 'revolutionize' its concepts and infiltrate it with terms of 'propaganda'. He expressed fears that in the end 'the result may be fine indoctrination' (1947, p. 99).

Also, carrying his logic to an extreme, Tappan flatly stated that the only persons who could be *scientifically* studied as criminals were those found guilty by the judicial system. He recommended that sociologists study prison inmates because these persons were truly representative of the total population of criminal offenders. By this logic, persons who had committed a robbery, rape or murder but had not been adjudicated were not criminals; therefore, they could not be part of a representative sample of criminals. Although there were, without question, more persons who had violated laws and had not been adjudicated for their violations, Tappan stubbornly argued that the traditional legal definitions of crime were more precise and objective than other definitions. Tappan's argument is obviously unjustified. However, it verges on the absurd when we add to the roster of criminals at large, those who have been falsely imprisoned. In the case of these guiltless victims, Tappan's argument, in its practical effects, is also pernicious: according to this argument Dreyfus and other less celebrated individuals should have been counted and considered among the criminal population merely because they had been adjudicated and found guilty by the institutions of criminal justice, for the duration of their lives or at least until the State admits that it has allowed a miscarriage of justice.

Although Tappan also characterized crime as social injury, he made no explicit attempt to follow up his criticism of others by indicating the nature of its defining criteria. He merely deferred to the officials of the State as the only persons who could legitimately decide this question and write it into law. Their decisions, therefore, in addition to determining the specific populations of criminals to be studied by criminologists, also determined the scientific definitions of crime and criminals. Any scientific convention contradictory to this rule was considered illegitimate.

d The legalistic compromise between traditionalists and reformists

The definition of crime and the criminal cannot be wholly separated on an abstract level because the criminal cannot be defined without a definition of crime. The sharp differentiation between definitions of crime and criminals has arisen because of the objections to the legal operational criteria which are part of the traditionalist definition of crime. Sutherland objected to these operational criteria, suggesting that researchers can consider persons as criminals even though they have not been found guilty of a crime by legal procedures.[4]

It has been indicated (Quinney, 1970b, p. 4) that Sutherland's definition of crime as a violation of the *criminal law* has been the most acceptable to sociologists in America. In various places he suggested that crime encompasses the concepts of 'social injury', 'injury to the State', and both the civil and criminal law. If his reformist preference is distinguished by the insistence that criteria such as 'social injury' be explicitly used to define crime, then it is more accurate to say that traditionalist definitions of crime are generally used by sociologists today. In regard to the definitions of *crime*, therefore, Tappan has won the day.[5] On the other hand, as we shall see, Sutherland's less restrictive definition of the individual *criminal* prevails over the traditionalist approach. In a sense, sociologists have made an ambiguous compromise between the traditionalist and reformist solutions to the definitional problem.

Nevertheless, although phrased differently, almost all American criminologists today define crime and the criminal by specific or abstract references to definitions and/or sanctions administered by *the State*.[6] Because of this, the term 'legalistic' will be used to refer to the variety of legal definitions; and 'legalists' refers to those social scientists assuming the legal definition, however reformist or traditional it may be. It has been observed that definitions of crime are ultimate standards for deciding whether a scholarly work should be considered criminological. By extension, therefore, it can be claimed that the domain of the science of criminology is still, in spite of Sellin and the reformist approaches, determined by agents of the political State because legalistic definitions of crime are formulated by these agents.

2 Scientific standards for evaluating legalistic definitions

Each one of the scholars involved in the thirty-year-old controversy preferred particular defining criteria. Sellin, for example, indicated that 'universal' or 'causal' relationships should be signified by the definition of crime. Sutherland noted that criteria based on the notion of 'social injury' and 'sanction' were adequate. Tappan argued for procedural criteria which included reference to the rules by which the criminal law is instituted. He also contended that the legal definition is more precise than others. In order to evaluate these different critical attributes of the definition of crime, it will be shown that it is necessary to distinguish standards held useful by philosophers of science for scientific concept formation.[7] Since criminology is above all, the *scientific* study of the causes, characteristics, prevention and control of the incidence of criminal behaviour, it is necessary to further note why scientific standards must take precedence over legal standards in evaluating the definition of crime.

a Scientists have many definitions of crime

When their definitional usages are examined, it is found that social scientists are not bound by a single definition of crime; whatever definition is employed depends upon the types of activity the scientist is engaged in, or the kinds of relationships he is interested in.[8] Some of these activities require replication by other scientists and the definitions produced for this purpose operate like a manual of instructions which specifies the procedures for measuring phenomena. When a scientist is concerned with choosing amongst procedures for measuring crime, whether based on personal observation, self-report questionnaires, interview responses, or administrative processes involving police, judges and juries, he becomes involved in making a choice of an *operational* definition of crime.[9]

Operational definitions, however, do not exhaust the kinds of definitions used by scientists. There are times when it is helpful to explicate the meaning of categories such as 'social control', 'anomie', 'predatory crimes', or 'crimes against property'. In this case, a second or analytic definition might be in order.

In formulating useful, parsimonious and workable theories of empirical relationships, scientists have also found it necessary to use abbreviated forms of already understood meanings or to single out a particular property, relationship or function for convenient reference. Definitions of this type are called *nominal* definitions, and are even used in textbooks where crime is abstractly but not causally defined by reference to such properties or relations as 'social injury', 'sanction' or the 'actor's relation to the State'.

Finally, amongst the most important definitions used by scientists are the *real* definitions which signify diachronic and synchronic relationships between variables.[10] Only one member of this class, causal definitions, which signify the necessary and sufficient conditions for the existence of a phenomenon, are real definitions. Causal definitions may be very complex and actually consist of a general theory of the phenomena in question. This may not be apparent in such statements as 'anomy is the contradiction of all morality' (Durkheim, 1933, p. 431), 'crime is a symptom of social disorganization (Sutherland and Cressey, 1960, p. 23), or 'delinquency is an expression of "unsocialized aggression"' (Jenkins and Hewitt, 1944). However these statements are actually abbreviated expressions of general theories of criminal behaviour such as social disorganization theories or psychoanalytic theories.

The operational, analytic, nominal and real definitions by no means exhaust the variety of definitional statements which characterize the work of scientists but they do indicate that the problem of selecting an appropriate definition of crime is not as simple as the legal scholars might suggest in their desire to achieve a universal definition of crime.

Historically, scholars involved in the study of theoretical explanations of human relationships have justifiably developed new modes of thought which depart greatly from customary ways of thinking in other professions. Perhaps the single most important feature of this perspective is the requirement that scientific categories must lead directly or indirectly to the formulation of empirically testable relationships. In light of this injunction, analytic or nominal categories may not be arbitrary; they must be heuristic and accurately descriptive and ultimately refer to accurate assumptions about the nature of the real world.

Sellin apparently challenged the notion that the *real* definition of crime must be derived from legal statutes, however narrowly or loosely this mandate is defined. To our knowledge, however, no modern sociologist has fully considered the degree to which the empirical thrust of his challenge resides most importantly within the principle of the *autonomy of scientific inquiry*.[11] This principle was first raised and named by John Dewey (1938) as the 'autonomy of enquiry'. In developing this principle, Dewey was primarily concerned with encroachments by logicians and philosophers of science in the 'logic in use' developed by scientists (Kaplan, 1964, pp. 3–11). However, as Abraham Kaplan (1964, pp. 3–6) has indicated, the act of encroachment can have its sources in other professions as well. For example, the insistence by members of the legal profession that the law provides the only possible definition of crime is an unjustifiable encroachment by lawyers on the autonomy of science. But this disregards the fact that legal definitions do not meet standards of scientific inquiry. Legal definitions have questionable heuristic value when used nominally or analytically. Operationally, these definitions are unreliable and invalid. Legalistic real definitions are sheerly descriptive; they play a trivial and commonsensical role in advancing theories of criminal behaviour. To demonstrate the validity of these evaluations, we will systematically compare defining criteria based on the notions of 'precision', 'procedural law', and 'sanctions', with the standards regulating the proper use of operational, real, analytic and nominal definitions.

b *What is precision? Or . . . 'Is there a lawyer in the house?'*

In the light of the variation in types of scientific definitions, it is difficult to comprehend from a scientific point of view what is meant when lawyers or sociologists claim that the legal definition of crime is the only 'precise' or appropriately 'technical' term available for defining crime.[12] What definitional usage is being referred to? If crime is to be defined in terms of its causal relationships, then it is important to reiterate that these real definitions which may consist of such abbreviated terms as 'anomie' or 'maladjustment' are actually theories of crime or criminals. The notion of 'precision' in relation to this kind of definition has little meaning because, in a causal enquiry, sensitizing concepts and hypothetical consructs[13] are not only permissible but are often absolutely necessary for achievement of explanations with high systematic (theoretical) import.

Legal scholars may agree on the importance of standardizing a *single* legal definition for every type of crime and criminal, but it can be flatly stated that the standardization of causal definitions in this manner would destroy the free marketplace of scientific ideas and the ability of scientists to advance the state of knowledge in the field.[14]

c *Are the legalists referring to precise, operational definitions?*

For purposes of scientific enquiry, the legal definition is a curious formulation which mixes normative, descriptive and operational meanings without regard to their very different functions. But the plain fact is that even if we differentiated these meanings and employed them separately, they would still be inadequate for scientific purposes. To illustrate this, let us assume, for example, that legalists are actually talking about the use of the legal definition for operational purposes when they insist on its 'precise' characteristics.[15] If used for operational purposes, then the key meaning of the legal definition would be the stipulation that administrative rules (i.e. procedural law) supply the procedures by which the amount of crime is to be measured. It should be noted that the only possible measurements which are permitted by these rules take the form of official enumerations of adjudicated cases. When criminologists derive their statistical rates from these enumerations, they operationalize criminal behaviour in the *only way made possible by the law*.

Although the legality of a proposed definition of crime may be determined by a majority in a parliamentary situation (and, therefore, as we shall see later, subsuming the activity of social scientists under the prevailing dominant ideology), operational definitions cannot be considered appropriate by a majority vote from an empiricist's point of view. Instead, standards based on the concepts of scientific reliability and validity are used to evaluate their worthiness. On the basis of these standards, social scientists have for decades[16] criticized the use of officially adjudicated data as invalid and unreliable measures of criminal behaviour. As a result, some research scientists have, in practice, abandoned the operative meanings contained in the legalistic definitions of crime irrespective of their own explicit commitments to these definitions. Even the substantive contents of these categories, which are stipulated in the legal code, are not used in the operational definitions in present practice. All that remains of legalistic definitions is the *formal* acquiescence, on the part of researchers, to such conceptual categories as robbery, rape or homicide.[17]

d Political power as a determinant of precision

Recent works on 'crimes without victims' (Schur, 1965) or 'crimes of consumption' (Glaser, 1970, p. 138) are good indicators of the considerable disagreement regarding *ethical* standards to be used in the definition of crime and criminals. (These standards are usually subsumed under such categories as 'social injury'.) As an outcome, in practice, administrative procedures and sanctions preempt 'social injury' by default. In comparison with this ethical category, these standards are allegedly *relatively* more precise because they are operationally more reliable. (At least scholars *know* what is meant by the terms 'procedures' and 'sanctions', but there may exist little understanding of 'social injury'.) But even though this is undoubtedly the case, it should not obscure the fact that the degree of linguistic precision (i.e. social determinacy and usage) of the meanings of 'procedures' and 'sanctions' in this case, is actually dependent upon political processes. Ultimately, legal definitions assume certain political conditions for optimum operational precision. These conditions can be *best* fulfilled by a *totally* controlled society such as Orwell's 'Oceania' in *1984*. The 'reliability' of the measurements or descriptive relationships which are directly or indirectly defined by reference to administrative procedures and sanctions, is dependent upon administrative purpose and expertise; but the completeness of its execution is dependent on political power. This is why it can be assumed that with regard to the legal definition: political power determines the precision of the definition and the measurement of the phenomena.

e The real definitions of legal definitions and legal definitions as real definitions

Towards the beginning of criminology textbooks, a legalistic-nominal definition is usually offered. In this statement the authors single out certain ethical properties of criminal behaviour and/or limit themselves to consideration of the relationships between criminal behaviour and sanctioning agencies. Although these nominal definitions are sometimes treated as real or causal definitions, there are a number of reasons why they are merely nominal. Behaviour which is legally defined as crime, according to the views of most persons trained in an empiricist tradition, had existed *before* its legal definition was formulated.[18] The *behaviour*[19] can, therefore, be justifiably regarded as a determinant and, as such, it is not the law which determines crime, but *crime which determines the law*.[20] In light of this, it is again highly misleading to use legalistic definitions (which refer, for example, to sanctions) as real definitions, in spite of the fact that sanctioning processes feed back and influence this behaviour over time.

Sociologists are explicating and redefining the legal definition for purposes that are quite foreign to its original, legalistic usage. One reason for this is that, once formed, legally established sanctioning processes do influence criminal behaviour. And the nature of this influence is being enquired into by sociologists today. The reworking of the definition is necessary because complex, and often discretionary, operational processes, which influence ongoing characteristics of criminal behaviour, are very inadequately symbolized in the original legal statement.[21]

Are legal definitions real, i.e. causal definitions? In the process of ascertaining the effects of the institutions of criminal justice on criminals, it has become imperative to differentiate criminals who have been sanctioned by law from those who have avoided sanctions. But this is not the only reason why this differentiation is important. The certain knowledge that there are vast numbers of criminals 'at large' has long generated serious questions about the adequacy of those theories which have only been confirmed by the use of official statistics. In light of this, scientists are fully justified in rejecting the logic of the argument that a criminal's status can only be defined legalistically. They are justified in viewing this matter as an *empirical* question in order to settle outstanding issues in their field. In the view of these scientists, the efficacy of calling 'criminal' those who have acted as such but who have not been adjudicated and found guilty of their violations can be substantiated by empirical test. Canons of logic cannot be substituted for empirical criteria in making this assessment.[22] Criminologists interested in the study of the *institutions of criminal justice* often use the notion of sanction to define crime. This notion is particularly plausible as a defining criterion because it is easily related to everyday experiences. One illustration of this is Austin T. Turk's explication of 'the sanctioning process' as 'generic'[23] to the word *criminal*. Turk (1969, p. 22) indicates that the sanctioning process is observed when 'somebody asserts a right-wrong; someone fails to conform; and some mode of coercion is used in the course of defining a violator and depriving him of something, even if it is little more than a few minutes spent in sending a lawyer to bat.' It is suggested here, however, that if social scientists are interested in real definitions of the institutions of criminal justice, that they organize their defining criteria with reference to a *general theory* of the State (particularly in capitalist and socialist societies) rather than simple properties of microscopic and often contractually governed interpersonal relationships.

In constructing real definitions of the causes or control of crime, therefore, there is no absolute necessity for utilizing the notion of sanction as a defining criterion. In light of this, a general definition which identifies crime as behaviour which is sanctioned by the State is highly misleading. Just as misleading, however, is the notion that sanction is intrinsically necessary for *any* type of scientific definition of crime.

f Are sanctions generic?

As we have noted, neither positivistic nor legalistic arguments can provide adequate explanations for the existence of a generally accepted notion that sanction is generic for defining crime. This notion, as we have seen, is certainly not necessary for scientific operational definitions of criminals. Nor is it necessarily essential to real definitions. It may be useful for defining particular kinds of relationships between the criminal and the State, but there are undoubtedly instances where sanctions are an incidental aspect of this relationship. If we think in terms of the general relationship between the State and crime, rather than the State and the individual criminal, sanctions may be even less significant than other kinds of relationships. To some extent this fact has been obscured by the unanalysed, metaphorical use of the term sanction to symbolize the extremely complex relationships between crime and the State.

Regardless of this unsubstantiated claim, authors of most textbook definitions identify crime by singling out sanctioning processes. To argue that crime must be defined in terms of sanction, however, is to insist that sanctions are absolutely necessary for understanding, predicting, preventing and/or controlling crime. Studies in the sociology of law and criminal behaviour indicate that this necessity may exist in some cases,[24] but it has never been demonstrated that it holds as a general rule.

Humanistic scholars, including scientists and non-scientists, have been tantalized by the possibility that behaviour which is injurious to the great majority of persons in society can be prevented or controlled by means other than punishment of individuals. Psychologists and psychiatrists have asked whether there are other re-educative or rehabilitative procedures which can replace sanctioning processes as we have traditionally come to understand them. Sociologists, from their perspective, have asked whether the radical restructuring of social institutions or systems can eliminate crime more effectively and fairly than traditional and repressive forms of social control. Whatever one may think of the efficacy of any one specific proposal in this respect, it is quite clear that most run counter to the legislative definitions regarding the treatment of crime. They, more often than not, also contradict standards which legislators currently employ in defining criminal behaviour. By contending that sanctions are generic to the definition of crime, legalists discourage the possibility of viewing crime from very different points of view and limit the definitions of crime to those established by the current occupants of the houses of political power. Political power, as we have seen, makes procedural criteria allegedly more 'precise' for scientific purposes than ethical criteria. As a parallel to this, power also seems to make sanctions generic to the definition of crime.

The differentiation of the empirical properties of social relationships is strongly dependent upon the theoretical intentions of the social scientist. Because of this, it can be said that just as the knowledge of the empirical properties of social phenomena does *not* arise (as Sellin contends) 'intrinsically from the nature of the subject matter', sanctioning processes are not more intrinsic to the definition of crime than any other possible relationship. This does not mean that sanctions are extraneous to all theoretical purposes. *This will always depend upon the theoretical perspective involved.*

g The critical role of ethical criteria in relation to sanctions

Sellin was concerned with developing a general strategy for explaining crime while Sutherland was interested in explaining a particular type of crime (i.e. white-collar crime). When Sellin's proposals in the controversy over the definition of crime are compared with Sutherland's, therefore, it can be shown that the differences between these scholars are due less to their general orientation than to their different purposes; they were concerned with problems on disparate levels of specificity. In other writings, Sutherland did propose a general, 'normative conflict'[25] theory of crime, which was derived from the same metatheoretical assumptions underlying Sellin's 'culture-conflict' theory. The similarities in orientation between these scholars also become salient when it is realized that Sutherland was not alone in singling out sanctions as an essential feature of the phenomena he was interested in. Sellin, it is true, was concerned with more inclusive normative phenomena than legally codified norms, but in turning his attention to the concrete problem of comparing legal and non-legal norms, he suggested that the degree of *sanction* be used as a *universal* standard of comparison (1938, pp. 23–45).

Perhaps the most revealing part of the controversy about the legal definition is the degree to which theoretical sociologists like Sellin and Sutherland avoided the confrontation with standards which could have been used in fully evaluating *the moral justifications* of legal codes. Even Sutherland, who did most to question the justification for the separation between civil and criminal codes, went to great pains to show that his interpretation of white-collar crime was in *accord* with established legal precedents. However, if ruling classes and powerful interest groups are able to manipulate legislators to their own advantage, isn't it possible that there are instances of socially injurious behaviour which have no legal precedents? Consider, further, the chance that there are practices by men of power which are highly injurious to most of mankind and which are neither defined nor sanctioned by civil or criminal laws, such as, for example, genocide and economic exploitation. Isn't it apparent, if Sutherland had consistently explored the use of ethical categories like social injury, that he would have concluded that there are, on one hand, socially non-injurious acts which are defined as crimes and, on the other, socially injurious acts which are nevertheless not defined as either civil or criminal violations?

It is in relation to these logical possibilities that the ideological function of legal sanctions (as a defining criterion) is fully exposed. If the *ethical* criteria of 'social injury', 'public wrong', or 'anti-social behaviour' are not explicated, then the existent *ethical standpoint of the State is taken as a given* when the criterion of sanctions by the State is also used in the definitions of crime. This is why the meanings of such categories as social injury are so critical for the definition of crime.

In light of this, it can be concluded that, in the controversy over the definition of crime, the only argument which transcended the State was ostensibly value-free,[26] whilst, in addition, the only argument which admitted moral criteria, considered these criteria applicable solely if they were embodied in the law. What explains the extreme selectivity which is manifest in the controversy over the definition of crime? Why hasn't any American sociologist proposed that these definitions of crime are *not* the only possible definitions? The answers to these questions and those raised at the conclusion of the previous section will be suggested in the form of a very terse review of the historical development of the *ideological* perspective which has unduly dampened the controversy over the legal definition of crime.

3 Ideological aspects of the controversy over the definition of crime

(*a*) *Ideological influences on the usage of categories*

It can be readily understood that, in the desire to examine and utilize apparently more precise categories, scholars might overlook the degree to which their own scientific behaviour is determined by the same political conditions which gave rise to legal definitions in use. But this is insufficient for explaining why conventional political categories have succeeded in superseding all other ethical, as well as professional, criteria for defining the nature of crime. Nor can inertia supply the reason for the supremacy of conventional political standards. These political standards are more than an encroachment on the autonomy of science. They are also in contradiction to the truly scientific and humanistic mandate that it is not the professional's function to be a mere technician who complies, wittingly or unwittingly, with established authorities. According to this mandate every professional is morally responsible for his own actions: this responsibility cannot be justifiably delegated to agents of the State.

(*b*) *Corporate liberalism and metatheoretical categories*

Are non-legal definitions of crime currently in use amongst sociologists? At one point in his argument, Sellin (1938, p. 8) declared that 'Innumerable definitions of crime have been offered which if not read *in their context* would appear to go beyond the legal definition. Upon examination, however, almost all of them prove to be the legal norms clothed in sociological language.' (Our emphasis.) This observation is as accurate and observable today[27] as it was in 1937. Less clear, however, is the degree to which highly formal and nominal definitions of crime have persisted even in cases where scholars have explicitly repudiated their use.

American sociology abounds in formal and nominalist categories which are metatheoretical in nature. It is often not realized that the most influential categories of this type have been generated only after scholars have reflected on the meanings of previous theoretical works and singled out properties or relationships which seem to have been used time and time again by different theorists. Therefore, although these properties or relationships are nominally defined, they are not to be considered arbitrary distinctions. Instead, they refer, indirectly, to the theories of human behaviour which have claimed the attention of sociological interest for some time. Such categories as 'conduct norms' or 'normative conflict' are the outcomes of this process. For purposes of analysis, they can be termed 'metatheoretical categories' because they are derived by abstracting relationships designated by theories.[28]

The metatheoretical categories which maintain legalistic definitions of crime were generated during the formative years of sociology. Works which mark the beginning and end of this period are Lester Ward's *Dynamic Sociology* (1883) and William F. Ogburn's *Social Change* (1922). During this time, traditional liberal assumptions as to the nature of man and society were substantially altered by leading scholars, not only in sociology and criminology but in every other discipline and professional field. As a consequence, a new variant of the liberal ideology, corporate liberalism, came into being.[29] In sociology, the leading American scholars[30] involved in the modern reconstruction of liberalism included besides the above-mentioned, Albion Small, Frank Giddings, Edward A. Ross, W. I. Thomas, Robert E. Park and Ernest W. Burgess, amongst others.

Particularly after the publication of a series of essays by Ross beginning in 1895,[31] scholars urged the study of every conceivable type of social relationship from within the framework of a liberal-functionalist metatheory of *social control*. These essays accelerated an intellectual development which culminated in the systematic combination of corporate liberal concepts of social control with those derived from the classical liberal notion of the harmony of interests.[32] This combination was utilized in order to solve what sociologists call the 'problem of social integration' or synonymously, 'the problem of *order*'.[33]

In formulating solutions to the problem of integration, American and European scholars were spurred by the extraordinary social instabilities which accompanied the rise of monopoly capitalism. During the last quarter of the nineteenth century, the USA, for example, sporadically experienced sixteen years of depressions and recessions (Mitchell, 1927). From the turn of the century until the First World War, the USA was still economically unstable (Kolko, 1967); it was characterized by extensive immigration and rapid industrial change. There was no diminution of industrial violence (Adamic, 1931), and the very foundations of American capitalism appeared to be threatened by the emergence of progressive movements, labour unions and socialist parties (Weinstein, 1968). Some, but not all members of these movements, were also militantly opposed to the new and aggressive foreign policies which were instituted by the American government (Preston, 1963). These policies vigorously supported the penetration of economic markets overseas with every means possible including armed forces (Williams, 1961).

American sociologists from Ward onwards utilized their theoretical ideas to criticize socialist doctrines, as well as the 'effete minds' (i.e. intellectuals)[34] who opposed American imperialist wars. They also attacked the laissez-faire capitalist ('the Robber Barons') and the older laissez-faire liberal theorists like Herbert Spencer, because they opposed political regulation of the economy. This proposal was substantiated by their new conceptions of man and society. These conceptions admitted the existence of 'the perpetual clash of interest groups' but suggested ways of stabilizing and restraining this conflict. The expanded powers of the State, it was claimed, would enable it to perform an effective role in reconciling or regulating conflicts between 'interest groups' within the framework of capitalism.

The American scholars also turned their attention toward ways of maintaining established institutions such as the family. In the process, they developed theories and metatheories focusing on solutions to the problem of integration from their new ideological point of view. In time, their efforts produced categories and generalizations which led directly to the modern liberal-functionalist orientations called pluralism and structural-functionalism.

Space limitations preclude an adequate discussion of these general developments or consideration of the role they played in contributing to Sellin's interpretation of the concept of norms. It can be demonstrated, however, that his concept was derived from a very general functionalist orientation which implicitly assumed that certain 'optimum' social relationships were functionally imperative to the associated life of man. These relationships were called 'natural' or 'normal' states. And the functional prerequisites for these states were utilized as criteria for evaluating all behaviour which was considered inimical to optimum functioning (i.e. a gradually changing but stable order). In theory, these prerequisites were usually hypostatized as 'norms'; and unnatural or *abnormal* conduct was perceived as a *normative* departure or deviation from 'normative expectations'.[35] Within this general perspective, normal societies were actually depicted as being repressive. They repressed and channelled the anarchic, egotistic tendencies allegedly inherent in the nature of man by the 'judicious' application of rewards and sanctions.

(*c*) *Technocratic doctrines*

Side by side with the development of basic corporate liberal orientations, the early American sociologists also professed and greatly elaborated the *technocratic doctrines* which were expressed in rudimentary form by Henri Saint-Simon.[36] These doctrines can be regarded as an independent system of ideas[37] but they were developed in conjunction with an intellectual tradition which can be called 'liberal syndicalism'.[38]

Basic to the definition of technology is the vision of a society managed not by common people but by experts or enlightened leaders who are highly informed by expert advisors.[39] Another hallmark of technocratic-doctrine is the implicit use of the norms of established institutions as standards for identifying 'abnormal', 'pathological' or 'deviant' behaviour. A further indicator of the use of technocratic doctrines is the contention that sociologists are involved in a *value-free* or ideologically neutral enterprise in the very shadow of their simultaneous subscription to established norms.[40]

What was the state of criminology almost two decades after the formative period? At the time when Sellin challenged the legal definition of crime, sociology had long been rooted in corporate liberal theories of human relationships. In addition, crime was perceived as but one instance of the structural relationships within the larger and more general culture. Criminal personalities were seen as little more than simple homologues of these social relationships.[41] Solutions to the problem of integration also encompassed the concepts of criminal behaviour. These stressed the creation and maintenance of normative consensus. (Conflict was to be minimized, reconciled or regulated; consensus was to be maximized because of its role as a functional imperative to the maintenance of a stable and socially integrated order.) Conflict and disorganization! These key words signified the preconditions for crime. Consensus, harmony and equilibrium! These terms referred to stability and order.

(*d*) *Value-free sociology*

In the light of these developments it is possible to understand the essence of Sellin's seemingly radical proposal, as well as his *complementary*, rather than contradictory, relation with Sutherland's legalistic position. Sellin proposed, in essence, that the organizing principles for examining and explaining the nature of criminal behaviour be derived from the highly general propositions and categories which were being used by sociologists at the time. By proposing that the concept 'conduct norm' be used instead of the legal definition, Sellin was simply advising sociologists that they would not get far with the highly descriptive contents of the legal definitions. If they wanted to explain crime, the notion of conduct norms was a key to unlocking a whole stockpile of axioms, mechanisms and categories derived from the theories which corporate liberal scholars had found useful for solving the problem of integration.

Armed with this strategy, Sellin did *not* advocate the elimination of the legal definition. On the contrary, he (1938, p. 367) specifically suggested that this definition be used to indicate *criminal* departures from the conduct norms of 'political groups'. (These norms, he observed, were different from other norms because they are legally codified.) But Sellin also suggested that the scientific explanation of these departures would have to take into account theoretical concepts which emerged from the study of both legal *and* non-legal norms. He proposed further that, since the relation between the criminal and civil law is ambiguous from this larger point of view, the criminologist's 'concern with *crime norms* and their violations may well be *broadened to include legal conduct norms* embodied in *the civil law*' (1938, p. 39, our emphasis). Thus, even though Sellin began his journey from a more abstract starting-point, he arrived at the same destination as Sutherland.[42] This is not surprising, considering that both scholars were using similar metatheoretical assumptions in approaching the subject of criminal behaviour.

At bottom, therefore, Sellin's argument reinforced rather than challenged the broader legalistic approach which had been developed by Sutherland. It did not challenge this approach because it was woven from the same corporate liberal and technocratic ideologies which had emerged amongst the founders of American sociology. These founders constructed a view of the world which was of service to the new corporate liberal State and implicitly justified the use of criteria which favoured the maintenance of established institutions. In the metatheory of social control, departures from norms of established institutions were 'abnormal' and conducive to social instability. Normative sanctions, therefore, were considered an important mode of social integration. Individual behaviour had to be controlled by these sanctions if the established institutions were to survive.

Guided by the metatheory of social control, many American criminologists functioned as technocratic 'consultants' who spent their lives gathering information which would be of use to the men who managed existing institutions, whether they were aware of this or not. The profession of ideological neutrality on their part was by no means a guarantee of this neutrality. Instead, it was one of the great myths which prevented principled scholars from being aware of the ideological character of their basic theoretical assumptions.[43]

4 A modern humanistic alternative

Because of space limitations, the final section of this chapter will not attempt a definitive alternative to the legal definition. Instead, there will be suggested, in desperate brevity, what is hoped will be useful points of departure for those interested in exploring new approaches to this problem. It is felt that this discussion will have served a useful purpose if it stimulates the development of a number of alternative approaches at this time,[44] when so many received doctrines are being called into question.[45]

(*a*) *Moral criteria for definitions of crimes*

No scholar involved in the controversy about the definitions of crime has been able to avoid direct or indirect use of moral standards in a solution to this problem. In spite of this, the choices of defining criteria have been accompanied by a technocratic incapacity to confront the moral implications of this selection. It is not clear, for example, that the acceptance of procedural law as a defining criterion delegates personal responsibility to agents of the State. But this delegation is no less a moral act and therefore cannot avoid complicity in the actual definitions made by official agents. Just as moral is the explicit use of sanctions or the implicit use of other defining criteria,[46] derived from functional imperatives of established institutions or political economies. In light of this, the claim that value judgments have no place in the formulation of the definition of crime is without foundation.

An alternative solution to the definition of crime should openly face the moral issues presented by this definitional dilemma. Traditionally, these issues have been inadequately represented by such unanalysed terms as 'social injury', 'anti-social act' or 'public wrongs'. But how does one confront the problem of explicating 'social injury' or 'public wrongs'? Is this done by reference to the functional imperatives of social institutions or by the historically determined rights of individuals? In our opinion, the latter is the only humanistic criterion which can be used for this purpose.

There has been an expansion of the concept of human rights throughout history. And political events have made it possible, at this time, to insist on the inclusion of standards clustered around modern egalitarian principles, as well as enduring standards such as the right to be secure in one's own person, the right to speak one's mind, and the right to assemble freely. We refer to these ideas as modern because they are to be distinguished from those fashioned in the eighteenth century when a rising middle class formulated a challenge to the economic prerogatives of feudal aristocracies. At that time, the functional imperatives of the patriarchal family, price-making market and political State were reified, by recourse to natural law, as basic human needs. In this reified form, equality was primarily perceived as the immutable right to compete *equally* with others for a position in social, economic and political spheres of life. In the context of our modern political and economic institutions, however, competitive equality has not had, as an empirical outcome, the furtherance of human equality. Instead, it has been used to justify inequalities between the sexes, classes, races and nations.

Life in industrialized nations over the last 200 years has clearly indicated that rhetoric regarding the equality of opportunities cannot preserve the spirit of the egalitarian credo. Nor can liberalism, the ideology which, above all others, has laid claim to the concept of equality of opportunity, be used in defence of egalitarianism. Liberalism is, at bottom, a highly élitist ideology. It has justified and helped perpetuate social inequality in the name of equality. It was in the name of free competition and laissez-faire liberalism, for example, that Western nations converted the people and natural resources in South America, Asia and Africa into sources of cheap labour and raw materials during the nineteenth and twentieth centuries.[47] Because of the use of the concept of equality of opportunity by liberals, ostensibly egalitarian notions cannot be taken for granted. They must be subjected to careful scrutiny.

When the concept of equality of opportunity is analysed, it is found that it does not refer to egalitarian principles at all. Instead, it refers to principles of equity or fairness which should govern the ways in which social *inequality* is instituted in our society. In its most defensible form it stipulates that meritorious standards rather than lineage, race or other 'natural' criteria should regulate the unequal distribution of the goods of life. But there is no society on the face of this earth which actually distributes the goods of life on the basis of differences in *natural* talents of individuals. The differences which actually determine the distribution of rewards are for the most part socially determined. As a consequence, even in democratic societies, the notion of equality of opportunity serves more as a justification for gross inequalities established on the basis of class, race, sex, ethnicity and other grounds. Within the framework of liberalism, moreover, equality of opportunity is merely one amongst many standards which justifies an élitist morality. This morality can rightfully claim that each individual should be treated equally, but, in practice, some preferred criterion is always inserted to guarantee that some men are treated more equally than others.[48]

In opposition to the ever-increasing demand for equaliterianism, élitist social scientists have formulated theoretical justifications for social inequality.[49] We deny the ethical and empirical validity of these theoretical justifications! Irrespective of claims to the contrary (Warner, 1949; Moore, 1963), there is no universal moral rule or empirical property which is inherent to man or society which makes social inequality a functional necessity. Above all, there is no valid moral or empirical justification for the outstanding forms of social inequality in existence today including economic, racial and sexual inequality. If the traditional egalitarian principle that *all* human beings are to be provided the opportunity for the free development of their potentialities is to be achieved in modern industrial societies, then persons must be regarded as more than objects who are to be 'treated equally' by institutions of social control. All persons must be guaranteed the fundamental prerequisites for well-being, including food, shelter, clothing, medical services, challenging work and recreational experiences, as well as security from predatory individuals or repressive and imperialistic social élites. These material requirements, basic services and enjoyable relationships are not to be regarded as rewards or privileges.[50] They are rights!

In formulating a conception of human rights which can be useful to criminologists, it is important to recognize the political *limits* of the ethical doctrine of *equal intrinsic value* when applied to human beings. This doctrine asserts generally that all men are to be regarded not as means but as *ends* in themselves. This doctrine has been found useful by philosophers and other scholars in formulating a logically consistent defence of egalitarian principles which subordinates criteria based on social expedience and utilitarian logic, to those based on some kind of 'ultimate', irreducible, 'natural' equality of men. However, although philosophers of ethics and legal scholars may require logically consistent and persuasive justifications for equality (and commonsense may contend that men are born free and equal), the plain fact is that throughout all history, equality has been decisively defended, not on the basis of formal logic but on *political* grounds. Most of the inhabitants of this earth, furthermore, have never been born free and equal. The achievement of freedom and equality has been won at great cost to individuals and their families.

By delineating the naturally intrinsic qualities of men, philosophers have attempted to transcend the politically controversial issues posed by the abrogation of human rights. Their natural-law principles, however, cannot be substituted for a substantive and historically relevant interpretation of human rights which takes into account the political ideals men have, as well as the kinds of social institutions which can nullify or realize these ideals. It is not enough to provide good reasons for the achievement of broader human rights or to catalogue these rights. Criminologists must be able to identify those forms of individuals' behaviour and social institutions which should be engaged in order to defend human rights. To defend human rights, criminologists must be able to sufficiently identify the violations of these rights – by whom and against whom; how and why.

This reconstruction of the definition of crime will entail the problem of priorities regarding different rights. This problem may be uniquely posed in varying types of political economies. In the Soviet Union, for example, the right to those basic conditions which allow for the fullest possible democratic participation in political life, such as free speech and assembly, would be given high priority. Likewise, in the USA the right to economic well-being for all men should be considered crucial. This priority will come into conflict with the prerogatives of governing social classes, economic strata or political élites. But this must be expected by humanistic criminologists. Also to be expected is the opposition from the legal interpreters of crime. If the right to be secure in one's own person is to have greater value than social inequalities based on the ownership of property, for example, then one should be prepared to define the use of deadly force on the part of police officers as unjustifiable homicide when this force is used in defence of property. (This would be the case, for example, were a thief to be slain by an officer while refusing to halt when ordered to do so.) There is no doubt that significant portions of the existing criminal law would overlap with the definition of crime on the basis of human rights. But on the other hand, it is also true that many forms of behaviour, including those now defined as crimes without victims or crimes of consumption, would not be defined as crimes within this new perspective.

(*b*) *There are criminal social systems*

Perhaps there are no statements more repugnant to traditional legal scholars than those which define social systems as criminal. But this repugnance reflects the antiquarian psychologistic and technocratic character of the legal tradition. This tradition is blind to the fact that extensive social planning makes it possible to evaluate, mitigate or eliminate the *social* conditions which generate criminal behaviour. It is no longer sufficient to justify the restriction of criminology to the study of those institutions which define, adjudicate and sanction *individual* criminals. It has become evident that any group which attempts to control or prevent criminal behaviour by the activity of the traditional institutions of criminal justice alone is incapable of accomplishing this end.

As a rule, criminal behaviour *does* involve individual moral responsibility and the assessment of psychological relationships, such as the motivated character of the criminal act. However, the science of crime has gone beyond the centuries-old notion that crime can be conceived as a function of the properties of atomistic individuals alone.[51] Social scientists today are intensely involved in scrutinizing social relationships which generate criminal behaviour. This activity is reflected in the *real definitions* of crime which have been and are being developed by sociologists, economists, anthropologists and political scientists.

The logical strictures on the definition of social systems or relationships as criminal are removed when it is realized that real definitions by social scientists establish a diachronic relationship between the notion of criminal rates, for example, and the *socially* necessary and sufficient conditions for these rates.

If crime is defined by scientists in terms of the *socially* necessary and sufficient conditions for its existence, what would be more logical than to call these social conditions criminal? After all, crime has been traditionally defined by legalists on the basis of nominalist definitions or descriptive definitions which refer to the ways in which agents of the State react to criminal behaviour. To be sure, some legalists have used ethical terms such as 'public wrongs' or 'social injury' in earmarking criminal behaviour. But isn't a real definition of crime vastly superior to a nominalist definition or a definition which does not even define crime but merely refers to how the State reacts to it? And isn't a scientist justified in making a logically implied, normative evaluation of what he considers to be the cause of crime? And given the acceptance of criminal institutions and social-economic relationships as real definers of crime, what more ultimate claim can social scientists use to justify their unique role as criminologists, than to use the term crime to identify social systems which can be regulated or eliminated in order to control or prevent crime? What better term than crime can be used to express their *normative* judgments of the conditions which generate criminal behaviour?

It can be argued that the term 'criminogenic' be used to designate the social conditions which cause crime. But this term obfuscates the main point being made here: that the *social conditions* themselves must become the *object* of social policy and that it is not an individual or a loose collection of atomistic individuals which is to be controlled, but rather the social relationships between individuals which give rise to criminal behaviour. (Even if we put everybody involved in criminal behaviour at any one time behind bars, there is no guarantee that a new generation of criminals would not emerge given the maintenance of social conditions which originally made these individuals criminal.) In this context, the term crime as a label for social systems becomes a warrant not for controlling atomistic individuals, or preventing an atomistic act, but rather for the regulation or elimination of social relationships, properties of social systems, or social systems taken as a whole.

(c) *Are imperalistic war, racism, sexism and poverty crimes?*

Once human rights rather than legally operative definitions are used to earmark criminal behaviour, then it is possible to ask whether there are violations of human rights which are more basic than others and to designate these rights as most relevant to the domain of criminology.[52] Basic rights are differentiated because their fulfilment is absolutely essential to the realization of a great number of values. Although the lower boundary of this number is not specified here, the sense of what is meant can be ascertained by considering security to one's person as a basic right. Obviously a danger to one's health or life itself endangers all other claims. A dead man can hardly realize *any* of his human potentialities.

Similar assessments can be made of the right to racial, sexual and economic equality. The abrogation of these rights certainly limits the individual's chance to fulfil himself in many spheres of life. These rights, therefore, are basic because there is so much at stake in their fulfilment. It can be stated, in the light of the previous argument, that individuals who deny these rights to others are criminal. Likewise, social relationships and social systems which regularly cause the abrogation of these rights are also criminal. If the terms imperialism, racism, sexism and poverty are abbreviated signs for theories of social relationships or social systems which cause the systematic abrogation of basic rights, then imperialism, racism, sexism and poverty can be called crimes according to the logic of our argument.

It is totally irrelevant, in this light, to consider whether leaders of imperialist nations are war-criminals by virtue of legal precedent or decisions by war-tribunals.[53] Nor is it relevant to make note of the fact that property rights which underlie racist practices are guaranteed by law. It is likewise unimportant that sexual inequality in such professions as sociology is maintained by references to the weight of tradition. Neither can persistent unemployment be excused because it is ostensibly beyond the control of the State. What is important is that hundreds of thousands of Indo-Chinese persons are being denied their right to live; millions of black people are subjected to inhuman conditions which, on the average, deny them ten years of life; the majority of the human beings of this planet are subjected because of their sex; and an even greater number throughout the world are deprived of the commodities and services which are theirs by right. And no social system which systematically abrogates these rights is justifiable.

Is there wonder why we have raised questions about the legalistic definitions of crime when the magnitude of 'social injury' caused by imperialism, racism, sexism and poverty is compared to that wrought by individual acts which the State legally defines as crimes? Isn't it time to raise serious questions about the assumptions underlying the definition of the field of criminology, when a man who steals a paltry sum can be called a criminal while agents of the State can, with impunity, legally reward men who destroy food so that price levels can be maintained whilst a sizable portion of the population suffers from malnutrition. The USA is confronted with a grave moral crisis which is reflected above all in the technocratic 'benign neglect' shown in the unwillingness to recognize the criminal character of great social injuries inflicted on heretofore powerless people, merely because these injuries are not defined in the legal codes.

(*d*) *Modern libertarian standards*

The limits of this chapter do not permit the detailing of operating standards[54] which might be useful for earmarking the kinds of behaviour which should be of central interest to criminologists, but neither these standards, nor the notion of basic human rights itself, are more difficult to define than the operating standards and notions underlying legal conceptions of 'social injury' or 'public wrong'. The solution to this problem is also no less political. Indeed, it is time to recognize that all of the above concepts are brought to light and operationalized by the political struggles of our time.

It is not claimed that a satisfactory solution to the problem of defining crime has been offered in this chapter. What is certain is that the legalistic definitions cannot be justified as long as they make the activity of criminologists subservient to the State. It is suggested that an alternative solution can be developed which is based on some of the traditional notions of crime as well as notions organized around the concept of egalitarianism. In this process of redefining crime, criminologists will redefine themselves, no longer to be the defenders of order but rather the guardians of human rights. In reconstructing their standards, they should make man, not institutions, the measure of all things.

Notes

* We wish to express our appreciation to Sheldon Messinger, Anthony Platt, Paul Takagi and Joseph Weis for their advice and criticism, and would like to thank, in particular, Menachem Amir and Anatole Shaffer for their detailed suggestions, which helped clarify this chapter.

1 Criminological studies, therefore, provide knowledge which is diachronically or synchronically related to *legally* defined crimes and criminals.

2 Because of this, Sutherland's discussions on this topic attempted to demonstrate the connection between criminal and civil violations via analogy, historical parallels, and certain similarities between civil and criminal procedures, etc. For example, he wrote, 'although many laws have been enacted for the regulation of occupations other than business, such as agriculture or plumbing, the procedures used in the enforcement of these other laws *are more nearly the same* as the conventional criminal procedures' (1945, p. 139, our emphasis).

3 The term 'agents' is used in the broad sense. It includes, for example, legislators, judiciary and police, because the definition and operative interpretation of crime are not restricted to law-makers.

4 Sutherland and Cressey (1960, p. 19) stated, 'However, for scientific purposes it is not necessary that every decision be made in court; the criminologist must only know that a certain class of acts is defined as crime and that a particular person has committed an act of this class. Just as there is justification for writing of 'unapprehended criminals' and 'criminals at large'.

5 Gresham Sykes's evaluation of Tappan's criticism of the use of ethical criteria is one example. Sykes (1961, p. 20) states, in regard to the attempts by sociologists to equate 'criminal' with 'anti-social' that "Paul Tappan, as a lawyer-sociologist, has carefully indicated the hazards surrounding this position: it invites subjective value judgements; it substitutes the rather vague category of anti-social behavior for the more precise category of crime; and what is perhaps more important, it is apt to make the social scientist forget that all social rules are "relative, impermanent, variable" '.

6 No better example can be given than Richard Quinney's meticulous definition of crime. Quinney (1970b, pp. 6–7) writes, 'Conduct is not regarded as criminal unless these conditions are present . . . (1) the label of crime has been officially imposed on conduct (2) by *authorized persons and agencies* (3) of a *politically organized society*. Crime is therefore a legal category that is assigned to conduct by authorized agents of a politically organized society. The criminal is, it follows, a person who is assigned the status of criminal on the basis of the official judgment that his conduct constitutes a crime.' (Our emphasis.)

7 For a perceptive discussion of the relation between definitions of crime, and scientific concepts, see H. Bianchi (1956, pp. 90–111).

8 For the meanings of such terms as 'operational', 'analytic', 'nominal' and 'real' definitions as well as the 'explication', see Carl G. Hempel (1952).

9 It should be noted in passing that Tappan's defence of the precision of the legal definition is inconsistent because he had been a foremost critic of the legal codes defining criminal behaviour amongst juveniles (Tappan, 1947).

10 Our interpretation of the real definition is broader than Hempel's. He generally restricts real definitions to causal definitions.

11 Sellin's criticism of the legal definition, as we shall note later, represents an unsuccessful and incomplete attempt to question this definition on the basis of the autonomy of science.

12 Michael and Adler (1932, p. 22) stated, 'The most *precise* and least ambiguous definition of crime is that which defines it as behaviour which is prohibited by the criminal code.' (Our emphasis.) Tappan also used the term precision in criticizing definitions of crime not grounded in the criminal law. In 1967, Leonard Savitz (1970, pp. 46–7) indicated that 'if the defendant is not convicted, or the conviction is not upheld by appellate courts, he is not a criminal'. Savitz added that 'it is disconcerting to note that often, even in serious research projects, the terms crime and criminals are used with considerable lack of *precision*. It seems to be often assumed that anyone who is arrested is necessarily a criminal. As these are basic concepts upon which the field of criminology is based, such casual indifference is somewhat difficult to understand.' (Our emphasis.)

13 These sensitizing concepts and hypothetical constructs appear vague because their meanings often vary, depending upon the usages to which they are put by different theorists and researchers. Furthermore, these categories are often reformulated in light of additional knowledge. But this very property of impermanence, and the rich connotations which are characteristic of these ideas, make them useful to scientists interested in the discovery of heretofore unknown empirical relationships. The fact that there are a number of these definitions at any one time cannot be taken as a sign of the inability of scientists to formulate 'precise' notions of criminal behaviour.

14 If Tappan's insistence that scientists use the legal definition instead of their own causal definitions is pushed to its logical limit, then it means that no other definitions of crime are warranted. This insistence, for

example, means that there should exist no competing causal definitions of crime in general or of any type of criminal behaviour.

15 For example, Michael and Adler state (1932, p. 23), 'However inadequate conviction of crime may be as a test of criminality, in no other way can criminality be established with sufficient certainty for either practical or scientific purposes. The criminologist is therefore quite justified in making the convict population the subject of his studies, as he does.' This reference obviously utilizes the legal definition to operationally define criminals.

16 In recent years, in particular, criminologists engaged in delinquency research have begun to systematically reject the use of official data altogether as measures of the actual distribution of delinquency in a community. By constructing measures of delinquency other than those prescribed by criminal law, they have suggested that the official, political procedures are invalid for scientific purposes (Cicourel, 1968; Nye, Short and Olsen, 1958; Dentler and Monroe, 1961; Empey and Erickson, 1966; Gold, 1966).

17 As an illustration of this discrepancy between formal and substantive contents, compare the instructions on any self-report delinquency questionnaire with the substantive contents of the statutes defining these same offences in the criminal law.

18 Although not sufficient, the behaviour is obviously necessary for the existence of the social processes which lead to a definition of crime.

19 Even with the possibility that 'labelling' theories of crime (Werthman, 1969; Becker, 1963; Kitsuse, 1963) are proven valid for some types of crime, it is doubtful that most crimes will ever be explained on this basis.

20 The determining relation between crime and the law has been noted by many criminologists, including, for example, H. Bianchi (1956, p. 97), and it is particularly apparent in the analysis of 'white-collar crime'.

21 Again we note the irony in Tappan's remarks to the effect that his orientation is an 'objective' one, and that sociologists are engaged in some sort of immoral or subversive enterprise when they do not use the traditional legal definition of crime. It is now a matter of record that modern research in delinquency (which is not dependent on official statistics) has produced clear evidence of class and racial bias in the administration of the law. It is curious how morally appropriate these 'immoral' sociologists can be.

22 From the empiricist point of view, the legal argument that criminal status is, by definition, necessarily determined by the criminal justice system leads to an empirically *unfalsifiable* corollary. It logically implies that *all* persons who actually violate a statute but are not adjudicated by these institutions are *not* criminals. (Such persons include, for example, those who have committed unsolved crimes.) This corollary, however, is scientifically unacceptable because its truth value is determined solely on logical grounds. If a scientific definition is meant to signify relations in the real world, there must be some empirical criteria by which it can be ultimately evaluated. In order to utilize these criteria,

the definition of criminal behaviour itself must be formulated so that it can be empirically tested. This formulation, it is argued, cannot be made without operationally defining criminal behaviour *independently* of the legal sanctions or procedures which are commonly used to identify crime.

23 Turk (1969, p. 22) states, 'Thus, anyone who is defined officially as a violator . . . is criminal in the *generic* sense, whatever he may be called in accord with the terminologies and assumptions currently in vogue. That there are differences in the ways in which authorities perceive and process violators does not negate the fact that . . . our observations are of the *sanctioning processes*.' (Our emphasis.)

24 An outstanding example of the determining relationship between the law and crime includes the development of criminal syndicates involved in the illegal production and sale of alcoholic beverages during the prohibition era. Today a similar relationship exists with respect to narcotics.

25 The term 'differential social organization' was also used to refer to this general theory of crime (Cressey, 1960).

26 The concept of 'value-free' sociology has been under sharp attack in recent years. For references to this controversy, see John Horton (1966) and Alvin Gouldner (1968).

27 In 1968, for example, Irving L. Horowitz and Martin Liebowitz (1968, p. 282) offered this 'radical' definition of deviancy: 'Deviancy is a conflict between at least two parties: *superordinates* who make and *enforce* rules, and subordinates whose behaviour violates these rules.' (Our emphasis.) The authors indicate that their definition is based on a 'conflict model'. When the context of this definition is examined, it is found that, in most cases, the authors refer to behaviour defined by law, involving prostitutes, homosexuals, drug addicts, illegal forms of civil disobedience, etc. The 'superordinates' in this case are therefore agents of the State and the reference to rule enforcement involves State sanctions. Finally, when the principles underlying Horowitz and Liebowitz's 'conflict model' are examined, they turn out to be old-fashioned, pluralist principles regarding the nature of social conflict and conflict resolution.

28 The prefix, *meta*, in this case symbolizes a process of abstracting relationships contained in theories. (The outcome of this process is a collection of formal categories, axioms and mechanisms which may or may not be systematically related in a general orientation or strategy of theory construction in specific types of enquiry.) The suffix, *theory*, indicates that the object of study is not the real world but theories of that world.

29 European scholars were also involved in this task, including Emile Durkheim and Sigmund Freud.

30 For discussions of the complex relations between the development of corporate liberalism and the social, political and economic changes during this period, see, for example, Williams (1961), Kolko (1962) and Weinstein (1968).

31 These essays appeared later in a single volume entitled *Social Control* (1901).

32 For an extended discussion of corporate liberal concepts of social control, see Schwendinger and Schwendinger (1974).

33 Scholars grapple with this problem when they are concerned with explaining the persistent features of social systems. How do social systems remain stable? What is at stake in achieving a stable social order in the midst of great conflicts or accelerated change? These are the kinds of questions which pose the problem of integration.

34 Long before Vice-president Spiro Agnew's reference to 'effete snobs', Ward (1903, p. 240) stated that most 'peace agitation is characterized by total blindness to all the broader cosmic factors and principles and this explains its complete impotence'. Identifying individuals who agitate for peace as 'effete minds' he noted that 'it is the mark of the effete mind to exaggerate small things while ignoring great things' and, reminiscent of contemporary references to 'silent majorities', he added, 'the crude instincts of the general public' are far safer guides to the evaluation of war than 'maudlin sentimentality and . . . certain minds which, from culture or advantage, gain the credit of constituting the cream of the most advanced intelligence'.

35 Sellin (1938, p. 6) states, for example, 'It would seem best, in order to avoid misunderstanding to speak . . . of normal and abnormal conduct, i.e. conduct in accord with or deviating from a conduct norm.'

36 American sociologists have generally mistakenly attributed the origins of technocracy and positivism to Comte. Although Comte insisted on the originality of his conceptions, most of them were plagiarized from Saint-Simon. In addition, technocratic doctrines were developed further by the disciples of Saint-Simon, such as Bazard, Laurent and Engantin (who were called the Saint-Simonians); although as George Iggers (1958) points out, these doctrines were made subservient to theocratic standards and principles.

37 The independence of technocratic doctrines from corporate liberalism is testified by the fact that socialist scholars have also subscribed to them.

38 In the USA, corporate liberal syndicalists included Small and Weatherly. In Europe, De Greef, Tarde and Durkheim were numbered amongst the outstanding liberal syndicalists. It is important to note that this type of syndicalist thought is most responsible for the later development of modern pluralism. For a discussion of some of the salient characteristics of this form of syndicalist thought, see Williams's (1961, pp. 356–60, 384–6) description of the development of 'American syndicalism'.

39 For a classic criticism of this approach, see Mills (1943; 1959, pp. 84–99).

40 Although Ward insisted on the doctrine of a value-free social science as early as 1883 (and symbolized this in his distinction between 'pure' and 'applied' sociology in a two-volume work in 1903), it was not until the 1920s that this doctrine took firm hold amongst the Americans. At that time, the scholarly academics opposing this doctrine were chiefly represented by the 'Christian sociologists'. Their influence on the way in which professionals defined the field disappeared after President Wilson's administration.

41 In this view, the 'abnormal' conditions which produced criminal

behaviour and criminals were, on the level of social relationships: culture *conflict* and social *disorganization*; on the level of personality relationships: personal *conflict* and personality *disorganization* (Blumer, 1937).

42 The differences between Sellin and Sutherland disappear altogether when Sutherland considers the definition of the 'nature of crime from a *social* point of view' (our emphasis). In the discussion of the 'social' nature of crime, Sutherland and Cressey (1960, pp. 14–15) use three criteria to distinguish crime: (1) values of a political group, (2) isolation or culture conflict and (3) sanctions. If the term 'conduct norms' were substituted for 'values', then this interpretation would be identical with Sellin's.

43 To a great extent, the ostensibly value-free character of criminology in the USA is derived from the fact that it developed historically under the aegis of sociology rather than law (as was the case in Europe). It is interesting to note in passing, however, that Tappan's argument supported a definition of crime which was actually posed by Michael and Adler, who edited a 1932 report by a committee under the auspices of the School of Law of Columbia University on the feasibility of an Institute of Criminology and Criminal Justice. Sutherland and Sellin were members of the committee's staff, and obviously objected to the narrowly stated legal definition of crime in the report. Their objections, emerging in 1937 and 1940, as noted, reflected a broader sociological approach to the statement.

44 There are scholars today who analyse legally defined relationships from a socially critical standpoint. It is not the purpose of this section to deny their humanitarian outlook. The logic of our previous argument, however, suggests that the humanistic content of their theories is not derived from their use of a value-free methodological perspective nor the use of a legal definition 'in-itself'. Instead, the humanistic content is derived from a concept of rights which tacitly regulates their scholarly activity. Because of this, it is felt that a definition of crime which is squarely based on conceptions of human rights will make explicit what is now inchoate, inconsistent and implicit. The charge will be made that our alternative to the legal definition will 'taint' the objective, scholarly character of criminology by bringing each scholar's political biases to the fore. The answer to this objection, is that a scrupulous inspection of theories in the field will indicate that individual ideological biases have always existed although the mystique of a value-free methodology has obscured their inexorable influence.

45 One cannot overestimate the degree to which even doctrinaire interpretations of the more humanitarian legal definitions of crime, which were originally extended as a result of the Second World War, are being rejected as a result of contemporary events. One example is the insistence of George Wald (Nobel Laureate in Physiology and Medicine) that the directors and managers of the Dow Chemical Corporation be held responsible for participating in a 'crime against humanity' by their production of napalm. A similar case against Dow is made with regard to herbicides and defoliants (Wald, 1970).

46 These other criteria usually define crime as a departure form 'normal' states, which may be vaguely signified by such exceedingly formal terms as 'the mores', 'the group', 'the political group', 'superordinates', 'the public', or 'society'.

47 The inequality inherent in the relation between the colonial and colonizer was, and still is, amongst the most profound of human inequalities. Nevertheless, during the second half of the nineteenth century and the beginning of this century, social Darwinism, propounded first and foremost by the famous liberal scholar Herbert Spencer, was used to justify the subjugation of peoples of colour on the grounds that they were genetically inferior; and the exploitation of domestic labour in the name of equality of competition between nations and equality of opportunity between individuals.

48 As Stanley I. Benn (1967, p. 68) has succinctly stated: 'Although the elitist would allow that ordinary men have interests deserving some consideration, the interests of the super-man, super-class, or super-race would always be preferred. Some men, it might be said, are simply worth more than others, in the sense that any claim of theirs, whatever it might be and whatever its specific ground, would always take precedence. Such a morality would maintain that there was some criterion, some qualifying condition of race, sex, intellect, or personality, such that a person once recognized as satisfying it would automatically have prior claim in every field over others.'

49 For a classic debate on this issue, see the discussion between Davis (1953), Moore (1953) and Tumin (1953a, 1953b).

50 The degree to which the fulfilment of basic human needs is equated with dollars in American society is revealed in the American Medical Association's persistent denial of the right of all persons to medical services. As John H. Knowles (1970, p. 74) states 'a significant group of doctors has the attitude as stated by a past AMA president, that health is a privilege, not a right. I think that health is as much a right as the right to schooling or decent housing or food, and the people have begun to perceive it as a right.'

51 The science of crime has gone beyond this even though the legalists may not have progressed this far. It is vital, however, that legalists be informed that social scientists are not merely interested in isolated criminal acts but in personality relationships, social relationships and systems of social relationships which generate a succession of criminal acts on the part of distinct individuals, on one hand, and socially distributed instances of criminal acts by many individuals, on the other hand. The psychiatrist or psychologist, for example, interested in the moral careers of individuals, has moved beyond the empirical issues which were traditionally addressed by legal scholars and which are still reflected in the way in which the criminal law is fashioned today.

52 The basic human rights, it should be reiterated, that are not being referred to here are those alleged rights which are intrinsic to the nature of man, or which are functionally imperative for social stability and order. A prime example of the reification of social imperatives is Garafolo's depiction of 'natural crimes' on the basis of basic moral

sentiments of *pity* (involving emphatic feelings) and *probity* (involving the rights of private property). These 'basic moral sentiments' are functionally necessary for the maintenance of 'modern societies'. Garafolo's theory was in the *reformist* Darwinist tradition initiated by early corporate liberals. This tradition was used to justify the expansion of the political power of the State in order to regulate the uncontrolled competitive processes represented by laissez-faire capitalism.

53 It is rather incredible to find sociologists publishing what appear to be poorly written legal briefs criticizing the war in Indo-China. We suggest that they spend their time explaining the imperialist nature of this war and leave the legal criticisms to lawyers who also recognize the unjust character of this war. Generally, sociologists have used legalistic justifications where the status of the behaviour in question is equivocally defined from the standpoint of the criminal law and, in practice, are usually concerned with the analysis of business and political crimes. But certain assumptions underly this legalistic mode of justifying the definition of behaviour as criminal. For example, when to call genocide a crime is justified on the basis of legal precedents, it is assumed that agreements arising out of a contractual relationship, 'freely' entered into by a group of nation States, provide the essential criterion for defining such a crime. As a result, the *procedural conventions* existing between these States are imposed as necessary conditions for deciding whether an indisputably grave injury to mankind has taken place in any specific case. Isn't this an absurd and arbitrary basis on which to identify a crime of such magnitude as genocide! This decision to use a procedural convention is an *ethical decision*. And the fact that contractual or other agreements are necessary to establish precedents for these conventions does not, by any means, make those agreements necessary for recognizing that genocide is a heinous crime or, on the other hand, that men are able to commit genocide without ever being charged with their crimes by the State.

Reliance on legal precedent elevates the importance of procedural standards, in spite of the fact that in following this approach one can just as easily contend (by tautological reference to these standards) that genocide did not exist before the Nuremberg trials; that the act of dropping 100,000 tons of bombs on a Vietnamese city is not sufficient proof of complicity in a war-crime on the part of American military personnel; that the Biafran people were not victims of genocidal acts; and that political leaders of powerful imperialistic nations cannot be considered war-criminals after ordering the devastation of smaller nations unless they are brought before an international tribunal and found guilty.

54 Such as infant mortality, length of life, quality of food, diets, medical and recreational services, employment opportunities, etc.

5 Misfit sociology and the politics of socialization

Geoff Pearson

> Today, difficulties that a mere two or three years ago would have passed for private matters – for conflicts between students and teachers, workers and employers, or marital partners, for conflicts between individual persons – now claim political significance and ask to be justified in political concepts. Psychology seems to turn into politics – perhaps a reaction to the reality that politics, insofar as it relates to the masses, has long been translated into psychology.
>
> The gentle social control exercised by the mass media makes use of the spectacle of an undermined private sphere in order to make political processes unrecognisable as such. The depoliticized public realm is dominated by the imposed privatism of mass culture. The personalization of what is public is thus the cement in the cracks of a relatively well-integrated society, which forces suspended conflicts into areas of social psychology.
> There they are absorbed in categories of deviant behaviour: as private conflicts, illness, and crime. These containers now appear to be overflowing.[1]

The area of slippage between deviant and political categories to which Jürgen Habermas draws attention here has, in a series of remarkable convergences, placed on the agenda the construction of a politics of socialization. What this chapter explores is a blend of 'radical' social science which is woven into the fabric of these convergences. Cutting through discipline boundaries, and incorporating the sociology of deviance, radical welfare strategy, anti-psychiatry, some version of politics, humanistic psychology and much more, and sometimes extending even into the broader expanses of popular culture and music, there has been a certain consistency of theme which I call 'misfit sociology'.[2]

It would be wrong to think of misfit sociology as merely an 'inter-disciplinary' exercise in the area of deviance. It is characterized primarily by an 'insider' perspective which many took for 'phenomenology', a ready sympathy for the underdog, and a theoretical tendency towards de-reification. But what holds misfit sociology together is sometimes less remarkable than what within it is at odds with itself. Thus, a brief mention of leading figures within the misfit paradigm – Howard Becker, Ronald Laing, Erving Goffman, Thomas Szasz – belies the appearance that a clear unifying tendency within misfit sociology is a left-wing political commitment. Here is an area where the theoretical air is thin, allowing a number of conflicting orientations to exist side by side. Similarly, a sort of popular front between 'Marxism' and 'phenomenology' has been achieved to the satisfaction of some, allowing people within this theoretical dispersion to plug into misfit sociology for many different purposes. Peter Sedgwick has recently lamented the scope of such indiscriminate popularity in the work of Laing,[3] but here it is not a problem: indeed, one of the most important features of misfit sociology is that it is not so much a bounded academic domain, as a *Zeitgeist* of sorts with close and intimate connections in some areas with broader social movements, principally the 'counter-culture'.

The radicalism of misfit sociology

The central unifying tendency within misfit sociology is the attempt *theoretically* to throw off the shackles of a pre-defined and officially categorized social reality; that is to say, there is a dissolution of *reification* in social science.[4] Whether the assault is on reified imagery, the given facticity of deviance rates, positivistic methodology or conceptions of mechanical causality, the refusal to regard human action and the social world as *out there* in the world of objects is the linchpin to the theoretical substance of this 'radical' scholarship, and also underlies the ambiguous relationship of 'Marxism' and 'phenomenology'. De-reification in the area of welfare and deviance threatens the professional's sense of competence and authority. The professional lays claim to his authority from two sources, other than those of office: he claims to possess a measure of *technical competence* in the sense of an armoury of technical skills, and he lays claim to some *moral veracity*; that is, to being a 'good person'. A reified morality is a major prop to these claims, and a cornerstone of professional ideology. Under the conditions of a reified morality, as Jack Douglas has argued, moral rules become: 'highly routinized [and] may even be progressively *absolutized* or *objectified*; that is, made independent and necessary . . . thinglike or objects not subject to individual interpretation.'[5]

While morality stands 'out there' it seems unquestionable: all one can do is obey, and that sense of duty lends an *absolute* legitimation to those who would maintain it. Furthermore, the act of maintaining and servicing non-human, non-humanizable, quasi-physical entities has more of the appearance of a *technical* and *morally-neutral* activity than a morally and politically committed *persuasion*. Here a distinction employed by Habermas is useful. He distinguishes between two classes of rule: those of a 'purposive-rational' character (*Zweck-rational*) and 'consensual norms'. Whilst the former depend for their validity on empirically grounded or analytically correct propositions, consensual norms are valid only in so far as there is intersubjectivity of mutual understandings.[6] Habermas goes on to consider violations of these different types of rule. In brief, the violation of technical rules he calls *incompetence* where punishment is 'built in' by failure and rebuff by reality. The violation of consensual norms he terms *deviant* behaviour, and in this case sanctions only operate through human agency and by convention. Habermas writes that 'learned rules of purposive-rational action supply us with *skills*, internalised norms with *personality* structures'.[7]

In these terms, it seems that a reification of social order causes *deviant* acts to take on the appearance of *incompetent* acts; that is to say, behaviour which is susceptible to change by *skilled* intervention as compared to persuasive, coercive or educative intervention. Furthermore, the intervener appears as if in possession of a technical armoury, rather than as someone *possessed by* a persuasion. Undergoing psychiatric treatment, claims one eminent psychiatrist, is a simple business: it is like having a man call to repair a TV set; when it is mended, he does not insist which channel you watch.[8]

De-reification subverts this technocratic conception of morality, deviance and order as social problems are rediscovered as moral dilemmas. Crucially, the welfare professional's reliance on publicly administered and tolerated definitions of 'need' as something given and objective is toppled: that old catchphrase 'you can't legislate morality' is dismembered. Morality can be, and is, legislated; moral crusaders *are* events in the world; patterns of stigma *are* invented by professionals and peddled to their clients who *do* conform.[9] In the de-reifying traditions of misfit sociology, 'deviance' is something *arrived at* and constructed in negotiations between deviants and audiences, thus directing attention to the understanding of welfare practices and ideologies as a vital component of any understanding of deviance.

The welfare professional is thus posed questions which by definition he cannot answer, for his authority is not morally grounded, but routinized. Recently, when one social-work educator, Munday, lamented the state of professional training programmes which were, as he saw it, overrun with students 'highly motivated by very left-wing values', he also placed 'sociology' centrally in his vision of professional hell. This sociology exposed students to 'general attacks on traditional beliefs in society', 'assailed . . . [them with] a variety of academic material that is threatening, undermining and often downright depressing', and 'teaches that it is our system that is at fault'.[10] One might imagine that the author had in mind a Marxist sociology, but he writes: 'The ideas of writers like Matza, Becker and Cicourel are intellectually fascinating and persuasive, but quite ominous for the social worker.'[11]

Here is the central *theoretical* element of misfit sociology's radicalism: it roots out the moral and political ambiguities of deviance control, and subverts the reasonable and unobjectionable face of its moral and technical authority.

One might also think that there is something of a misreading involved in this reaction to the writings of some of the godheads of misfit sociology. I would argue that a second feature of the misfit paradigm which gives it an appearance of radicalism is not so much what it places on offer, as what is taken from its ambiguities by its audience. What misfit sociology's reading audience consistently takes from it is that here in the preoccupation with how social control ideologies frame and determine the form, rate and imagery of deviance is a turning of the guns of social science on to the establishment. There is something more than the mere expression of an unconventional sentimentality: the aggressive noises which misfit sociology makes towards the social-control apparatus takes on the appearance of a politics, and misfit sociology becomes transformed into a theoretical conception of deviance and deviance control as politics, even if it is not altogether clear as to what kind of a politics this is.

The sense that misfit sociology makes a politics available has been strengthened formidably by its affinities with innovatory client organizations, and with the libertarian New Left. Central to both of the latter is the preoccupation with how men and women are oppressed by the subtle violence of everyday life. Here there is a meeting-ground and a mixing of themes between misfit sociology and the New Left so complete that it sometimes becomes difficult to know where to draw the line between the two. Consequently, apparently easy movement of concepts and imagery has been enjoyed: sometimes conceived of as a form of crypto-political primitive rebellion,[12] deviance was embraced as a means of fighting against 'the system', breaking down power-invested taboos, and even as freedom itself. Working, as Herbert Marcuse depicts the social function of art, 'in the established reality against the established reality',[13] deviance seemed to suggest a means of fighting for a subversive human freedom. Obscenity is thus for both Marcuse and Rubin a means of claiming back language from the oppressors.[14] What madness is for David Cooper – an awakening to a personal and political salvation – so the liberation of the mind and body through the use of drugs is regarded by Leary.[15] Sometimes the links operate at the level of suggestive metaphor: just as for Peter Berger a de-reifying social science is a 'political dynamite' which de-legitimates the taken-for-granted programmes of everyday life, thus 'unthinking' the legitimating props to social institutions and vested interests, so would the New Left think itself free, transcend the straitjacket of a socialized imagination in a chemical revolution, or fuck its way to freedom.[16] Everywhere, it was the joyless quality of life which was understood as the core feature of the deviant rebellion. No longer conceived of as a marginal conglomerate of hooligans, Paki-bashers, telephone-kiosk wreckers and feckless psychopaths, the problem of 'juvenile delinquency' was grasped thus: 'The revolt of youth was the first burst of anger at the persistent realities of the new world – the boredom of everyday existence, the *dead life*.'[17]

The politics of misfit sociology

In this manner in its broadest conception misfit sociology adopts the form of, and lays some grounds for, a *theoretical politicization of everyday life*. To suggest that, however, is already to leap far ahead of what misfit sociology actually accomplishes into the land of promises. Hints of moves towards a politics of socialization revealed in the choice of *titles* of recent contributions to the literature suggest only what people would *like* to be in a position to offer: namely, a politics of the family, a politics of child-rearing, a politics of sexuality, vandalism, pornography, shop-lifting, play, sexual deviancy and soccer hooliganism; a body politics, a hormonal politics and a politics of ecstasy. Ronald Laing may talk of a politics of experience, but it is not at all clear that he provides one.

Here is found the most consistent and easily justified criticism of the political radicalism of misfit sociology: simply, that it is short in substance. Hidden within this criticism is also a sense of outrage. The appeal could almost be, 'how could one mistake *that* for radicalism!'

It is Alvin Gouldner who offers the sharpest formulation of the non-radical nature of misfit sociology, and he argues that it is a mask for liberalism and an avoidance of erect commitment. Thus, characterizing Goffman's social psychology as one where there is no 'metaphysics of hierarchy' and where all social claims, however eccentric, disreputable or lowly, are 'endowed with a kind of equal reality', Gouldner argues that whilst 'some among the rebellious young' may see this unconventionality as having a radical potential, it represents, if ambiguously, 'an avoidance . . . [and] an accommodation to existent power arrangements'.[18] Gouldner's criticism of the sociology of Howard Becker is comparable, if more fierce. Becker, Gouldner argues, provides the basis only for a new kind of careerism:[19]

> It is a sociology of and for the new welfare state. It is the sociology of young men with friends in Washington. It is a sociology that succeeds in solving the oldest problem in personal politics: how to maintain one's integrity without sacrificing one's career, or how to remain liberal although well-heeled'.

The ideology of Becker's sociology, writes Gouldner, is an enlightened liberalism, critical of a mismanaged, ineffectual and callous welfare system, but effectively a criticism only of the *low-level* officials who manage care-taking institutions, and not of high-level officialdom which shapes the character of these institutions, welfare budgets and research-funding. Writing of Becker's paper 'Whose Side Are We On?', he says: 'Becker's theoretical school is indeed taking sides; it is a party to the struggle between old and new elites in the caretaking establishments'.[20]

Without more specific evidence as to the stratification of welfare élites which he has in mind, it is difficult to judge Gouldner's argument. Superficially, however, his remarks, whilst they may, or may not, accurately locate Becker's position and that of other élite sociologists, fall short of the mark in accounting for the more global critical sense of the misfit sociology depicted here. The concern is not with malpractices, nor with ineffectual techniques; in an early contribution, the sense of 'violence' in psychiatry which Cooper wished to depict had, as he put it, 'little to do with people hitting each other on the head with hammers . . . [it] is the subtle, tortuous violence that other people, the Sane Ones, perpetrate against the identified mad-men'.[21]

Similarly, Ingleby writes in his account of the ideological roots of psychology and psychiatry: 'we are not primarily interested in outrages – in scientists who tell lies, in rigged experiments, or in mental hospitals which institutionalise the sort of violence against patients about which you can set up a Government Enquiry'.[22]

Misfit sociology's sense of wrong is to be found in homely comforts and in self-evident truths. Thus, Richard Sennett talks of the 'brutalization' of the suburban family,[23] and David Cooper, who had already described the family as a 'gas chamber', in his later writing leaves no room for doubting the sentiments of the position: 'The most benevolent institutions of our society become our oppressors in a way that relegates the gas chambers of Auschwitz to the level of a *naif*, fumbling attempt at massacre.'[24]

However extravagantly, Cooper expresses the central sentiment of misfit sociology, namely that the welfare institutions in their most benign form are oppressive: it is not only the 'bent' copper who is scrutinized. Gouldner's position here is confused, and to some extent inexplicable,[25] the main clue to his actions being the persistent manner in which he attempts in his discussions of misfit sociology to establish the links between this brand of 'radicalism', its essential bankruptcy as he understands it, and the 'know nothing New Left' for which he does not hide his distrust. Constantly peering beyond immediate appearances, and attempting to discern the form of some 'unreliable' political prescription, Gouldner's fire is drawn, one suspects, because for him there is more at stake than a radical careerist here or there. His treatment of Becker, of Goffman, and of Garfinkel, is a play with shadows, the real substance of the matter being the 'Ideas' of political debate. His dismissal of Garfinkel's ethnomethodology as a 'sociology of happenings',[26] whilst it does, as Mungham and I have suggested,[27] touch a nerve of the joy of methodological ecstasy which ethnomethodology offers to some, is nevertheless an underestimation of the position and says less of which Garfinkel has on offer, and rather more of what he, Gouldner, is prepared to tolerate. What is at issue for Gouldner is not 'radical social science' – not matters of partisanship, objectivity, and scholarship – but politics, dressed as rationality. In his sometimes indiscriminate, but always passionate denunciation of Becker, Goffman and Garfinkel, there is always the impression that the conviction came first, and then, however Gouldner may attempt to present the matter as otherwise, argument followed after.

If there is a clear relationship, however, as Gouldner implies there is, between emergent forms of sociological theory and changes in the nature and politics of industrial societies, then he is clearly correct in attempting to understand those theories in those terms. However, his grudging attitude towards the 'New Left' limits his appreciation of the nature of misfit ideology. Thus, in his account of Goffman, the ideology of 'dramaturgy' is presented only as an elaborate deception which, although taken as a 'rebel vision' of society by some, is in the final analysis a 'cool-out' and a dupe:[28]

> The dramaturgical model allows us to bear our defeats and losses, because it implies that they are not 'for real' . . . winning and losing become of lesser moment. It is only the game that counts. . . . The dramaturgical model invites us to carve a slice out of time, history, and society. . . . Rather than offering a world view, the new model offers us 'a *piece* of the action'.

There is, however, an alternative view of the ideology embodied in Goffman: take, for example, *Asylums*, a key text in misfit sociology.

Here, in the hidden agenda of his book, Goffman offers the image of society as a 'total institution' – a prison, a mental hospital, a factory for breaking heads. As 'inmates', members of society have only the remnants of an identity and suffer invasion of their speech, dress and manners, and colonization of their habits. At the same time, their oppressors pose as nurses, doctors and 'helpers' of various kinds, and further undermine and mystify the last shreds of inmate ambition with this 'repressive tolerance'. Nevertheless, if Goffman's portrayal of the total institution can be taken as the depiction of an oppressive society, it is also an optimistic portrayal: all is not lost, for the inmates can, and do, fight back. By means of 'removal activities'[29] and other guerrilla tactics, the fight for human freedom goes on: the total institution may be a 'dead sea', but it is 'a kind of dead sea in which little islands of vivid, encapturing activity appear'.[30] Sometimes, what are officially categorized as 'symptoms' are in Goffman's accounts the tactics whereby identity is salvaged in the oppressive ambit of the asylum, and primitive acts of rebellion and insurgency against the ruling order. Thus:[31]

> In mental hospitals, one of the most dramatic instances of establishment alienation is provided by the patient who is appropriately oriented in the situation in all visible ways while calmly doing a single thing that sets him quite outside the present reality. . . . I have observed an otherwise well-demeaned (albeit mute) youth walking down the ward halls with a reasonably thoughtful look on his face and two pipes in his mouth; another conducting himself with similar nicety while chewing toothpaste; another with soap on his shaved head . . . another with a ball of paper screwed into his right eye as a monocle; another with a foot-long strip of woven newspaper dangling from his pocket. One patient would graciously accept tobacco for his pipe and then pop the offering into his mouth with a continued artful gesture of gratefulness for the smoke; another would quietly enter the cafeteria and eat his meals peacefully, departing when told to, and manage all his compliant behaviour with a dinner-roll balanced on his head. . . . And frequently, patients would lie on benches in an ordinary relaxed manner while keeping a few fingers or an arm extended and stiff, showing that they were not giving in to actual relaxation . . . these proclamations were made with a sly look on the patient's face, so that it appeared that he was more than ordinarily aware of the implications of his acts and was performing them with these implications in mind . . . this situational self-sabotage often seems to represent one statement in an equation of defence. It seems that the patient sometimes feels that life on the ward is

> so degrading, so unjust, and so inhuman that the only self-respecting response is to treat ward life as if it were contemptibly beyond reality and beyond seriousness. . . . In short, the patient may pointedly act crazy . . . to make it clear to all decent people that he is obviously sane.

If we understand Goffman's *Asylums* and associated work as politics, then it clearly is a 'non-rational' politics, open to the play of libido, and offering a perspective of optimism which puts social structure up for grabs at the drop of a hat. In proposing an alternative reading of Goffman to that offered by Alvin Gouldner, I am suggesting that the answer to the question 'Who, and under what conditions, would read it in that way?' is supplied by placing it in the contexts of the 'new politics' and the end of the end of ideology. Set against those contexts, the basis of the 'radicalism' of Goffman – the freeing of thought for action – becomes apparent where it is not apparent in Gouldner's version. As with Berger who would have us 'unthink' social institutions, and Garfinkel in whose world – despite his own substantial arguments to the contrary – social structures seem to crash down almost of their own accord, Goffman's sense of the world as a man-made 'script' rings with a zest and confidence which opposes the oppressive gloom of the corridors of power where access to leverage on social structure is closed off: misfit sociology offers a politics which 'faces down the Man'. It is not surprising, then, that 'some among the rebellious young' embrace, and are turned on by it.

If, however, we part company with Gouldner in his inability to make the radicalizing influence of misfit sociology intelligible, we nevertheless rejoin him in asserting that it is incomplete. Goffman's mental patients can only dismiss the social structure of the total institution by a gesture because Goffman has already banished social structure *conceptually*. If we understand *seriously* matters of social structure, power, culture and history, we cannot grant Goffman's inmates the credibility which he allows them. The de-legitimation of power-invested structures is a precondition of their criticism and removal, and the tactics of Goffman's patients, like the 'retreatist' politics of libertarian expression, may be necessary, but they are not self-evidently sufficient. If we follow this line of thinking, then power-invested structures demand to be *removed*, not shrugged off, blown, nor spirited away:[32]

> Men make their own history, but they do not make it just as they please; they do not make it under circumstances chosen by themselves, but under circumstances directly encountered, given and transmitted from the past. The tradition of all the dead generations weighs like a nightmare on the brain of the living.

Goffman's men, on the contrary, make their own history, *and* they make it just as they please, although they appear to sleep no more easily for all that.

A major criticism of Gouldner's appraisal of misfit sociology is, to summarize, that whilst recognizing the links between its ideology and that of the 'rebellious young', he does not confront the matter directly in terms of political theory, strategy and tactics, thereby blunting his argument as a one-sided criticism. The second area of weakness, shared by Paul Walton's important criticisms of this field of scholarship, is that its 'radicalism', although denied, is also taken for granted. Walton thus writes that, 'labelling theory, which appeared to many of us to offer a radical promise, seems to fall short', and that, 'the social reaction approach is as profoundly un-radical as its predecessors',[33] but says nothing of how this appearance of radicalism emerged.

Walton's arguments are concerned specifically with the work of Lemert, Becker and others which he accepts as 'the Social Reaction Approach' to deviance, otherwise known as 'Social Control Theory, Labelling Theory, Transactionalism, Interactionism, etc.',[34] and the main thrust of his criticism is to point to the absence of consideration of power, interest and social structure in this perspective. For him the social reaction approach is a 'one-sided exercise in the de-mystification of some of the faults of earlier sociologies of crime and deviance'.[35] Walton raises fundamental objections to the emphasis on audience reaction, arguing correctly that the question of the origins of *initial* deviance is side-stepped, and that the existence of core sentiments and meanings which are widely shared by members of society and enforced by ruling élites is denied.[36] So far so good; Walton further holds that: 'Much deviancy must be viewed as a struggle, or reaction, against "normalized repression", a breaking through, as it were, of accepted, taken-for-granted, power-invested commonsense rules'.[37]

If that is so, however, then the 'social reaction approach' must be seen as part of that struggle since, as argued above, and as Walton clearly recognizes, it involves a de-legitimation and challenging of the taken-for-granted quality of rules as applied to deviants, and the recovery of a de-reified conception of deviance (as enforced rules), drawing attention to the negotiation of those definitions, and the power differentials in those negotiations.

It is precisely this which Walton assumes, however, and does not attempt to make accountable. To do that would demand taking the analysis beyond the simply internal-theoretical aspects of one perspective ('social reaction') and would require that we look at *contexts*. First amongst these contextual sitings which must be considered are the disciplinary 'bedfellows' of labelling theory, and the considerable theoretical dispersion of this area which leads here to the subsumption of the whole under 'Misfit Sociology'. Second, as begun here, it requires some indication of what it is that misfit sociology confronts – routine professionalism and moral absolutism – and the nature of its explosive role in these confrontations. Given this second consideration, the relativistic pluralism of misfit sociology, for example, cannot be seen in nearly such an unambiguous fashion as some critics within the misfit paradigm seem to imply, as a sort of limp liberalism.[38] Rather, it is rescued as something which bursts the husks of the reasonable soft machine of the social-control apparatus.[39] Pluralism does not understand the deviant as a man whose 'coping mechanisms' have failed, or as an inept performer, unnatural and other-worldly: rather, it allows the deviant credibility; unearths *his* rationality as opposed to ours, and discovers that there is 'method in his madness'. It reveals a morally organized world, and not one where ideology is at an end, and where human beings are calculating machines exercising technical operations, who, when they disagree, have 'gone wrong' in their workings. In the third place, and finally, it necessitates an account of the users, and the mechanics of the uses made of misfit sociology, recognizing that under the conditions here summarized there are possibilities of a number of competing abstractions to be made from the misfit paradigm. What I am suggesting is that only when these conditions are satisfied can misfit sociology be comprehended as a *radicalizing* influence, for we must arrive at an understanding of the radicalism of theory (the flow and interchange of scholarship and action) by understanding scholarship and action concretely in their relations. Both Gouldner and Walton approach the matter abstractly, ripping the 'social-reaction approach' (Walton) and 'the Becker School' (Gouldner) out of their contexts, and attending to them only as internally-rational theory. But that is just what misfit sociology is not, as Walton recognizes: 'The task is made difficult by the fact that this approach to the sociology of deviance encompasses a variety of theorists who, although they share many assumptions in common, hold to these assumptions with differing degrees of subtlety, sensitivity, and sophistication'.[40]

Clearly, if one takes into account not only that 'theoreticians' are men, but also that 'practitioners' and 'clients' have attached their own 'non-scholarly' meaning to misfit sociology, this rings even more true. One hears, for example, complaining voices in the *British Journal of Psychiatry*:[41]

> Bright young schizophrenics, like bright young people generally, are interested in reading about their condition. From the vast and varied selection of literature available to them, they appear to show a marked preference for R. D. Laing's *The*

> *Politics of Experience*. The present authors . . . are of the opinion that they know what is best, and that this book is not good for these patients.

Here Laing is seen not simply as a theorist, but as someone offering rules by which to play the game, a prescriptive model of the being of madness which competes with the established medical model and makes patients ('like bright young people generally', one wonders) less amenable. Compare the following translation, as 'theory' is put into 'practice' in the pages of the underground newspaper *International Times*:[42]

> If you are admitted [to a mental hospital] you have to play their game . . . be cool. Brighten up or calm down, as the case may be. Tell the nurse and psychiatrist how much better you feel. Start looking in the paper for a job, or get the psychiatric social worker to find one, you can always leave it. Agree about how pointless or unstable your life has been.

Here is a further twist of the screw: whatever its intentions, misfit sociology has been often taken as a prescription for deviant acts and deviant rebellion.

Walton and Gouldner, thus, afford misfit sociology a rationality which it does not have, and then, not surprisingly, find it lacking in those respects. From our perspective this shortage of consistency is not a difficulty standing in the way of giving an account, but is a crucial feature of misfit sociology which makes it possible to become such a ubiquitous radicalism. Indeed, Walton quite possibly demonstrates that it is precisely when 'labelling theory' is given a rigorous formulation that it stops being radical.

The objection is that Gouldner and Walton proceed to understand a social movement as if it were a calculus, thereby treating theory abstractly in isolation from its sitings. That is, of course, a perfectly legitimate enterprise under some conditions, but it is not the only way of proceeding. Moreover, there is a peculiar arrogance in insisting that a reading audience should only take from what one writes what one *thinks* one offers. Indeed, the rise and popularity of misfit sociology can simply not be understood in such terms; for many, to give an example, it takes the form of a reaction against styles and traditions of social scientific inquiry which they barely understood. What seems to be required, therefore, is that we attempt to understand misfit sociology as a moment of the *imagination*, and in particular, as a moment of the political imagination. And in the realm of imaginative discourse, rather than attend simply to the internal calculation of theory, one must place thought firmly in the world and join with someone, perhaps, like Hesse who puts the matter succinctly when he writes in a late note to his *Steppenwolf* that:[43]

> Poetic writing can be understood and misunderstood in many ways. In most cases the author is not the right authority to decide on where the reader ceases to understand and the misunderstanding begins. Many an author has found readers to whom his work seemed more lucid than it was to himself. Moreover, misunderstandings may be fruitful under certain circumstances. . . .
>
> I neither can nor intend to tell my readers how they ought to understand my tale. May everyone find in it what strikes a chord in him and is of some use to him!

The question is how thought comes alive in the world. One thing we know: ideas do not simply translate themselves into action. Ideas are transformed into action, and are taken as justification for action (or inaction) *by men*. My account of these matters has been brief and necessarily speculative: there is a distaste, if quite understandable, amongst social scientists to explore the mechanics of such a position and take seriously its implications, which are that men will take what they want, and make what they choose out of what they take. Perhaps, having laboured long and hard over the intricacies of scholarship, it is difficult to accept that the most important, and possibly only, impact of thought comes from 'vulgarization'.

Perhaps because Walton's analysis regards the dispersal of theory as troublesome, but does not set out to look at its workings and function in the world, he appears to remain *within* that dispersal, expressing some of its contradictions. Thus, he requires both that deviance 'must . . . be viewed as ultimately predetermined by structural inequalities and ideologically enforced consensus, *no matter how complex the mediatory variables*';[44] Whereas: 'we want to argue that many people commit deviant acts as a result of making choices . . . deviants are always rational creatures, for like any other persons, they engage in choice and evaluation'.[45]

Giving voice here both to theoretical confusion, and to competing ideologies within deviant minorities that deviants are on the one hand 'victims', or on the other, 'rebels', Walton appears locked within the contradictions of the misfit paradigm. At the same time, however, there is a rationality here: how to develop the understanding of *power* and *determination*, whilst at the same time salvaging the concept of a *person* who exercises *choice*. In the final analysis there is no argument with Gouldner and Walton. Or rather, differences recede in the face of the shared ambition of understanding the workings of power and interest in the lives of subjects. Here is the growing edge of misfit sociology.

Growing pains: power, deviance and reasonableness

Clearly, to be a good friend to the deviant one must do more than give him choice and rationality 'like any other person', in that such a position fails to recognize that often what the deviant suffers from is a *lack of choices* (determination). If the misfit is to do more than 'make out', or retreat into a dubious pluralism of 'you're all right if you think you are', then he must recognize that; and if we are interested in him, then so must we.

What is at stake here is not simply how power distributes itself externally – in social structures – but, crucially, how it is represented *internally*. The heavy reliance in this area on a *sociology*, however, with its consequences of a too easy acceptance of the disciplinary fragmentation of knowledge, stands in the way of this project. There is an unwitting tendency in any sociology to deny actors an *inside* and an *impulse*, and to refuse *our view* of that impulse as 'unsociological', and there are reflections of this tendency in the writings of some of the most important critics within the growing edge of misfit sociology. Although the matters are nowhere addressed in a rigorous fashion, when they are discussed at all approaches to the deviant's insides are rejected by *fiat* as demonic, psychologistic and biological mystification. Whilst we may argue that there are good reasons, given many correctional practices grounded in psychological explanation, for lumping together psychology with demonology,[46] the question of whether a sociological, psychological or biological theory reveals, or masks, 'reality' is not the fundamental issue. In a very important sense these questions are simply irrelevant: it is not important who is right or wrong about deviance, but rather, who has the right to say what is right. Psychological, or even 'constitutional' accounts for that matter, of deviant enterprise are not in themselves absurd; nor are they in themselves repressive. What can be repressive is what men make of individually-oriented, psychological-constitutional accounts of deviance. If the homosexual, for example, is a 'social problem', then he is a social problem irrespective of whether his genes are bad, his mothering too 'good', or he has chosen to be that way. He is a 'problem' because in our society sex roles are structured in such a way as to make the homosexual appear as repulsive and menacing. But this should not be mistaken for a 'sociological' explanation of homosexuality: what matters is not what the homosexual *is*, but whether I want to change him, and whether I have the means to ensure that I get my way.

If the intention is to defend the deviant, then what is required is a defence of his *unreasonable* nature, and not a demonstration – scientific or otherwise – that he could be like any one of us, given the constitutional, psychological or social breaks. We may characterize such defences as liberal, and they must always fail, for the deviant, whatever else, *is* different. At the same time, questions of aetiology are irrelevant not because they are 'wrong', but because they miss the point: the basic human issue which is obscured is that either we respect the deviant's style, or we do not; and if his 'bent' frightens us, then he is 'abnormal'. Who cares if 'mild ill-manners' are biologically, socially or psychologically determined as long as they are inoffensive and unwilled? But, let them be volitional and they are a *scandal*: what is at stake in the defence of the deviant is the *control* of morality.

Thus, misfit sociology stands at a growth-point, usually conceived of as a transition into a more general cultural criticism which leaves the mundane matters of welfare far behind. The exercises of misfit sociology, and the things at which it was so good – computing 'guilt' with regard to society's creation of stigma, stereotypical blind men, sick junkies, or 'screaming queers' – recede in importance as 'secondary deviation' is understood as the superficial appearance of power, and as it is seen that much of the compelling quality of 'labels' derives from their wider roots in key moral meanings and should be understood in such terms. The temptation to follow this thinking is supported by the manner in which the misfit paradigm is so easily truncated into a narrow welfare critique, conceiving of misfit sociology as a politicization of social work which reflects some crisis in social welfare, when it signals as much as anything else a crisis in politics and social science. Nevertheless, there is danger also in the flight into the realm of a high theory of culture, on the one hand, ignoring the deviant's insides, and the politics of socialization, or of 'reasonableness'; and on the other hand, ignoring the growing power of welfare élites, and the dissemination of welfare ideologies into wider expanses of our culture, with the power to define organizational, structural and political issues as personal and psychological – not only in social work and psychiatry, but also in organization-management theory, and in political debate.[47] A critique of culture must take as one major task a critique of welfare. Where, to rephrase Wilhelm Reich, social science focuses on why the hungry man steals, rather than on the more remarkable problem that his hungry brother does not, the politics of reasonableness are central.[48]

Images of freedom

From many perspectives it has been suggested that the study of deviance is, at one and the same time, the study of respectability, rules and order. What is neglected in these accounts is that the other side of order is freedom. Hidden within the images of deviance are images of freedom, and there is a cultural equation running between the two; we play out our relationship to certain forms of freedom in our relationship to the imagery of deviance.

The deviant is, in one widely popularized argot, a 'villain': he does not get the shakes; he tests nerve and skill; he is the 'hard man'; his rebellious nature is saturated with *risk*. *The deviant is the man who tests his freedom to the limits*. The 'madness inside us all' is the terrible vision of Blake. Blake's vision rebels against straitjacketed sensibilities: 'the man who turns his back on society', whether he be vagrant, idiot, psychotic, thug or petty thief, is equated with what our 'freedom' would look like if we dared to chance our arm.

But this vision of freedom is not itself free. In his valuable analysis of the Manson Family, Stuart Ewan suggests as much; here is a freedom which depicts itself as an abyss of ungirded sensuality, thrusting men back into the arms of order, for 'too much freedom is a dangerous thing'.[49] The charge must be laid at the door of the *sociology* of deviance that it fails to recognize that what stands in our imagery opposed to order is not chaos, but freedom, and that in this mis-representation of freedom as chaos our freedom is contained: it is something we may 'hanker after', but will under no circumstances *want*. Countless crime movies where, until the final frames, the audience is encouraged to identify with the villain, simply lose their point if this is not grasped. In the cops-and-robbers game we glimpse our freedom, and then taste its containment. As Scott has argued, although to what purpose it is not entirely clear, the relationship between deviance and social order here has an added twist: deviance literally 'rejuvenates' society. Noting how deviants, although threatening to social order, are *tamed* rather than *destroyed*, he writes:[50]

> To contain and control deviance, and thereby master it, is to supply fresh and dramatic proof of the enormous powers behind the social order. The visible control of deviance is one of the most effective mechanisms by which a social order can tangibly display its potency. The act of harnessing things which are dangerous helps to revitalize the system by demonstrating to those who live within it just how awesome its powers really are.

Placed in these contexts, misfit sociology can only move forward as part of a wider attempt to understand how men grasp their freedom; it is the other side to the orientation which understands the problem of deviance as the problem of how men construct and maintain order.

I am suggesting, then, a formulation which rescues the study of deviance from a narrow concern with practical welfare matters, whilst at the same time salvaging the cutting-edge of misfit sociology which was its capacity to engage in moral–political enquiry without consigning deviance to a marginal status, or to a theoretical preoccupation with the 'problem of order'. It is as well to reflect again that the rise of the misfit paradigm must be firmly situated historically. Much of misfit sociology's capacity to say so much to so many flows from its links with historically situated social movements, sharing and expressing a number of currents within the radical intelligentsia, the student protest movement of the 1960s and the awakening struggles of oppressed minorities: it struck, as Stanley Cohen puts it, 'a political chord'.[51] The sense of 'politics' to which it has lent itself is that which understands *personal* liberation as a necessary feature of, and prelude to, the more distant *political* liberation, thus turning to youth politics, hippies, drug politics and the various 'freaks' who were kicking through cultural taboos as the location of truly liberating social change: misfit sociology's 'research data' are also its political heroes. Misfit sociology enables the social scientist to do the impossible: remain a social scientist within a theoretical mood which is highly suspicious of academicism; engage in deviance-welfare concerns despite *radical* opposition to much welfare ideology; engage in action which appears 'relevant' whilst maintaining distance from traditional and 'discredited' political channels. Reflecting in an autobiographical mood on the origins of the National Deviancy Conference as a growing away from political orthodoxy, Cohen writes:[52]

> Going through various degrees of disillusionment with such activities . . . talking or doing something about deviance seemed to offer – however misguided this may look to an outsider – a form of commitment, a way of staying in, without on the one hand selling out, or on the other hand playing the drab game of orthodox politics.

Most importantly, misfit sociology enabled individuals to solve the problem of the relationship of their lives as social scientists and their lives as men and women: it allowed them to put together in their lives *politics*, *social science*, and *compassion*. However, to the extent that the political optimism which lay at the back of these currents appears to be in decline,[53] so a key aspect of allegiance to misfit sociology fades, and the apparent ease of movement from scholarship to action, and back again, becomes more tortuous. Speculatively, it is possible that we must understand misfit sociology as a historically limited solution to some of the problems of radical social scientists *qua* social scientists: the days of faith in 'chemical revolution', for example, are passed.

In a most perceptive critique of Laing, Richard Sennett puts his finger on the problem when he asks: 'If I, a sane man, want to wake up, and I can't will myself into mental illness, what am I to do?'[54] The lesson is that deviance is not itself freedom, and that misfit sociology has not yet provided the key to the politics of socialization. But equally, a vital and enduring insight secured both in misfit sociology, and in the politics of the New Left, was that deviant behaviour could not simply be comprehended as residual, or as only a *distorted* form of personal expression. One of the few attempts to really grapple with the substance of the experiences which lay at the back of this convergence of politics, deviance and reasonableness is provided by Jeff Nuttall's *Bomb Culture*. It is, amongst other things, an exploration of the human potential which lies behind the doors of order:[55]

> Sickness . . . the confrontation of taboo, daring the uncountenanceable. . . . The feeling of exhilaration following the first act which violates the previous restriction, the moment after leaving the Church, committing buggery, making love to one's own sex, when new areas of freedom open out limitlessly like vast meadows. How Leonardo must have felt dissecting his first procured corpse, or Renaissance dukes defying the Pope.

If I am right, then a crucial task of any cultural criticism must be to wrest the images of freedom out of their constraining sockets. In that context, criminology becomes recognizable as not simply an attempt to offer men the means whereby to live as they please, but perhaps also to help them live as they choose. Such a criminology will contribute to the construction of utopias, rather than the confinement of dystopias. As part of a wider enterprise, it will emerge from under the wraps of professional expertise into the world. For, as Ernest Becker has put the matter (my emphasis):[56]

> To opt for a theory of human ills is not only to opt for the kind of person one is going to have to pay deference to professionally; it is also to opt potentially for the kind of world *one is going to wake up in*, the kinds of human beings that one will have *to come across in the street.*

Notes

1 J. Habermas (1971a, pp. 42–3).
2 G. Pearson (1972).
3 P. Sedgwick (1972, pp. 646–8).
4 For accounts of reification, see Marx, *Capital*, vol. 1 (1867, p. 72); P. L. Berger and S. Pullberg (1966, pp. 56–71); P. L. Berger and T. Luckmann (1967, p. 106 and *passim*).
5 J. D. Douglas (1970, pp. 19–20), original emphasis.
6 Habermas (1971a, pp. 91–4).
7 Ibid., original emphasis.
8 D. Stafford-Clark and P. Winch (1970, pp. 88–101).
9 See, for example, T. Duster (1970); H. S. Becker (1963, pp. 121–63); R. A. Scott (1970, pp. 255–90); E. Goffman (1961); J. Young (1971b).
10 B. Munday (1972, pp. 3–6).
11 Ibid., p. 4.
12 The central statement is provided by I. L. Horowitz and M. Liebowitz (1968, pp. 280–96). See also S. M. Lyman (1970, pp. 21–34); F. Davis (1967, pp. 10–18); and, for some suggestions on crypto-political aspects of vandalism, I. Taylor and P. Walton (1971, pp 8–9).
13 H. Marcuse (1969, p 46).
14 Ibid., p. 42; and J. Rubin (1970, pp. 109–10).
15 See D. Cooper (1971, pp. 106ff.); and T. Leary (1970).
16 See P. Berger (1971, pp. 1–5).
17 Situationist International (1967, p. 12).
18 A. W. Gouldner (1971, p. 379).
19 A. W. Gouldner (1968, pp. 103–16).
20 Ibid., p. 107. This finds an echo in C. Cannan (1970).
21 D. Cooper (1965, pp. 18–24).
22 D. Ingleby (1970, p. 161).
23 R. Sennett (1970, pp. 29–37).
24 Cooper (1971, p. 103).
25 Cf. T R. Young (1971, pp. 276–81); and J. O'Neill (1972, pp. 209 ff.).
26 Gouldner (1971, pp. 390–5).
27 G. Mungham and G. Pearson (1972).

28 Gouldner (1971, p. 385).
29 Goffman (1961, pp. 60–5, 67–8).
30 Ibid., p. 68.
31 Goffman (1963, pp. 224–5).
32 Marx (1853, p. 15).
33 Walton (1973).
34 Walton (1972, p. 1).
35 Ibid., p. 10.
36 Cf. C. A. B. Warren and J. M. Johnson (1972, pp. 69–92).
37 Ibid., p. 11.
38 See, for example, I. Taylor (1972, pp. 633–40).
39 The idea of the social-control apparatus as a Soft Machine belongs to Jock Young (1972b, p. 11).
40 Walton (1972, p. 1).
41 M. Siegler, H. Osmond and H. Mann (1969, p. 947).
42 *International Times* (1969, p. 7).
43 H. Hesse (1965, pp. 5–6).
44 Walton (1972, p. 11).
45 Ibid., p. 9.
46 For example, T. S. Szasz (1970).
47 See, for different perspectives on this theme, P. Halmos (1970); H. Marcuse (1964); M. North (1972); and J. O'Neill (1972).
48 See, W. Reich (1972, p. 19).
49 S. Ewen (1972, pp. 33–45).
50 Scott (1972, p. 29).
51 S. Cohen (1971, p. 32).
52 Ibid., p. 33.
53 See, for example, the considerable caution with which Herbert Marcuse approaches the matter in his *Counter-Revolution and Revolt* (1969), and compare the earlier optimism of *An Essay on Liberation* (1969).
54 Sennett (1971, p. 40).
55 J. Nuttall (1970, p. 132).
56 Becker (1968, p. 364).

6 The political economy of crime: a comparative study of Nigeria and the USA

William J. Chambliss

Criminology shares in common with all other social thought the fact that the research we do and the explanations we divine flow from and reflect the general theoretical perspective within which we work. In the social sciences two perspectives dominate our work. These are commonly referred to as the 'functional' and 'dialectic' models of society.[1] In the study of crime these two models are intimately associated with the work of Emile Durkheim and Karl Marx.

The starting-point for both Marx and Durkheim is that we can understand crime (or any social phenomenon for that matter) only if we can articulate and describe the consequences which the event has for the larger set of social relations in which the event is implicated. In this sense, then, both perspectives are 'functional',[2] though the dialectic argues that the equilibrium produced by functional interrelation is necessarily a temporary state of a changing historical process and *not*, as the functional perspective suggests, an 'ingredient of all healthy societies'.[3] For Marx, a 'healthy society' would be one free of class conflict and therefore free of crime.

The dialectic and functional models diverge rather sharply on the issue of what exactly is contributed by crime to 'all healthy societies'. For Durkheim, crime's most important function (i.e. consequence) in society was its role in establishing and preserving the moral boundaries of the community:[4]

> Crime brings together upright consciences and concentrates them. We have only to notice what happens, particularly in a small town, when some moral scandal has just been committed. They stop each other on the street. They visit each other. They seek to come together to talk of the event and to wax indignant in common. From all the similar impressions which are exchanged, for all the temper that gets itself expressed, there emerges a

> unique temper . . . which is everybody's without being anybody's in particular. That is the public temper.

For Marx, the most important contribution made by crime to society (or function of crime in society) is its contribution to temporary economic stability in an economic system that is inherently unstable:[5]

> Crime takes a part of the superfluous population off the labour market and thus reduces competition among the labourers – up to a certain point preventing wages from falling below the minimum – the struggle against crime absorbs another part of this population. Thus the criminal comes in as one of those natural 'counterweights' which bring about a correct balance and open up a whole perspective of 'useful' occupations . . . the criminal . . . produces the whole of the police and of criminal justice, constables, judges, hangmen, juries, etc.; and all these different lines of business, which form equally many categories of the social division of labour, develop different capacities of the human spirit, create new needs and new wages of satisfying them. Torture alone has given rise to the most ingenious mechanical inventions, and employed many honorable craftsmen in the production of its instruments.

In addition, Marx viewed crime as contributing to political stability by legitimizing the State's monopoly on violence and justifying political and legal control of the masses.[6]

More specifically the two perspectives suggest the following different interpretations of crime:

Functional hypotheses	*Dialectic hypotheses*
1 Acts are criminal because they offend the morality of the people.	1 Acts are criminal because it is in the interests of the ruling class to so define them.
2 Persons are labelled criminal because their behaviour has gone beyond the tolerance limits of the community's conscience.	2 Persons are labelled criminal because so defining them serves the interests of the ruling class.
3 The lower classes are more likely to be arrested because they commit more crimes.	3 The lower classes are labelled criminal and the bourgeoisie is not because the bourgeoisie's control of the means of production gives them control of the State and law enforcement as well.
4 Crime is a constant in societies. All societies need	4 Crime varies from society to society depending on the

and produce crime.	political and economic structures of the society.
5 As societies become more specialized in the division of labour, more and more laws will reflect contractual disputes and penal laws will become less and less significant.	5 As capitalist societies industrialize, the division between social classes will grow and penal laws will increasingly have to be passed and enforced to maintain temporary stability by curtailing violent confrontations between social classes.
6 Socialist and capitalist societies should have the same amounts of crime where they have comparable rates of industrialization and bureaucratization.	6 Socialist and capitalist societies should have significantly different crime rates since class conflict will be less in socialist societies and therefore the amount of crime lower as well.
7 Crime makes people more aware of the interests they have in common.	7 Defining certain people as criminal permits greater control of the proletariat.
8 Crime creates a tighter bond between and leads to greater solidarity amongst members of the community.	8 Crime directs the hostility of the oppressed away from the oppressors and towards their own class.

Elsewhere I have investigated the extent to which the two paradigms are compatible with data on the creation of criminal laws.[7] In this chapter I hope to shed light on the relative utility of the two models in explaining the distribution and content of criminal behaviour. To do this I will report on the results of a comparative study of crime and criminal law enforcement in Nigeria and the USA.

Data collection

Our data comes from research in the USA – principally Seattle, Washington – and in Nigeria, principally Ibadan. The research methods employed are mainly those of a participant observer. In Seattle the research spanned almost ten years (1962–72), and in Ibadan the research took place during 1967–8. In both cities the data were gathered through extensive interviewing of informants from all sides of the criminal law – criminals, professional thieves, racketeers, prostitutes, government officials, police officers, businessmen and members of various social-class levels in the community. Needless to say, the sampling was what sociologists have come to call (with more than a slight bit of irony) 'convenience samples'. Any other sampling procedure is simply impossible in the almost impenetrable world of crime and law enforcement into which we embarked.

Nigeria and the USA share in common the fact that they inherited British common law at the time of their independence. Independence came somewhat later for Nigeria than for the USA but the legal systems inherited were very similar. As a result both countries share much the same foundation in statutes and common law principles. Whilst differences exist, they are not, for our purposes, of any great significance.

In both Nigeria and the USA it is a crime punishable by imprisonment and fine for any public official to accept a bribe, to solicit a bribe or to give special favours to a citizen for monetary considerations.

It is also against the law in both countries to run gambling establishments, to engage in or solicit for prostitutes, to sell liquor that has not been inspected and stamped by a duly appointed agency of the government, to run a taxi service without a licence, etc.

And, of course, both nations share the more obvious restrictions on murder, theft, robbery, rape and the standard array of criminal offences. In both countries there is a striking similarity in the types of laws that do not and those that do get enforced.[8]

Crime and law enforcement in Nigeria

In both Nigeria and the USA many laws can be and are systematically violated with impunity by those who control the political or economic resources of the society. Particularly relevant are those laws that restrict such things as bribery, racketeering (especially gambling), prostitution, drug distribution and selling, ursury and the whole range of criminal offences committed by businessmen in the course of their businesses (white-collar crimes).

In Nigeria the acceptance of bribes by government officials is blatantly public and virtually universal. When the vice president of a large research organization that was just getting established in Nigeria visited the head of the Nigerian Customs he was told by the Customs Director that 'at the outset it is important that we both understand that the customs office is corrupt from the top to the bottom'. Incoming American professors were usually asked by members of the faculty at the university if they would be willing to exchange their American dollars on the black market at a better exchange-rate than banks would offer. In at least one instance the Nigerian professor making this request was doing so for the military governor of the States within which the university was located.

Should the incoming American fail to meet a colleague who would wish to make an illegal transfer of funds he would in all likelihood be approached by any number of other citizens in high places. For example, the vice-president of the leading bank near the university would often approach American professors and ask if they would like to exchange their money through him personally and thereby receive a better exchange-rate than was possible if they dealt directly through the bank.

At the time of my study, tithes of this sort were paid at every level. Businessmen desiring to establish businesses found their way blocked interminably by bureaucratic red-tape until the proper amount of 'dash' had been given to someone with the power to effect the result desired. Citizens riding buses were asked for cigarettes and small change by army soldiers who manned check-points. The soldiers, in turn, had to pay a daily or weekly tithe to superior officers in order to be kept at this preferential assignment. At the border one could bring French wine, cigarettes and many other prohibited commodities into Nigeria, so long as prior arrangements had been made with the customs officers either in Lagos (the capital of the country) or at the check-point itself. The prior arrangements included payment of a bribe.

As a result of bribes and payoffs there flourished a large and highly profitable trade in a wide variety of vices. Prostitution was open and rampant in all of the large cities of Nigeria – it was especially well developed in those cities where commerce and industry brought large numbers of foreigners. Gambling establishments, located mainly in large European-style hotels, and managed incidently by Italian visitors, catered to the moneyed set with a variety of games of chance competitive with Monte Carlo or Las Vegas. There was a large illicit liquor trade (mostly a home-brewed, gin-like drink) as well as a smaller but nevertheless profitable trade in drugs that received political and legal protection through payoffs to high-level officials.

In at least Ibadan and Lagos gangs of professional thieves operated with impunity. These gangs of thieves were well organized and included the use of beggars and young children as cover for theft activities. The links to the police were sufficient to guarantee that suspects would be treated leniently – usually allowed to go with no charges being brought. In one instance an entire community within the city of Ibadan was threatened by thieves with total destruction. The events leading up to this are revealing. The community, which I shall call Lando, had been victimized by a gang of thieves who broke into homes and stole valuable goods. The elders of Lando hired four men to guard the community. When thieves came one evening the hired guards caught and killed three of them. The next day the Oba of the community was called on by two men from another part of the city. These men expressed grave concern that some of their compatriots had been killed in Lando. The Oba informed them that if any other thieves came to Lando they would be dealt with similarly. The thieves' representatives advised the Oba that if such a thing happened the thieves would burn the community to the ground. When the Oba said he would call the police it was pointed out to him that the chief of police was the brother-in-law of one of the thieves. Ultimately an agreement was reached, whereby the thieves agreed to stop stealing in Lando in return for the Oba's promise that the thieves could sell their stolen property in Lando on market day.

Ibadan is a very cosmopolitan city which lies in the Yoruba section of western Nigeria. Although dominated by the Yoruba, there are nonetheless large numbers of Hausa, Ibo and other ethnic groups in the city. The Hausa, who are strongly Muslim, whilst the Yoruba are roughly 50 per cent Christian, occupy a ghetto within Ibadan which is almost exclusively Hausa. Despite the fact that the Hausa are an immigrant group where one might expect the crime rate to be high, there are very few Hausa arrested for crime. This is particularly impressive, since there is a general belief that the Hausa are responsible for some of the more efficient and effective groups of professional thieves in the area. The explanation for this apparently lies in the fact that the Hausa have a strong leadership which intervenes with payoffs and cash to government and police officials, whenever a member of their community is in any difficulty.

Payment of bribes to the police is usually possible whenever an arrest is likely. An incoming American who illegally photographed an airport was allowed to go (without even destroying his film) upon payment of fifteen dollars to the arresting officer. Six dollars was sufficient for the wife of an American professor to avoid arrest for reckless driving. A young son of a wealthy merchant was arrested on numerous occasions for being drunk, driving without a licence, stealing and getting into fights. On every occasion the police returned him to the custody of his parents without charges being filed when the father paid the arresting officer (or the policeman on the desk) thirty to forty-five dollars.

Such practices were not atypical, but were instead the usual procedure. It was said, and research bears this out, that one with money could pay to be excused from any type or amount of crime.

Who, then, did get arrested? In general those who lacked either the money or the political influence to fix a criminal charge. The arrest rates for the immigrant, indigenous and Hausa areas are shown in Table 1. The most common arrest of youth was for 'street trading' – that is, selling items on the street. The second most frequent offence was 'being away from home' or 'sleeping out without protection'. Amongst adults, 'suspiciousness', public indecency, intoxication and being with no visible means of support were the most common offences. Although robbery, theft and burglary were common offences (in a sample of 300 residents of Ibadan, 12·7 per cent reported having been the victim of burglary), arrests for these offences were much less frequent.

Anyone who has lived or travelled in foreign countries will not be surprised by these findings. What is usually not recognized, however, is that these same kinds of things characterize crime and criminal law enforcement in the USA (and possibly every other nation) as well.

TABLE 1 *Arrest rate for 1,000 population*

	Ibadan, Nigeria, 1967	
Immigrant areas	*Indigenous area*	*Hausa area*
1·41	0·61	0·54

Crime and law enforcement in Seattle

Seattle, like Ibadan, is a city of 1,000,000 people with its own police, government and set of laws inherited from Britain. In Seattle, as in Ibadan, one can find any type of vice that suits the palate. One must travel away from the middle- and upper-class suburbs that ring the city and venture into the never-never land of skid-row derelicts, the black ghetto or a few other pockets of rundown hotels, cafés and cabarets that are sprinkled along freeways and by the docks.

Here one can find prostitution, gambling, usury, drugs, pornography, bootleg liquor, bookmaking and pinball machines. Simply in terms of profit, gambling and usury are most important.

Gambling ranges from bookmaking (at practically every street corner in the centre of the city) to open poker games, bingo parlours, off-track betting, casinos, roulette and dice games (concentrated in a few locations and also floating out into the suburban country clubs and fraternal organizations) and innumerable two- and five-dollar stud-poker games scattered liberally throughout the city.

The most conspicuous card-games take place from about ten in the morning (it varies slightly from one 'fun house' to the next) until midnight. But there are a number of other twenty-four-hour games that run constantly. In the more public games, the limit ranges from one to five dollars for each bet; in the more select games that run twenty-four hours a day there is a 'pot limit' or 'no limit' rule. These games are reported to have betting as high as 20,000 and 30,000 dollars. I have seen a bet made and called for 1,000 dollars in one of these games. During this game, which was the highest stakes game I witnessed in the six years of study, the police lieutenant in charge of the vice squad was called in to supervise the game – not, need I add, to break up the game or make any arrests, only to insure against violence.

Prostitution covers the usual range of ethnic group, age, shape and size of female. It is also found in houses with madames *à la* New Orleans stereotype, on the street through pimps, or in a suburban apartment building or hotels. Prices range from five dollars for a short time with a street walker to 200 dollars for a night with a lady who has her own apartment (which she usually shares with her boyfriend who is discreetly away during business operations).

High-interest loans are easy to arrange through stores that advertise 'your signature is worth $5,000'. It is really worth considerably more; it may in fact be worth your life. The interest rates vary from a low of 20 per cent for three months to as high as 100 per cent for varying periods. Repayment is demanded not through the courts but through the help of 'The Gaspipe Gang' who call on recalcitrant debtors and use physical force to bring about payment. The 'interest only' repayment is the most popular alternative practised by borrowers and is preferred by the loan sharks as well. The longer repayment can be prolonged the more advantageous it is to the loan agents.

Pinball machines are readily available throughout the city and most of them pay off in cash.

The gambling, prostitution, drug distribution, pornography and usury (high-interest loans) which flourish in the lower-class centre of the city do so with the compliance, encouragement and co-operation of the major political and law-enforcement officials in the city. There is, in fact, a symbiotic relationship between the law-enforcement–political organizations of the city and a group of *local* (as distinct from national) men who control the distribution of vices.

The payoffs and briberies in Seattle are complex. The simpler and more straightforward are those made by each gambling establishment. A restaurant or cabaret with cardroom attached had to pay around 200 dollars each month to the police and 200 dollars to the 'syndicate'. In reality, these were two branches of the same group of men but the payoffs were made separately. Anyone who refused these payments was harassed by fire inspectors, health inspectors, licensing difficulties and even physical violence from enforcers who worked for the crime canal in the city. Similarly, places with pinball machines, pornography, bookmaking or prostitution had to pay regularly to the 'Bagman' who collected a fee for the police.

Payoffs to policemen were also required of tow truck operators, cabaret owners and other businesses where police cooperation was necessary. Two truck drivers carried with them a matchbox with three dollars in it and when asked for a light by the policeman who had called them to the scene of an accident they gave him the matchbox with the three dollars. Cabaret owners paid according to how large their business was. The police could extract payoffs because the laws were so worded as to make it virtually impossible to own a profitable cabaret without violating the law. For example, it was illegal to have an entertainer closer than twenty-five feet to the nearest customer. A cabaret, to comply with this ordinance, would have had to have a night-club the size of a large ballroom at which point the atmosphere would have been too sterile as to drive customers away, not to mention the fact that such large spaces are exceedingly expensive in the downtown section of the city. Thus, the police could, if they chose to, close down a cabaret on a moment's notice. Payoffs were a necessary investment to assure that the police would not so choose.

The trade in licences was notoriously corrupt. It was generally agreed by my informants that to get a tow-truck licence one had to pay a bribe of 10,000 dollars; a cardroom licence was 25,000 dollars; taxi-cab licences were unavailable as were licences for distributing pinball machines or juke-boxes. These licences had all been issued to members of the syndicate that controlled the rackets and no outsiders were permitted in.

There were innumerable instances of payoffs to politicians and government officials for real-estate deals, businesses and stock transactions. In each case, the participants were a combination of local businessmen, racketeers, local politicians and government officials.

Interestingly, there is also a minority ghetto within Seattle where one would expect to find a high crime rate. In Seattle this is the Japanese-American section of the city.

It is widely believed that the Japanese-Americans have a very low propensity to crime. This is usually attributed to the family-centred orientation of the Japanese-American community. There is some evidence, however, that this perspective is largely a self-fulfilling prophecy.[9] Table 2 shows a comparison between the self-reported delinquency and arrest rates of Japanese-American youth for a selected year. The data suffers, of course, from problems inherent in such comparisons, but none the less the point cannot be gainsaid that the actual crime rate amongst Japanese-American youth is considerably higher than the conventional view would suggest.

Thus, we see that in both the Hausa area of Ibadan and the Japanese-American section of Seattle there is reason to suspect a reasonably high crime rate but official statistics show an exceptionally low one. When discussing Hausa crime earlier, I attributed this fact to the payoffs made by Hausa leaders to the police and other government officials.

TABLE 2 *Comparison of arrests (for 1963) and self-reported delinquency involvement, by racial groups*[a]

Racial group	*Per cent arrested*	*Per cent self-reporting high delinquency involvement*[b]
White	11	53
Negro	36	52
Japanese	2	36

[a] Based on data from Richard H. Nagasawa, *Delinquency and Non-Delinquency. A Study of Status Problems and Perceived Opportunity*, unpublished M.A. thesis, University of Washington, 1965, p. 35.

[b] A self-reported delinquency scale was developed and the respondents were divided so that 50 per cent of the sample was categorized as having high and 50 per cent as having low delinquent involvement.

Somewhat the same sort of system prevails in Seattle as well, especially with regard to the rackets. Whereas prostitutes, pornography shops, gambling establishments, cabaret operators and tow-truck operators must pay off individually to the police and the syndicate, the Japanese-American community did so *as a community*. The tithe was collected by a local businessman and was paid to the police and the syndicate in a group sum. Individual prostitutes and vice racketeers might at times have to do special favours for a policeman or political figure but by and large the payoffs were made collectively rather than individually.

This collective payoff was in large measure a result of the same characteristic of both the Hausa and the Japanese-American communities, namely the heterogeneous social-class nature of the community. Typically, wealthy or middle-class members of the lower-class white slum or the black ghettos moved out of these areas as rapidly as their incomes permitted. So too with Yoruba, Ibo or other ethnic groups in Ibadan. But many, though certainly not all, upper- and middle-class Hausa in Ibadan, and Japanese-Americans in Seattle retained their residence in their respective communities. As a result the enforcement of any law became more problematic for law-enforcement agencies. Arrests made of any youth or adult always carried with it the possibility that the suspect would have a politically influential parent or friend. There was also the possibility that a payoff of some sort (including political patronage) would override the policeman's efforts. Since there was also the necessity to hide from the middle and upper class the extent to which the police closed their eyes to the rackets, it was then convenient to avoid having many police in the Hausa and Japanese-American community. The myth of these areas as 'no crime' sections of the city was thus very convenient. By contrast, since only those members of the middle- and upper-class who were seeking the vices would come to the skid-row area or the black ghetto, then the presence of the police was not problematic and in fact helped to assure the 'respectable' citizen that he could partake of his prurient interests without fear of being the victim of a robbery or of any violence.

As in Nigeria, all of this corruption, bribery and blatant violation of the law was taking place, whilst arrests were being made and people sent to jail or prison for other offences. In Seattle over 70 per cent of all arrests during the time of the study were for public drunkenness.[10] It was literally the case that the police were arresting drunks on one side of a building whilst on the other side a vast array of other offences were being committed.

Discussion

What, then, are we to conclude from these admittedly brief sketches of selected aspects of crime and law enforcement in Nigeria and America? The most obvious conclusion is that these law-enforcement systems are *not* organized to *reduce crime* or to enforce *the public morality*. They are rather organized to *manage* crime by cooperating with the most criminal groups and enforcing laws against those whose crimes are a minimal threat to the society. In doing so the law enforcers end up as crime producers. By promising profit and security to those criminals who engage in organized criminal activities from which the political and legal systems can profit, law enforcement practices produce crime by selecting and encouraging the perpetuation of criminal careers.

This general conclusion is clearly in line with the postulates we earlier derived from the dialectic perspective. The findings are incompatible with the relevant postulates derived from the functional perspective. Particularly relevant are postulates 1–3 (p. 168). The data from this comparative study clearly support the argument that criminal acts which serve the interests of the ruling class will go unsanctioned whilst those that do not will be punished. It seems likely, although not necessarily proven by these data, that we can much better explain the propensity to violate the law as a consequence of economic interests than we can explain it as a consequence of socialization into particular value-sets of normative systems. The lawyers in the prosecuting attorney's office, the judges on the bench as well as the policeman on the beat all shared an anti-criminal set of values and norms, but they nonetheless took bribes and encouraged racketeering because it was in their economic interests to do so.

The question as to whether crime contributes to social solidarity (the functional argument) or is an economic product (the dialectic argument) is difficult to untangle because of the vagueness of the claims. 'Social solidarity' would, presumably, suggest that crime increases consensus. But the prevalence of widespread graft and vice in Nigeria and the USA would seem to reflect the perpetuate dissensus rather than consensus. It would seem that a much more plausible characterization derives from the dialectic position that crime is an economic product in view of the intimate tie-in between businessmen, politicians, law enforcers and racketeers that has been discovered.

The present study does not bear directly on the other propositions outlined above. We can nonetheless speculate on the relative merits of the two perspectives. A few years ago Kai Erikson published an extremely imaginative account of the causes and effects of crime on the Puritan communities of New England.[11] His data showed quite clearly that the leaders of the community (that is, those who controlled the political and economic resources of the community) used crime as a convenient label to pin on groups who threatened their position. By this technique, there was a semblance of peace immediately following each of the 'crime-waves'. The peace, needless to say, was gained at the expense of those individuals and groups who had previously threatened the monopoly on power that the entrenched power-holders had. Erikson interprets the results of these encounters between various groups and social classes as leading to increased social solidarity. This may be the case; however, it is equally clear that the increased solidarity was short-lived for, by Erikson's own account there were three major crime-waves produced by the leaders of the community within a relatively short period of time.

Postulates 4–6 (pp. 168–9) deal with expected differences between societies. The functional argument implies that societies at comparable levels of industrialization should share comparable crime rates. Crime statistics are notoriously unreliable, so we are really whistling in the dark on this issue. It is, however, worth noting that if we were to rank other societies according to the degree to which the resources of the society have been distributed throughout the population, we might find some interesting comparisons. The crime rate in the USA is probably amongst the highest in the world and its resources the most concentrated in the hands of a few. China's resources seem to be far more equitably distributed and their crime rate correspondingly lower. Sweden and Norway are, if my impression is correct, somewhere in between the extremes of China and the

USA on both variables. And one gets the impression that crime in East Germany is far less prevalent than is the case in West Germany. But lacking reliable data, these are only highly impressionistic observations.

Summary

Comparative data from research on crime and law enforcement in Nigeria and the USA has been used to shed light on the relative utility of postulates derived from the functional and dialectic theoretical models. The existence of widespread corruption in the political and legal systems of both countries and the prevalence of vices coupled with the fact that most of the law-enforcement energy is devoted to the arrest and processing of minor offences committed by persons at the bottom of the social-class hierarchy, suggests the superiority of the dialectic model.

Notes

1 I have chosen to use the term 'dialectic' rather than the more familiar 'conflict model' because the latter has unfortunately been used to include pluralist models which are quite incompatible with the more routine viewpoint which divides social thought along the most important dimension of criticism.

2 Pierre L. Van den Berghe (1964, pp. 695–705).

3 Émile Durkheim (1958, p. 67).

4 Émile Durkheim (1960, p. 102).

5 Karl Marx (1969, pp. 375–6).

6 Karl Marx (1964b, pp. 225–30).

7 William J. Chambliss (1974, chapter 1).

8 Throughout the chapter we rely on data from Ibadan and Seattle as a basis for discussing the patterns of both countries. This leap may disturb some and if so then you may consider the study as speaking only to the two cities with only a promise of application more generally. From a variety of research studies and my own impressions, I am convinced that what is true of Ibadan and Seattle is also true throughout both countries; but whether or not this is the case should not affect the overall conclusions of this enquiry.

9 Richard H. Nagasawa (1965). See also William Chambliss and Richard Nagasawa (1969, pp. 71–7).

10 James P. Spradley (1970, p. 128).

11 Kai Erikson (1965).

7 Crime control in capitalist society: a critical philosophy of legal order

Richard Quinney

I begin with the contention that we do not adequately understand our contemporary existence. Our comprehension of the present, as well as the past, is mystified by a consciousness that only serves to maintain the existing order. And if we are ever to remove the oppression of the age, we must critically understand the world about us. Only with a new consciousness – a critical philosophy – can we begin to realize the world of which we are capable.

My position is thus a critical one: critical not only in an assessment of our current condition, but critical in working toward a new existence, in a negation of what *is* by thinking about and practising what *could be*. And to follow the argument to its conclusion, any possibility for a different life will come about only through new ideas that are formed in the course of altering the way to think and the way we live. What is involved here is no less than a whole new way of life. What is necessary is a new beginning – intellectually, spiritually and politically.

Understanding legal order

Nowhere is the inadequacy of our understanding more apparent than in the thoughts and lives we lead in relation to legal order. Our thinking about law and crime only confirms an official ideology that supports the existing social and economic order. As long as we fail to understand the nature of law in contemporary society, we will be bound by an oppressive reality. What is urgently needed is a critical philosophy of legal order.

I am attempting to develop a critical philosophy of legal order that will allow us to contemplate and act toward the fulfilment of a new reality. In order to accomplish this, it is necessary to understand where we have been in regard to our thinking about the legal order and the relation of our thoughts and actions to the official reality.

In order to understand where we have been and where we are going, several modes of thought must be distinguished. Each mode embodies its own epistemology and ontology, its own way of thinking and its own assumptions about reality. Each mode of thought takes a particular stance toward the philosophical issues of objectivity, reflexivity and transcendence. Furthermore, each mode carries with it a specific relation to the dominant order. Each way of thinking has its own potential for either oppressing us or liberating us.

I will present the four modes of thought as follows: (1) the positivistic, (2) the social constructionist, (3) the phenomenological and (4) the critical. My objective is to develop a critical philosophy of legal order. The result will be a Marxist theory of crime control in capitalist society.

Positivism

The positivistic mode of thought begins with the realist assumptions about existence. These assumptions are shared by anyone who has not reflected about the problems of perception and experience. At best, there is only a naïve acquaintance with epistemological and ontological concerns. Rather, 'methodology' is the chief concern of the positivist. How to develop a method to grasp or 'discover' the laws of the physical world occupies the attention of the positivist.

Positivism follows the simple epistemology that absolutely separates the knower from the known. Objectivity is assumed possible because of the belief that an order exists independent of the observer. The observer's cognitive apparatus supposedly does not affect the nature of what is known. Given enough knowledge, accumulated systematically, the scientist could predict future events and control their occurrence. An orderly universe could be established through man's knowledge and manipulation of the external world.

The overriding emphasis of positivistic thought is on the *explanation* of events. And in following a mechanistic conception of the relation of social facts, the positivist usually couches his explanations in terms of causality. What is ignored in this approach to explanation is an *examination* (even an awareness) of the philosophical assumptions by which the observer operates (Louch, 1969). Nor is there a recognition that the nature of explanation depends upon the kinds of things investigated, nor that explanation requires a description of the unique context in which events occur. Likewise, the positivist refuses to recognize that to assess and make statements about human actions is to engage in a moral endeavor. Instead, the positivist regards his activity as being 'value-free'.

The intellectual failure of positivism is that of not being reflexive.

There is little or no attempt to examine or even question the metaphysics of enquiry, to turn the activity of explanation back upon itself. The positivist refuses to be introspective. His concern is to get on with the task of explaining, without considering what he is doing. Positivistic thought is of a particular kind; it is calculative thinking as Heidegger has described: 'Its peculiarity consists in the fact that whenever we plan, research, or organize, we always reckon with conditions that are given' (Heidegger, 1967, p. 46). In other words, there is little time to ask the crucial philosophical questions that ultimately affect the operations of investigation. 'Calculative thinking races from one prospect to the next. Calculative thinking never stops, never collects itself. Calculative thinking is not meditative thinking, not thinking which contemplates the meaning which reigns in everything that is' (ibid.).

The political failure of positivist thought, as related to its intellectual failure, is its acceptance of the *status quo*. There is no questioning of the established order, just as there is no examination of scientific assumptions. The official reality is the one with which the positivist operates – and the one that he accepts and supports. The positivist takes for granted the dominant ideology that emphasizes bureaucratic rationality, modern technology, centralized authority and scientific control (Schaar, 1970, pp. 303–8). Positivistic thought, in fact, naturally lends itself to the official ideology and the interests of the ruling class. Little wonder that the talents of positivistic social scientists are in such demand by those who rule. Social scientists have failed to break out of the interpretations and practices of the official reality. The official reality is the reality within which the positivist comfortably operates, not asking what could be and never seeking to transcend the established order.

Most of the research and theoretical developments in the sociology of law have been dominated by the positivistic mode of thought.[1] The legal order is taken for granted, with research directed toward an understanding of *how* the system operates. Little attention is devoted to questions about why law exists, whether law is indeed necessary, or what a just system would look like. If the value of justice is considered at all, the concern is with the equitability of the system, rather than whether the system should exist in the first place. Suggestions may be made for changing particular laws, but the outlines of the legal system are to remain intact (Morris and Hawkins, 1970). Inadequacies in the administration of justice may be noted, but prescriptions for change are in terms of more technical and efficient procedures.

Likewise, the efforts of criminologists have been devoted almost solely to the most conservative interests. Attention traditionally has been on the violator of criminal law, rather than on the legal system itself (Jeffery, 1956, pp. 658–72). Solution of the crime problem has been in terms of changing the law-breaker rather than altering the legal system. Only recently have some criminologists realized that law is problematic, turning their attention to a study of criminal law. But, for the most part, these studies have been based on the positivistic mode of thought (Quinney, 1969).

The conservative nature of most research and theory on law and crime is logically related to the social scientist's emphasis on social order. In the search for the natural laws of society, social scientists have favoured any existing arrangements that would assure an orderly society. Anything that would threaten the existing order has been regarded as a violation of natural order, thus a social pathology to be eradicated, ameliorated or punished in some way. Social scientists have formed an easy alliance with the ruling class that profits from the preservation of the existing capitalist order.

Thus, in following the positivistic mode of thought, social scientists (and especially those concentrating on the study of law and crime) have developed a particular kind of wisdom regarding social and political life. Research and theory in criminology and the sociology of law have done little more than provide a rationale for the established order. A social theory that would allow for human liberation has been excluded. It now seems evident that positivistic thought cannot provide a liberating conception of human existence. Instead, we must turn to alternative modes of thought.

Social constructionism

Social constructionist thought begins with a recognition of philosophical idealism. Social constructionists work with an ontology that questions the existence of an objective reality apart from the individual's imagination. Whether there are universal essences is, indeed, problematic. What can be assumed is that objects cannot exist *independently* of our minds, or at least that any such existence is important only as long as it can be perceived.

The epistemological assumption of social constructionist thought is that observations are based on our mental *constructions*, rather than on the raw apprehension of the physical world. The concern of the social constructionist is not primarily with the correspondence between 'objective reality' and observation, but between observation and the utility of such observation in understanding our own subjective, multiple worlds.

Hence, following these assumptions, the social scientist's constructs have to be founded upon the world created by social actors. As Schutz conceptualized the problem: 'The constructs of the social sciences are, so to speak, constructs of the second degree, that is, constructs of the constructs made by the actors on the social scene, whose behavior the social scientist has to observe and to explain in accordance with the procedural rules of his science' (1963, p. 242).

The world that is important to the social constructionist, then, is the one created by the social actions of human beings, through interaction and intercommunication with others. This *social reality* involves the social meanings and the products of the subjective world of actors (Schutz, 1962; Berger and Luckmann, 1966). Persons, accordingly, construct activities and patterns of action as they attach meanings to their everyday life.

The social constructionist mode of thought makes a major advance over positivistic thought in respect to the crucial matter of reflexivity. The social constructionist questions the process by which he knows, instead of taking it for granted. In the course of this consideration, the social constructionist reflects on his activity as observer, using to advantage the social and personal nature of his observation. That this reflexivity does not extend to a political stance, and possibly political action, is a shortcoming inherent in the social constructionist mode of thought.

Further, social constructionist thought generally concentrates on the world of meanings created by social actors. Emphasis, especially in ethnomethodological studies, is on the construction of social order. Such concentration tends to ignore a world of events and structures that exist independent of the consciousness of social actors. This is the conservative side of social constructionist thought, making it inadequate for a critical perspective. As Lichtman has written about this inadequacy: 'It is overly subjective and voluntaristic, lacks an awareness of historical concreteness, is naïve in its account of mutual typification and ultimately abandons the sense of human beings in struggle with an alien reality which tends to dissolve the concept or 'ideology' or 'false consciousness' and leaves us, often against the will of its advocates, without a critical posture toward the present inhuman reality' (Lichtman, 1970–71, pp. 75–94).

Therefore, it is often necessary to revise or reject the world as some social actors conceive it. To accept the world that the social actors portray is often to accept the view of reality that the ruling class perpetuates to assure its own dominance. Social constructionist thought fails to provide a stance that would allow us to transcend the official reality – and ultimately, our current existence. Whilst social constructionists furnish us with the beginnings for an examination of multiple realities, they fail to provide a yardstick for judging the goodness of one reality over another. Social relativism prevails at the expense of a critical understanding of the social world.

The social constructionist perspective, however, has given new vitality to the study of crime and the law. In departing significantly from positivistic studies, social constructionists have turned attention to the problematic nature of the legal order. Crime and other forms of stigmatized behaviour are viewed first as categories that are created and imposed upon some persons by others (Becker, 1963). Crime thus exists because of the social construction and application of the label of crime.

Similarly, criminal law is not autonomous to society, but is itself a construction, created by those who are in positions of power. The administration of justice is a human, social activity that is constructed as various legal agents interpret and impose their order on those they select for processing (Cicourel, 1968). The social reality of crime is thus a constructive process whereby criminal laws are established and administered, behaviours are developed in relation to these criminal definitions, and conceptions of crime are always being constructed (Quinney, 1970a).

The legal order, accordingly, is a human activity. It is an order that is created for political purposes, to assure the hegemony of the ruling class. However, social constructionist thought stops at this point. To be sure, there are critical implications. There is the libertarian ideal that individuals should not be controlled by others, that persons must be free to pursue their human potential. But there is, nevertheless, a failure to provide an image of what a new world should look like. Without such an image of what could be, an understanding of the current reality lacks a critical perspective. The ideal of liberation may be present, but unless that ideal is accompanied by a critique of the present and an image of an authentic existence, transcendence of the existing order is unlikely. Critical thought and action must be informed by a critical philosophy.

Phenomenology

Phenomenological thought departs markedly from positivistic and social constructionist thought in its basic intention. Whilst the other modes of thought are concerned with the explanation of social life, phenomenological thought begins by examining the process by which we understand the world. Explanation as a form of thought is itself examined. Hence, the philosophical problems of epistemology and ontology are a major concern of the phenomenologist.

Phenomenologists, whilst differing considerably amongst themselves, generally agree that our knowledge of the physical world comes from our experiences. But, they continue, when we talk about the physical world we are not limited by our experiences. That is, we are not limited by our actual experiences; we are able to talk about *possible* experiences, thus altering our perception of things in the world. As long as a physical object exists in the world, it is possible to experience it. What is important is that an object is perceivable. We are thus capable of perceiving the essence of things.

The phenomenologists may proceed by 'bracketing' the questions of objective reality in order to turn attention to the reality in *consciousness*. The phenomenon in question, then, is that which manifests itself immediately in consciousness. Following Kant's distinctions, the phenomenologist is primarily concerned with *phenomenon*, or the appearance of reality in itself (Lauer, 1965, pp. 1–2; Thevenaz, 1962, pp. 42–3). Yet, it is possible to think about what is not known, the 'thing-in-itself,' or the *noumenon*, of which the phenomenon is the known aspect. Hence, our knowledge of phenomena is always subject to revision.

Consciousness itself is thus the course of our understanding of the world. Knowledge about the world cannot stand apart from our sense of things. Any understanding of an objective thing can come about only through our consciousness of the thing. Reality is not to be found existing independently of our consciousness.[2] Essence, or the essential, is thus what the human mind understands through its consciousness, in the course of its experiences in the world. Any objectivity is to be achieved by means of our own subjectivity – that is, through our consciousness.

Phenomenological thought is thought in its purest form. Following Kant's further distinction between thinking and knowing, phenomenologists are engaged in thinking beyond the limitations of knowledge. There is the urge to think and understand in contrast to solely construct verifiable knowledge (Kant, 1929). Whilst knowledge is not denied, room is made for thinking, for thinking about the possibilities. This allows the phenomenologist to think about such otherwise unthinkable topics as the meaning of our existence.

The urge to think forces us to transcend our conventional knowledge about the world and our place in it. It allows us to momentarily remove ourselves from our concrete experiences. This is, as Heidegger has termed it, meditative thinking: 'Meditative thinking demands of us not to cling one-sidedly to a single idea, nor to run down a one-track course of ideas. Meditative thinking demands of us that we engage ourselves with what at first sight does not go together at all' (Heidegger, 1966, p. 53). A comportment which enables us to keep open the meaning hidden in the world, in the arrangements of modern society, is what Heidegger further described as the 'openness to the mystery'. Related to this is a 'releasement toward things'. Through the two, in the course of meditative thinking, we seek our own true nature. And, as Heidegger writes, 'They grant us the possibility of dwelling in the world in a totally different way. They promise us a new ground and foundation upon which we can stand and endure in the world of technology without being imperilled by it' (ibid.).

The idea of some form of transcendence has been basic to most phenomenological thought. For Kant the phenomenological method was transcendental in that we attend to our experiencing of an object, rather than to the object directly, that all existing ideas be placed in abeyance. Therefore, to be transcendental is to be reflexive. Phenomenology, as Zaner has recently written, 'is "transcendental" because it is *foundational*, seeking to encover and explicatively analyse the necessary presuppositions of every actual and possible object and process of consciousness, leading ultimately to the grounds for philosophical reflection itself (reflexivity)' (Zaner, 1970, p. 203). The essence of a thing can be attained only, accordingly, through a transcendental philosophy – by being reflexive.

It is in the transcendental thinking of some of the phenomenologists that we find the inspiration for moving beyond the conventional wisdom of the age, including our contemporary knowledge of the legal order. Instead of reifying the social order, or giving an account of ordered existence, the movement is toward a transcendence of our experience. This is a necessary step as we begin to act in a way that will demystify the social world. Our primary interest is not in the development of a new social science (still a reified science), but in the creation of a new existence, an existence that is free of all reifications.

Phenomenological thought by itself, however, is incomplete for obtaining our objectives. Although it provides a drastic and necessary move beyond the other modes of thought, it lacks the critical edge that would allow us to truly transcend the present, in life as in mind. Phenomenology does make us question the assumptions by which we know and by which we live. This is its major achievement. But what is needed is a philosophy that would allow us to actively transcend the existing order, one that would allow us to be committed. We thus turn to the development of a critical philosophy.

Critical philosophy

A critical philosophy is one that is *radically* critical. It is a philosophy that goes to the roots of our lives, to the foundations and the fundamentals, to the essentials of consciousness (ibid., pp. 112–13, 117, 196, 203). In the rooting out of presuppositions we are able to assess every actual and possible experience. The operation is one of demystification, the removal of the myths – the false consciousness – created by the official reality. Conventional experience is revealed for what it is – a reification of an oppressive social order. The underside of official reality is thereby exposed. The liberating force of radical criticism is the movement from revelation to the development of a new consciousness and an active life in which we transcend the established existence. A critical philosophy is a form of life.

Thinking in itself is the beginning of a critical philosophy. For in the act of thought we engage in a particular kind of life, a reflective life that liberates us from preconceptions. Such theorizing, Blum contends, expresses self, is a display of mind. Furthermore: 'This "calling to mind", following an interpretation of Wittgenstein, is a way of recovering what one has all along, it is a way of seeing and as such it is inextricably tied to a way of living. More than this, it is to reconstitute or recreate out of one's life and history of a society another possibility for seeing. To theorise is to re-formulate one's self' (Blum, 1970, p. 305). The theorist is thus showing another possibility for seeing and living. Such theorizing has the potential of allowing us to comprehend a version of a possible society. Our selves are transformed in the course of theorizing.

The concept of thought in relation to a form of life is firmly based in the classic philosophical tradition. This is the theoretical attitude that ideas are to inform actions, that life is to be enlightened by thought. A critical philosophy, as Habermas (1971a, pp. 301–17) has suggested, is one that destroys the illusion of objectivism (the illusion of a reality apart from consciousness). Conceived in this way, thought itself is necessarily critical. In demystifying our lives of all presuppositions, our attention is directed to a critique of our current existence. In a critical philosophy truth is linked to the intention of the good and true life.

Thus, thinking's chief characteristic, as Hannah Arendt (1971, pp. 417–46) notes in an essay on thinking and moral considerations, is that it interrupts all doing, all ordinary activity. We are momentarily removed from our worldly associations; it is as though we entered into a different existence. Arendt adds that 'thinking, the quest for meaning – rather than the scientist's thirst for knowledge for its own sake – can be felt to be "unnatural", as though men, when they begin to think, engage in some activity contrary to the human condition' (ibid., p. 424). Arendt then concludes that only with thought that is aimed toward certain ideals (with the desiring of love, wisdom, beauty and justice) are we prepared with a kind of thought that promotes a moral existence. Only when we are filled with what Socrates called *eros*, a love that desires what is not, can we find what is good.

Without critical thought we are bound to the only form of social life we know – that which currently exists. We are not then free to choose a better life; our only activity is in further support of the system in which we are enslaved. Our current cultural and social arrangements, supported as they are by a bureaucratic-technological system of production and distribution, are a threat to individual freedom – including the freedom to know that this system is oppressive and may be altered. Such a system tends to preclude the possibility of an opposition from emerging within it. In aspiring to the rewards that the system holds out to us, we are unable to consider an alternative existence. Such is the message of Marcuse (1964, p. 9) in his discussion of the 'one-dimensional' character of our present reality. Only in a negation of the present can we experience something else.

It is apparent, then, that what prevents us from seeing clearly is the ideology of the age. The modern institutional order finds its legitimation in an ideology that stresses the rationality of science and technology (Habermas, 1970, pp. 81–121). A generalized belief in the importance of controlled scientific-technical progress gives legitimacy to a particular class – the one that utilizes science and technology. The extent to which this ideology pervades the whole culture limits the possibility of emancipation, even for the perceived need for this liberation. Moreover, the technocratic consciousness prevents a critical philosophy. Our understanding about the legal order, to be concrete, is limited by the ideology on which the legal order itself rests. That is, the legal order is founded on the rationality of science and technology, and the dominant mode of thought in understanding that order is based on this same ideology. Little wonder that we have been unable to break out of our conventional wisdom.

It is in a critical philosophy that we are able to break with the ideology of the age. For built into the process of critical thinking is the ability to think negatively. This dialectical form of thought allows us to question current experience (Marcuse, 1960, pp. vii–xiv, 3–29). By being able to entertain an alternative, we can better understand what exists. Rather than merely looking for an objective reality, our concern is with the negation of the established order. Through this negation we are better able to understand what we experience. Possibly, only by means of this dialectic can the present be comprehended. Certainly, the present cannot be surpassed until the dialectic is applied to our thought.

But more than negative thinking is required in a philosophy that will move us to a radical reconstruction of our lives – indeed, to revolution itself. In order to reject something we must have some idea of what things could be like. It is at this point that a critical philosophy must ultimately develop a Marxist perspective. In the Marxist notion of the authentic human being we are provided with a concrete image of the possible. Current realities are judged in terms of how they alienate human beings. Only in the conscious grasp of the world can we change the world. The process is a collective one, consciousness and action developed in association with others. The imagery is transcendental, to attain what is natural to us by removing that which obstructs our lives. It is in the contradiction of an oppressive existence, between what exists and what is authentically human, that we understand our reality and act to bring about a liberating existence.

To think in a Marxist fashion is to be genuinely critical, requiring the fullest extent of our critical resources. For most of us, however, Marxist thought has been presented in two forms: either in the liberal reactionary version, as a response to the Cold War mentality of the last twenty years, or in the orthodox realpolitik version. That we accepted these versions, and resorted to positivistic-pluralist thought, is the stark measure of the lack of critical facilities.

In contrast, what we are experiencing today is the creation of an underground Marxism (Klare, 1971–2, pp. 15–45). In the course of developing our critical capacities, we are rediscovering and recreating a form and body of thought that finds its grounding in Marxist analysis. Marxism is the one philosophy of our time that takes as its focus the oppression produced by a capitalist society. It is the one form of analysis that is historically specific and locates the problems of the age in the economic-class relations.[3] A Marxist critique provides, most importantly, a form of thought that allows us to transcend in thought and action that kind of existence.

Contrary to both liberal and orthodox interpretations, Marxism is highly creative thought, open to the interpretations of each generation. And with the changes in capitalism itself, from industrial capitalism to advanced monopoly capitalism, new and critical readings of Marx are necessary (Baran and Sweezy, 1966). Critical thought makes possible a new understanding of Marx in each age. Which is also to say, a new understanding of Marx makes critical thought possible.

All thinking, all life, is thus subject to critical philosophy. A critical philosophy of legal order, in particular, allows us to understand what has been otherwise unexamined. In an understanding of the true meaning of the legal order, in a Marxist critique, we are able to transcend the present and create an alternative existence. Liberation is the ultimate objective of a critical philosophy of legal order.

A critical-Marxist theory of crime control

To summarize thus far, I have argued that current modes of thought have prevented us from understanding the legal order. The dominant modes of thought, including the positivistic, social constructionist, and much of the phenomenological, have been tied to an age that can do little more than oppress, manipulate and control human beings as objects. The legal order has thus been viewed in the social sciences as a necessary force to assure order in capitalist society. Positivists have regarded law as a natural mechanism; social constructionists have viewed law relativistically, as one of man's conveniences; and many of the phenomenologists, whilst examining underlying assumptions, have done little to provide or promote an alternative existence. Hence, the conclusion reached is that our thoughts and our ways of thinking are wanting, are inappropriate and inadequate.

With a sense of the possible, I am suggesting a critical philosophy for understanding the legal order. That philosophy is based on a critical development of a Marxist thought for our age. Only a Marxist critique allows us to break out of the ideology and conditions of the age.

On the basis of the above discussion, a critical theory of crime control in capitalist society can now be presented. Marx had little to say about criminal law and crime control. The purpose here, then, is to develop a critical-Marxian analysis of crime control in capitalist society.

Whilst the legal order consists of more than criminal law, criminal law is the foundation of that order. A critical theory of crime control in capitalist society thus views criminal law as the coercive instrument of the State, used by the State and its ruling class to maintain the existing social and economic order. Therefore, in the development of a critical-Marxist theory of crime control we must consider the following topics: (1) crime and the ruling class, (2) crime control in the capitalist State, and (3) demystification of criminal law. The objective is a critical understanding of the modern legal order.

Crime and the ruling class

According to liberal intelligence, the State exists to maintain stability in civil society. Law is regarded, accordingly, as a body of rules established through consensus by those who are governed, or rather by the 'representatives' of the governed. Such a notion of the State and its law presents a false reality, but one that serves those who benefit from such a conception – those who rule.

An alternative position gets to the deeper meaning of the existence of the State and the legal order. Contrary to the dominant view, the State is created by that class of society that has the power to enforce its will on the rest of society. The State is thus a real, but artificial, political organization created out of force and coercion. The State is established by those who desire to protect their material basis and have the power (because of material means) to maintain the State. The law in capitalist society gives political recognition to powerful private interests.

Moreover, the legal system is an apparatus that is created to secure the interests of the dominant class. Contrary to conventional belief, law is a tool of the ruling class. The legal system provides the mechanism for the forceful and violent control of the rest of the population. In the course of battle, the agents of the law (police, prosecutors, judges, and so on) serve as the military force for the protection of domestic order. Hence, the State and its accompanying legal system reflect and serve the needs of the ruling class. Legal order benefits the ruling class in the same course of dominating the classes that are ruled. And it may be added that the legal system prevents the dominated classes from becoming powerful. The rates of crime in any State are an indication of the extent to which the ruling class, through its machinery or criminal law, must coerce the rest of the population, thereby preventing any threats to its ability to rule and possess. Criminal law as a coercive means in establishing domestic order for the ruling class thus becomes a basic assumption in a radical critique of crime.

That American society can best be understood in terms of its class structure violates conventional knowledge. It still comes as a surprise to many citizens that 1 per cent of the population owns 40 per cent of the nation's wealth, indicating that the liberal perspective dominates, just as the ruling class which profits from the prevailing view. Yet the evidence now overwhelmingly supports the radical critique of American society (Edwards *et al.*, 1972; Christoffel *et al.*, 1970). The liberal assumption of a pluralistic American economy – with corporation as just one kind of interest group amongst others – is negated, however, by the fact that the major portion of the wealth and nearly all the power in American society are concentrated in the hands of a few large corporations. Furthermore, those who benefit from this economy make up a small cohesive group of persons related to one another in their power, wealth and corporate connections. In addition, the pluralistic conception ignores all the manifestations of the alliance between business and government. From the evidence of radical scholarship, government and business are inseparable.

A critique of the American political economy thus begins with the now examined assumption that life in the USA is determined by the capitalist mode of production. And as a capitalist society, a class division exists between those who rule and those who are ruled. As Miliband writes, in reference to the class structure of capitalist societies (1969, p. 16):

> The economic and political life of capitalist societies is *primarily* determined by the relationship, born of the capitalist mode of production, between these two classes – the class which on the one hand owns and controls, and the working class on the other. Here are still the social forces whose confrontation most powerfully shapes the social climate and the political system of

> advanced capitalism. In fact, the political process in these societies is mainly *about* the confrontation of these forces, and is intended to sanction the terms of the relationship between them.

Whilst there are other classes, such as professionals, small business-men, office workers and cultural workmen, some of these either within or cutting across the two major classes, it is the division between the ruling class and the subordinate class that establishes the nature of political, economic and social life in capitalist society.

The ruling class, therefore, in capitalist society is 'that class which owns and controls the means of production and which is able, by virtue of the economic power thus conferred upon it, to use the state as its instrument for the domination of society' (ibid., p. 23). The existence of this class in the USA, rooted mainly in the corporations and financial institutions of monopoly capitalism, is well-documented (Kolko, 1962; Domhoff, 1967, 1970). This is the class that makes the decisions that effect the lives of those who are subordinate to this class.

It is according to the interests of the ruling class that American society is governed. Whilst pluralists may suggest that there are diverse and conflicting interests amongst groups in the upper class, what is ignored is the fact that members of the ruling class work within a common framework in the formulation of public policy. Superficially, groups within the ruling class may differ on some issues. But in general they share common interests, and they can exclude members of the other classes from the political process entirely (Kolko, 1969, pp. 6–7):

> If powerful economic groups are geographically diffuse and often in competition for particular favors from the state, superficially appearing as interest groups rather than as a unified class, what is critical is not who wins or loses but what kind of socioeconomic framework they *all* wish to compete within, and the relationship between themselves and the rest of the society in a manner that defines their vital function as a class. It is this class that controls the major policy options and the manner in which the state applies its power. That they disagree on the options is less consequential than they circumscribe the political universe.

In contrast to pluralist theory, radical theory notes that the basic interests, in spite of concrete differences, place the élite into a distinct ruling class.

In a radical critique of American society we are able, in addition, to get at the objective interests that are external to the consciousness of the individuals who compose them. We are able to suggest, furthermore, normative evaluations of these interests. Pluralists, on the other hand, are bound by the subjective interests of individuals (Balbus, 1971, pp. 151–77). The critical perspective allows us to understand the actual and potential interests of classes, of the ruling class as well as those who are ruled. What this means for a critique of legal order is that we can break with the official, dominant ideology which suggests the diversity of interests amongst numerous competing groups. We are able to determine the interests of those who make and use law for their own advantage.

The primary interest of the ruling class is to preserve the existing capitalist order. In so doing, the ruling class can protect its existential and material base. This is accomplished ultimately by means of the legal system. Any threats to the established order can be dealt with by invoking the final weapon of the ruling class, its legal system. Threats to American economic security abroad are dealt with militarily; an arsenal of weapons manned by armed forces is ready to attack any foe that attempts (as in a revolution) to upset the foreign markets of American capitalism (Horowitz, 1969). American imperialism fosters and perpetuates the colonial status of foreign countries, securing American hegemony throughout as much of the world as possible. This has been the history of American foreign relations, dominated by the corporate interests of the ruling class (Williams, 1969).

Similarly, the criminal law is used at home by the ruling class to maintain domestic order. Ruling-class interests are secured by preventing any challenge to the moral and economic structure of the ruling class. In other words, the military abroad and law enforcement at home are two sides of the same phenomenon: the preservation of the interests of the ruling class. The weapons of control are in the hands of the ruling class. Their response to any challenge is force and destruction. The weapons of crime control, as well as the idea and practice of law itself, are dominated by the ruling class. A stable order is in the interest of the ruling class.

From this critical perspective, then, crime is worthy of the greatest consideration. To understand crime radically is to understand the makings and workings of the American empire.

Crime control in the capitalist State

That the legal system does not serve society as a whole, but serves the interests of the ruling class is the beginning of a critical understanding of criminal law in capitalist society. The ruling class through its use of the legal system is able to preserve a domestic order that allows the dominant economic interests to be maintained and promoted. The ruling class, however, is not in direct control of the legal system, but must operate through the mechanisms of the State. Thus, it is to the State that we must turn in further understanding of the nature and operation of the legal order. For the role of the State in capitalist society is to defend the interests of the ruling class. Crime control becomes a major device of the State in its promotion of a capitalist society.

Criminologists and legal scholars generally neglect the State as a focus of inquiry. In failing to distinguish between civil society and the political organization of that society, they ignore the major fact that civil society is secured politically by the State and that a dominant economic class is able by means of the State to advance its own interests. Or when the State is admitted into a criminological or legal analysis, it is usually conceived as an impartial agency devoted to balancing and reconciling the diverse interests of competing groups in the society. This view, I am arguing, not only obscures the underlying reality of advanced capitalist society, but is basically wrong in reference to the legal order. In a critical analysis of the legal order we realize that the capitalist State is a coercive instrument that serves a particular class, the dominant economic class.

Several basic observations must be made in a critical analysis of crime control in the capitalist State. First, there is the question of the nature of the State, that is, the complexity of that which we call the State. Second, is the problem of how the dominant economic class relates to the State, that is, how that class becomes a ruling class and how the state governs in relation to the ruling class. Third, we must observe the development of the State in reference to capitalist economy.

'The state', as Miliband notes, is not a thing that exists as such. 'What "the state" stands for is a number of particular institutions which, together, constitute its reality, and which interact as parts of what may be called the state system' (Miliband, 1969, p. 49). Miliband goes on to observe that the State, or State system, is made up of various elements: (1) the government, (2) the administration, (3) the military and the police, (4) the judiciary and (5) the units of subcentral government (ibid., pp. 49–55). The administration of the State is composed of a large variety of bureaucratic bodies and departments concerned with the management of the economic, cultural and other activities in which the State is involved. The directly coercive forces of the State, at home and abroad, are handled by the police and the military. They form that branch of the State which is concerned with the 'management of violence'. The judiciary is an integral part of the State, supposedly independent of the government, which affects the exercise of State power. Finally, the various units of subcentral government constitute the extension of the central government. They are the administrative devices for centralized power, although some units may exercise power on their own over the lives of the populations they govern.

It is in these institutions that State power lies, and it is in these institutions that power is wielded by the persons who occupy the leading positions within each institution. Most important, these are the people who constitute the *State élite*, as distinct from those who wield power outside of State institutions (ibid., p. 54). Some holders of State power, members of the State élite, may also be the agents of private economic power. But when members of private economic power are not members of the State élite, how are they able to rule the State? Somehow the interests of the dominant economic class must be translated into the governing process, in order for that class to be a true ruling class.

Miliband has observed the essential relation between the dominant economic class and the process of governing (ibid., pp. 66–7):

> What the evidence conclusively suggests is that in terms of social origin, education and class situation, the men who have manned *all* command positions in the state system have largely, and in many cases overwhelmingly, been drawn from the world of business and property, or from the professional middle classes. Here as in every other field, men and women born into the subordinate classes, which form of course the vast majority of the population, have fared very poorly – and not only, it must be stressed, in those parts of the state system, such as administration, the military and the judiciary, which depend on appointment, but also in those parts of it which are exposed or which appear to be exposed to the vagaries of universal suffrage and the fortunes of competitive politics. In an epoch when so much is made of democracy, equality, social mobility, classlessness and the rest, it has remained a basic fact of life in advanced capitalist countries that the vast majority of men and women in these countries has been governed, represented, administered, judged, and commanded in war by people drawn from other economically and socially superior and relatively distant classes.

The dominant economic class is thus the ruling class in capitalist societies.

Viewed historically, the capitalist State is the natural product of a society divided by economic classes. Only with the emergence of a division of labour based on the exploitation of one class by another, and with the breaking-up of communal society, was there a need for the State. The new ruling class created the State as a means for coercing the rest of the population into economic and political submission. That the American State was termed 'democratic' does not lessen its actual purpose.

Hence, the State, as Engels observed in his study of its origins, has not existed in all societies. There have been societies which have had no notion of State power. Only with a particular kind of economic development with economic divisions, did the State become necessary. The new stage of development, Engels observes, called for the creation of the State (1942, p. 97):

> Only one thing was wanting: an institution which not only secured the newly acquired riches of individuals against the communistic traditions of the gentile order, which not only sanctified the private property formerly so little valued, and declared this sanctification to be the highest purpose of all human society; but an institution which set the seal of general social recognition on each new method of acquiring property and thus amassing wealth at continually increasing speed; an institution which perpetuated, not only this growing cleavage of society into classes, but also the right of the possessing class to exploit the non-possessing, and the rule of the former over the latter.
>
> And this institution came. The *state* was invented.

And the State, rather than appearing as a third party in the conflict between classes, arose to protect and promote the interests of the dominant economic class, the class that owns and controls the means of production. The State continues as a device for holding down the exploited class, the class that labours, for the benefit of the dominant class. Modern civilization, as epitomized by capitalist societies, is thus founded on the exploitation of one class by another. The State secures this arrangement, since the State is in the hands of the dominant economic, ruling class.

And law became the ultimate means by which the State secures the interests of the ruling class. Laws institutionalize and legitimize the existing property relations. A legal system, a public force, is established (ibid., p. 156):

> This public force exists in every state; it consists not merely of armed men, but also of material appendages, prisons and coercive institutions of all kinds, of which gentile society knew nothing. It may be very insignificant, practically negligible, in societies with still undeveloped class antagonisms and living in remote areas, as at times and in places in the United States of America. But it becomes stronger in proportion as the class antagonisms within the state become sharper and as adjoining states grow larger and more populous.

It is through the legal system, then, that the State explicitly and forcefully protects the interests of the capitalist ruling class. Crime control becomes the coercive means of checking threats to the existing economic arrangements. The State defines its welfare in terms of the general well-being of the capitalist economy. Crime control in the capitalist State is the concrete means for protecting the interests of the capitalist economy.

Demystification of criminal law

The purpose of a critical understanding of crime control is to expose the meaning of criminal law in capitalist society. The false reality by which we live, the one that serves the established system, must be understood. To demystify law in the USA is the goal of a critical theory of criminal law.

The above critical discussion of criminal law can be summarized in the following assertations:

1 *American society is based on an advanced capitalist economy.*
2 *The State is organized to serve the interests of the dominant economic class, the capitalist ruling class.*
3 *Criminal law is an instrument of the State and ruling class to maintain and perpetuate the existing social and economic order.*
4 *Crime control in capitalist society is accomplished through a variety of institutions and agencies established and administered by a governmental élite, representing ruling-class interests, for the purpose of establishing domestic order.*
5 *The contradictions of advanced capitalism – the disjunction between existence and essence require that the subordinate classes remain oppressed by whatever means necessary, especially through the coercion and violence of the legal system.*
6 *Only with the collapse of capitalist society and the creation of a new society, based on socialist principles, will there be a solution to the crime problem.*

Thus, criminal law in the USA can be critically understood in terms of the preservation of the existing social and economic order. Criminal law is used by the State and ruling class to secure the survival of the capitalist system. And as capitalist society is further threatened by its own contradictions, criminal law is increasingly used in the attempt to maintain domestic order. The underclass, the class that must remain oppressed for the triumph of the dominant economic class, will continue to be the object of criminal law as long as the dominant class seeks to perpetuate itself. To remove the oppression, to eliminate the need for further revolt, would necessarily mean the end of the ruling class and its capitalist economy.

Criminal law continues to secure the colonial status of the oppressed in the social and economic order of the USA. The events of the last few years relating to crime, including both 'disruption' and repression, can be understood only in terms of the crisis of the American system. Moreover, the oppression within the USA cannot be separated from American imperialism abroad. The crisis of the American empire is complete. The war waged against people abroad is part of the same war waged against the oppressed at home. The ruling class, through its control of the State, must resort to a worldwide counter-revolution. A counter-insurgency programme is carried out – through the CIA abroad and the FBI, the Law Enforcement Assistance Administration, and local police at home. A military war is being fought in Asia, while a war on crime with its own weaponry is being fought within the USA. All of this to avoid changing the capitalist order, indeed to protect it and to promote its continuation.

The consequences are revolutionary. Crime and the criminal law can be understood only within the context of this crisis (Horowitz, 1969, pp. 257–8):

> By posing on the national level the central issues of the international conflict, by linking the international struggle for self-determination with the internal quest for social equality and social control, the crisis of democracy increasingly presents itself as the revolutionary crisis of the epoch. The movement for the sovereignty of the people within the imperial nation coincides with the struggle for self-determination in the international sphere. Just as domestically the demand for domestic power is a demand to overthrow the corporate ruling class and to make the productive apparatus responsive to social needs, so internationally the precondition of democratic sovereignty and inter-state coexistence is the dissolution of the government of the international corporation and financial institutions which have expropriated the sovereignty of nations in order to appropriate the wealth of the world.

Never before has our understanding of legal order been so crucial. Never before has our understanding been so related to the way we must live our lives. To think critically and radically today is to be revolutionary. To do otherwise is to side with oppression. Our understanding of the legal order and our actions in relation to it must be to remove that oppression, to be a force in liberation.

Conclusion

The theoretical and research implications of a critical theory of law for the sociologist are far-reaching. The meaning of the above discussion is that everything we have done in criminology and the sociology of law has to be redone. A critical examination of law means uncovering all the orthodox assumptions we have held about law and crime control. Thus, both theoretically and empirically, we must reconsider everything that has preceded us. But more important, a whole new range of problems is now open to us. In the course of developing a critical imagination, we are thinking about things that never appeared to us under previous wisdom. To the question of where a critical theory of legal order will lead, we answer that it will take us to places no one has been before. In thought and in action, we are entering new realms of life, imagination and human possibility.

Notes

1 For example, see the issues of the Journal of the Law and Society Association, *Law and Society Review*, 1, 1, to 7, 1, November 1966–August 1972.

2 Kant made this clear, and on this Husserl agreed (see Lauer, 1965, p. 21).

3 Horowitz (1971–2, p. 57) writes in this regard (See also Sartre, 1963): 'There already exists, of course, a traditional *corpus* of Marxian theory which logically form the starting point of any new analytical approach. But revision of the analytic tools and propositions of traditional Marxist theory is inevitable if the theory is to develop as an intellectual doctrine, and not degenerate into mere dogma. In principle, it may even be possible to create a theory which is 'Marxist' in the restricted sense urged here, but which has little surface relation to the traditional Marxist categories and conclusions. Nonetheless, at this historical juncture, the traditional Marxist paradigm is the only economic paradigm which is capable of analyzing capitalism as an historically specific, class-determined social formation. As such it provides an indispensable framework for understanding the development and crisis of the present social system and, as an intellectual outlook, would occupy a prime place in any scientific institution worthy of the name.

8 Marx and Engels on law, crime and morality

Paul Q. Hirst

1 Radical criminology and Marxist theory

Many radical criminologists and deviance theorists in their opposition to orthodox studies of deviance, crime and law enforcement are turning toward 'conflict' approaches to this phenomenon, and towards Marxism, which they regard as embodying in a powerful and coherent way the 'conflict' approach to social phenomena.[1] This tendency in sociology reflects two very general approaches to Marxism in the social sciences which are shared by radicals and conservatives alike. First, the identification of the conceptual structure and analytic content of Marxist theory stems less from a thorough knowledge of Marxism itself than from the 'Marxism' that forms the basis of debates in the established social sciences. This 'Marxism' reflects far more the epistemological concerns of the established social sciences, the debates about the validity of Marx's so-called 'predictions' in relation to the changes in social structure since Marx's day, and the ideological opposition to Marxism of the professional anti-communists, than it does the positions of Marx, Engels and the orthodox Marxists. Secondly, in their eagerness to adopt a Marxist 'conflictual' position, the radicals seldom question their own theoretical-ideological point of departure and its relation to Marxist theory. They do not pose or think of posing the questions crucial to any application of Marxism to this non-Marxist debate between radicals and conservatives in the social sciences. These questions are two-fold. On the one hand, is the given field, criminology, and the object of study it presupposes, compatible with the object of study and conceptual structure of Marxism? On the other hand, what is the specific epistemological difference between the position of the radicals and the conservatives in criminology?

Radical and conservative theories of deviance take as their point of departure the given actuality of crime and the law, and of ideological conflicts reflecting standpoints within that actuality. Radical deviancy theory takes as its scientific point of departure the desire to develop a critique of the orthodox positions in the field. It seeks to explain and justify the criminal as a product of social relations, to situate the criminal as the victim of processes of labelling and punishment which serve the interests and represent the values of the establishment, and to question the nature of laws and values as the property of that establishment. Radical deviancy theory, therefore, questions the value assumptions, underlying justifications of establishment interests, and the ideological stand of orthodox criminology, but it very rarely questions its own position, assumptions and interests.

It is the aim of this chapter to demonstrate that Marxism has a quite different view of crime and 'deviancy' from that of the radicals; a view that abolishes this field as a coherent object of study. There is no 'Marxist theory of deviance', either in existence, or which can be developed within orthodox Marxism. Crime and deviance vanish into the general theoretical concerns and the specific scientific object of Marxism. Crime and deviance are no more a scientific field for Marxism than education, the family or sport. The objects of Marxist theory are specified by its own concepts: the mode of production, the class struggle, the state, ideology, etc. Any attempt to apply Marxism to this pre-given field of sociology is therefore a more or less 'revisionist' activity in respect of Marxism; it must modify and distort Marxist concepts to suit its own pre-Marxist purpose. 'Revisionism' should be seen to be done: it is the aim of this chapter to demarcate the Marxism of Marx and Engels from the 'Marxism' of the radicals.

2 The development of Marxist theory

The question of orthodoxy and revisionism raises the problem of which 'Marx' and which 'Marxism' we accept as the norm. Many sociological radicals seek to return to the themes of the 'young' Marx, to a Marxism free of 'monistic' and 'totalitarian' tendencies, to a Marxism concerned with man's alienation and human self-emancipation. The status of the work of the 'young' Marx, and of Marxist concepts in general, cannot be determined by a free-ranging and arbitrary choice based upon contemporary 'relevance' or the *post-hoc* political-ideological judgments which stem from the subsequent history of the workers' movement, in particular, from the history of the Communist Party of the USSR. Marx's own positions have much to tell us about the relevance of what is considered 'relevant' today. The validity of the concepts and the conceptual structure of Marxist theory cannot be determined by reading them in the future anterior, that is, of playing off the Marx of the 1844

Manuscripts against the Marx of *Capital*, against Lenin, or against Stalin.

It is the view of the author that Marx's theoretical development should enlighten these questions. Marx's later works (i.e. those works post-1844, that is, beginning with *The German Ideology*) contain a consistent and developed critique not only of bourgeois authors, Hegel, Feuerbach, Proudhon, Smith, Ricardo, etc., but also of the 'young' Marx who shared their theoretical positions. The author further considers that these differences can be revealed by the study of Marx's writings. These writings contain at each of the different periods a definite conceptual structure and enforce certain definite protocols on the reader. The notion that Marx's writings are open to any 'interpretation' we care to impose upon them is patently false and can be demonstrated by detailed reference to, and analysis of, the texts themselves.

It is to these texts that we now turn. Marx's positions on law and crime are of three distinct kinds and are directly related to his general theoretical position in three different periods. These periods are: (a) 1840–2, the Kantian critique of law, (b) 1842–4, the Feuerbachian period, and (c) 1845–82, the formation and development of Historical Materialism.

(a) *The Kantian-liberal critique of law*

> The speculative use of reason in *regard to nature* leads to the absolute necessity of some supreme cause of the *world*; the practical use of reason *with respect to freedom* leads also to absolute necessity – but only to the absolute necessity of *the laws of action* for rational being as such (Kant, 1948, p. 123).

Marx's writings in 1842, in the *Rheinische Zeitung* and other works, are part of a practical-polemical struggle for democracy and genuine liberalism against the cowardly liberals of the Rhenish Parliament and the Prussian State authorities. These writings are concerned with the nature of law, the freedom of the press and 'official' morality.

Marx's theoretical standpoint in these texts is a Kantian rationalism and universalism. His political standpoint is that of a radical democrat and egalitarian. Marx adopts broadly Kantian positions; that reason is the attribute of a free being, that reason is universal and is distinct in essence from all empirical particularity (the 'positive'), of which it is the critique. Marx, therefore, contrasts mere positive law and official morality founded upon mundane interests with the true, universal and free necessity of laws and morality founded upon reason (1842a, p. 35):

> Thus so far from a law on the press being a repressive measure directed against the freedom of the press, simply a means to

> deter by penalties the repetition of a crime, the lack of a law dealing with the freedom of the press should rather be seen as an exclusion of freedom of the press from the sphere of legal freedom, for legally recognised freedom exists in the state as law. Laws are as little repressive measures directed against freedom as the law of gravity is a repressive measure directed against movement. . . . Laws are rather positive, bright and general norms in which freedom has attained to an existence that is impersonal, theoretical and independent of the arbitrariness of individuals. A peoples' statute book is its Bible of freedom. . . .
>
> Where law is true law, i.e. where it is the existence of freedom, it is the true existence of the freedom of man. Thus the laws cannot prevent man's actions, for they are the inner laws of life of his action itself. . . . Thus a positive law is a meaningless contradition.

The Marx of this passage thinks his opposition to censorship through a critique founded upon a transcendental conception of reason and law. Law and freedom are anthropological categories in so far as they are human attributes, but *man* is defined by his status as a free and rational being. In the last instance, these attributes of man are his attributes only in so far as he partakes of qualities extrinsic to himself, reason and freedom, which have an existence independent of him and define him. For Kant these attributes are truly transcendental, in that man is human (has the attributes which mark him off from the beasts) in that he partakes, partially and blindly, of the nature of God.

Thus, the theoretical position of Marx in this period is quite distinct from his position in the Feuerbachian period. Feuerbachian anthropology conceives man not through transcendental attributes but through the concrete reality of his biologically-based species characteristics. Man's species being is that of a unique *animal*, an animal conscious of itself and of its species. For the Feuerbachian man is a universal being because the individual is able to appropriate through species self-consciousness the infinite possibilities of the species.

Marx in 1842 rejects all religious systems as a limitation of freedom and reason, as the dogmatic subordination of morality to interest and to specific conceptions derived from the particular (1842b, pp. 29–30, original italics):

> The specifically Christian law-giver cannot recognise morality as a sphere *sacred* in itself and independent for he vindicates its inner universal essence for religion. Independent morality violates the universal bases of religion and the particular concepts of

> religion are contrary to morality. *Morality knows only its own universal and rational religion*, and religion only its particular positive morality. Thus according to this instruction the censorship must reject all the intellectual heroes of morality – Kant, Fichte, Spinoza, for example, as irreligious and violating discipline, morals and exterior respectability.

The contradiction of a transcendental ethic apart from empirical religion, which is itself a religion of ethics, and the practical anti-clericalism and atheism of Marx, clearly drove him to accept the Feuerbachian foundation of ethics and religion on a 'concrete' anthropology. Marx's strictly idealist and speculative position in the Kantian period leads him to place the independent existence of the idea above all particular empirical existence and all concrete struggles (1842b, p. 48):

> We are firmly convinced that the true danger does not lie in the practical attempt to carry out communist ideas but in their theoretical development; for practical attempts, even by the masses, can be answered with cannon as soon as they become dangerous, but ideas that have overcome our intellect and conquered our conviction . . . are chains from which one cannot break loose without breaking one's heart.

No wonder, then, that Marx expressed 'embarassment' when he was forced to deal with 'economic questions' in the case of the abolition of the feudal rights of the Rhenish peasants to take wood from the forests. Marx here conceives economic relations as legal rights, from the standpoint of the distributive justice of absolute egalitarianism (1842d, p. 49):

> If every violation of property without differentiation or further definition is theft, would not private property be theft? Through my private property do I not exclude a third party from this property?

Marx bases his argument on the theory of natural rights; private property violates the natural rights of others, it is a *theft* of their rights, and it destroys the natural equality of men. This argument carries the egalitarian tendency in natural rights theory further than Rousseau's *Discourse on the Origin of Inequality Among Men.* In this doctrine that property is theft Marx echoes Proudhon, who he was later to castigate for this very moralism in *The Poverty of Philosophy.*

The Rhenish liberals are condemned for capitulating to particular interests; to an inequality between the poor and the privileged which destroys the essence of law. The origin of this privilege is conceived of as an historical fact, as the result of a past conquest (ibid., p. 50):

> Mankind appears as disintegrated into particular animal races who are held together not by equality but by an inequality that regulates the laws. A universal lack of freedom requires laws that lack freedom, for whereas human law is the existence of freedom, animal law is the existence of a lack of freedom. The rights of aristocratic custom run counter by their content to the form of general law. They cannot be formed into laws because they are formulations of lawlessness.

Marx rejects the dictates of aristocratic custom as a form of slavery; as a form contradictory in its essence with the form of law, for the form of law can only answer to that necessary principle of morality established by Kant: 'Man, and in general every reasonable being, *exists* as an end in itself, *and not merely as means*.'

(b) *The Feuerbachian period*

> Thus in the first part I show that the true sense of Theology is Anthropology, that there is no distinction between the *predicates* of the divine and human nature, and, consequently, no distinction between the divine and the human *subject*: I say *consequently*, for wherever, as is especially the case in theory, the predicates are not accidents, but express the essence of the subject, there is no distinction between subject and predicate, the one can be put in the place of the other (Feuerbach, 1841, p. 37).

Marx's *Economic and Philosophic Manuscripts of 1844* are the key texts of this period, the specific bone of contention between those who assert the continuity of Marx's work, or who counterpose the theory of alienation to the 'alienating' abstractions of *Capital*, and the orthodox Marxist position.

However, those who wish to found a theory of law and crime upon these texts face two serious obstacles: (a) law ceases to be an important element in Marx's argument; (b) the conceptual structure of the theory of the *Manuscripts* produces the reduction of all particular phenomena, law, the State, the family and religion, to the essential contradiction in society, that between the essence of labour as a self-realizing human activity and its alienation in an object, private property.

For Marx, as for Feuerbach, the existence of definite spheres of life, or social institutions apart from concrete human sensuous activity represents an alienation of the essential predicates of the human subject. Man has a specific essence, or nature, a set of predicates which constitute his species being, and man is the existence of the species in the individual, a conscious concrete subject.[2] Alienation represents the externalization of these predicates in an object which becomes independent of the subject and which subordinates the subject to his own externalized essence. This essence, separated from the subject, is no longer recognized by him, in its objectified form, as his essence, but as an independent principle which governs his own existence. Man is estranged from himself and subordinated to his own essence.

The object of the human sciences, of philosophy, is the critique of this separation of man from his essence; the revelation of the contradiction between the subject and its essential predicates. Religious and speculative anthropology makes this separation a part of the essential human condition, an ineradicable contradiction in man's being. For Feuerbach and Marx it is a specific separation which is the product of definite real-historical conditions which are bound up with the development of humanity itself and can be overcome at a particular stage in the development of humanity. Marx criticizes Feuerbach for having stopped in his critique at the point of demonstrating the foundation of religious alienation in human relations, at the point of revealing the Holy Family as an alienated form of the human family, and God as an alienated form of the essence of Man. He further criticizes Feuerbach for having stopped at a speculative critique, which remains within the idea, and therefore of having failed to recognize the necessity of a 'practical criticism' of alienation, the overcoming of alienation in the real by revolutionary practical activity.

Marx's theoretical critique in the *Manuscripts* necessarily reduces all particular social forms to the essential contradiction between the alienated form of man's essence in private property and estranged labour, and the concrete human subject who labours. The alienated predicates must be returned to the subject, hence no social relation can exist apart from the subject, and social relations are dissolved into the activity of the subject. Communism is the union of the subject and his essence, the practical abolition of the separation. Communism is the dissolution of all institutions into human self-realizing activity. Nothing exists apart from subjects, free relations one with another. Since all social relations are the spontaneous free actions of subjects, which entail no contradictions each with the other, law has no basis or reason for existence; even 'natural' laws become void in the union of nature and human practice (1844, p. 95):

> This communism, as fully developed naturalism, equals humanism, and as fully developed humanism equals naturalism; it is the *genuine* resolution of the conflict between man and nature and between man and man – the true resolution of the strife between existence and essence, between objectification and self-confirmation, between freedom and necessity, between the

individual and the species. Communism is the riddle of history solved, and it knows itself to be this solution.

The meaning of alienation in the *Manuscripts* is quite specific and is specified by a particular conceptual structure. Alienation, anthropology and man's being-toward-communism are inseparably linked by Marx's concepts. Thus to use 'alienation' as an explanation of a particular phenomenon, crime, for example, would be quite absurd for Marx, since alienation is a concept in a theory whose object is the dissolution of all phenomena. To prove the existence of alienation by interviews, indices, scales, X-rays or whatever, would be, for the Marx of 1844, an absurd alienation in itself. To introduce the concept of alienation into the modern social sciences is, therefore, either to abandon the concept of the *Manuscripts*, or to transform those social sciences into a practical-critical philosophy whose object is communism.

(c) *The formulation and development of Historical Materialism*

Marx and Engels's specific positions on law and crime in this period will be discussed in the following sections (3–4); the purpose of this section is merely to demonstrate the difference between Marx and Engels's later writings and those of Marx in the earlier periods. This difference will be demonstrated as follows: (i) the difference of the Historical Materialist conception of the social formation, cryptically stated in Marx's 1859 *Preface*, from Marx's conception of society in 1844; (ii) the difference between Marx's natural rights conception of human equality in 1842 and Marx's positions on this form of rationalist egalitarianism in the *Critique of the Gotha Programme*, 1875 (1859, p. 361):

> In the social production of their life, men enter into definite relations that are indispensible and independent of their will, relations of production which correspond to a definite stage of development of their material productive forces. The sum total of these relations of production constitutes the economic structure of society, the real foundation, on which rises a legal and political superstructure and to which correspond definite forms of social consciousness. . . . At a certain stage of their development, the material productive forces of society come into conflict with the existing relations of production, or – what is but a legal expression of the same thing – with the property relations within which they have been at work hitherto. . . . In considering such transformations a distinction should always be made between the material transformation of the economic conditions of production, which can be determined with the precision of natural

science, and the legal, political, religious, aesthetic, philosophic – in short ideological forms in which men become conscious of this conflict and fight it out.

The 1859 *Preface* has been regarded as the most reductionist of Marx's writings; as the text most open to an economic determinist reading. But, when we compare it with the thoroughgoing reductionism of the critique of separation in the *Manuscripts*, this text reveals a surprising complexity.

The social relations of production '*correspond*' to a 'definite stage of the development of . . . [the] material productive forces'. The economic structure is the '*foundation*' on 'which rises a legal and political superstructure' to which '*correspond* definite forms of social consciousness'. The economic structure of society is the condition of existence of the superstructure, it is the foundation on which this superstructure rests, and therefore prescribes certain definite limits to what can be erected upon it.

No more than this can be deduced from Marx's statements. Indeed, the very notion of 'foundation' prohibits any attempt to think the content or form of the superstructure as having a direct economic *causation* in the traditional sense (the sense of polemics which regard Marxism as a factorial theory of history). Rather, it suggests a determination of the limits of variation of the superstructure by the economic structure and says nothing about the *causation* or *origin* of superstructural forms or the ideologies which correspond to them.[3] The existence of distinct levels in the social formation, of distinct and irreducible forms of social relations, is entailed in this formulation.

This conception of the social formation would be anathema to the Marx of the *Manuscripts*. It entails the existence of distinct levels which demand the admissibility of social relations which are in no sense reducible to the practice of human subjects; the social relations of production are 'indispensable and independent of their will'. In no sense are these relations deducible from the human essence; it is not the case that 'the one can be put in the place of the other' since social relations independent of human wills, which are in no sense the *product*, even the *alienated* product, of those wills, cannot be deduced from the subject as its predicates. There is no *separation* in the existence of these distinct levels since their referent is not the human subject but their mutual articulation into a social totality. The reference of the levels is their relation each to the other. The relation of the social formation to the subject is completely different in 1859 from 1844. The social formation produces specific subjects with specific conditions of existence and a specific place in that formation. The social position, material conditions of existence, and forms of thought of the subjects ('definite forms of social consciousness') are effects of the structure of the social formation.

Moreover, Marx nowhere in this text suggests that these invariant characteristics of the social formation will vanish with communism. Indeed, we are left with no option but to recognize the existence of structure and superstructure as the necessary form of all human societies. The spontaneously social self-realization of human subjects, conceived as the form of communism in the *Manuscripts*, is no longer the conception of communism in 1859. In communist society, like any other, there are structural forms independent of and indispensable to the human subjects. Communism cannot know 'itself to be . . . the solution' to the riddle of history, since it is neither a unity of individual subjects, nor is it itself a subject. Social formations do not 'know' anything, and the subjects to which they give rise, even communist subjects, only know through 'definite forms of social consciousness', that is, they know as subject only through the forms of ideology which correspond to the relations that produce them as subjects. Communist societies obey the invariant laws of the social formation.

Thus, the epistemological basis of the critique of separation in the *Manuscripts* and the goal of the critique, spontaneous communism, are ruled out by the epistemological positions of the *Preface*. The *Preface* has a scientific *object*, the social formation, but no *goal*, since the new science does not identify its knowledge of its object with an end immanent in the real. It proscribes any reference to a telos; it rejects the basis of any telos, the union of social relations and the human subject, the union which enables us to read in history the ends of man. There is in the *Preface* no essential contradiction between alienated essence and the concrete subject which is resolved of anthropological necessity. The 'separation' of structure and superstructure is no contradiction but the invariant structure of the social formation.

It will be remembered that Marx, in his first essay into 'economic questions', depended upon a natural rights conception of equality. His arguments were those of distributive justice in respect of a given quantum of 'property' and the rights of each and all in respect of that quantum. His positions here can be regarded as: (i) absolute egalitarianism, equality of 'right'; and (ii) that the 'social question' is a matter of the just and equitable distribution of property, in this case, common ownership.

In his *Critique of the Gotha Programme*, 1875, Marx was confronted with very similar positions to the above in the programme of the German Worker's Party (1875, pp. 18, 21):

1. Labour is the source of all wealth and all culture, and *since*

> useful labour is possible only in society and through society, the proceeds of labour belong undiminished with equal right to all members of society. . . .
>
> 3. The emancipation of labour demands the promotion of the instruments of labour to the common property of society and the co-operative regulation of the total labour with a fair distribution of the proceeds of labour.

In his reply Marx castigates the abstract moralism and ethical universalism of these passages and thereby measures out for us the difference between Scientific Socialism and the Kantianism of his 1842 positions.

Marx rejects the notion that socialism is a matter of distributive justice.[4] Scientific socialism is founded on an analysis of the mode of production, the production relations and the productive forces, which enforce a definite mode of distribution in a given social formation. It is the economic structure of society which establishes a definite distribution of the conditions of production which governs the distribution of the means of consumption (1875, pp. 21, 25):

> What is 'a fair distribution'?
> Do not the bourgeois assert that the present-day distribution is 'fair'? And is it not, in fact, the only 'fair' distribution on the basis of the present day mode of production? Are economic relations regulated by legal conceptions or do not, on the contrary, legal conceptions arise from economic ones?
>
> Any distribution whatever of the means of consumption is only a consequence of the distribution of the conditions of production themselves. The latter distribution, however, is a feature of the mode of production itself. The capitalist mode of production, for example, rests on the fact that the material conditions of production are in the hands of non-workers in the form of property in capital and land, while the masses are only owners of the personal condition of production, of labour power. If the elements of production are so distributed, then the present-day distribution of the means of consumption results automatically.

In addition, Marx rejects the egalitarianism of 'equal rights'. Marx is not interested in ethical abstractions like 'equality', abstractions marked on their very character as ideological elaborations of bourgeois relation of production, but in the social relations pertaining in capitalist and socialist societies. The problem of 'equality' under socialism is not an ethical problem but a problem enforced by the mode of production; the measurement of the value of labour, the representation of the concrete labour of members of society by an equal standard. Thus in a socialist society, given deductions for depreciation, the development of the productive forces, administrative costs and common social needs, the worker: 'draws from the social stock of means of consumption as much as costs the same amount of labour'. The direct exploitation of labour no longer exists, but the mode of production still demands the determination of rewards by labour-time (ibid., p. 24, my emphases):

> In spite of this advance, this equal right is still constantly stigmatised by a bourgeois limitation. The right of the producers is *proportional* to the labour they supply; the equality consists in the fact that measurement is made with an equal standard, labour.
>
> But one man is superior to another physically and mentally and so supplies more labour in the same time . . . and labour, to serve as a measure, must be defined by its duration and intensity, otherwise it ceases to be a standard of measurement. This *equal* right is an unequal right for unequal labour. It recognises no class differences, because everyone is only a worker like everyone else; but it tacitly recognises unequal individual endowment and thus productive capacity as natural privileges. *It is therefore, a right of inequality, in its content, like every right.* Right by its very nature can consist only in the application of an equal standard; but unequal individuals . . . are measurable only by an equal standard in so far as they are . . . taken from one *definite* side only, for instance in the present case, are regarded only as *workers*.

The ruling principle of *communism* utterly rejects egalitarianism, it demands that individuals work to their specific capacities, and allocates means of consumption to units of consumption solely on the basis of need: 'from each according to his ability to each according to his need.' It is the communist mode of production which gives rise to such a principle, and those social relations and ideologies which it embraces form the superstructure of communist society.

It has been the subject of section 2, above, to demonstrate a very real difference between the theory of Historical Materialism and the positions of the young Marx. This difference is not the simple dissimilarity of positions of equivalent epistemological validity but 'incommensurable' assumptions; of different 'paradigms' or *Weltanschauung* which admit of a choice between them based upon ideological premises. It is a difference measured by a critique; a difference in which one theory rigorously demarcates itself from others by concepts which demonstrate their erroneous and unscientific character. It is a difference in which Historical Materialism demonstrates, by means of its scientific concepts, the ideological character of the philosophical anthropologies which underlay the positions of the Young Marx.

The remainder of the paper is devoted to an explication of Marx and Engels' post 1844 positions on law and crime; positions which derive from the concepts of Historical Materialism and the political theory of Scientific Socialism. This will be discussed as follows:

3 Crime, the law and Marxist politics
4 Organized crime and production relations.

3 Crime, the law and Marxist politics

(a) *The lumpenproletariat*

> The 'dangerous class', the social scum, the passively rotting mass thrown off by the lowest layers of the old society, may, here and there, be swept into the movement by a proletarian revolution, its conditions of life, however, prepare it far more for the part of a bribed tool of reactionary intrigue. (Marx and Engels, 1848, p. 44).

Marx and Engels's pronouncements on the criminal classes often appear savage, harsh and unthinking. It is often assumed that these views represent no more than the prejudices of two Victorian gentlemen and are passed off as expressing merely the conventional morality of their day. But Marx and Engels were rather extraordinary 'Victorian gentlemen'; they were atheists, they called for the abolition of the bourgeois family, and they castigated the very bourgeois cant which the hasty observer may attribute to them. To brush off Marx and Engels's remarks on these matters as 'bourgeois moralism' is radically to misconceive their standpoint and the reasons for these positions. Their standpoint was uncomprisingly political and based on the proletarian class position. Marx and Engels ask of any social class or socio-political activity, what is its effectivity in the struggle of the proletariat for socialism, does it contribute to the political victory of the exploited and oppressed?

Marx and Engels always stressed that capitalist society is complex, that any specific capitalist society represents the combination of different modes of production, and that it produces class relations which are not reducible to any simple opposition between proletariat and bourgeoisie. The proletariat alone is incapable of overthrowing the political rule of the bourgeoisie and its class allies; if it does attempt to carry through a political revolution in isolation, that is, without class alliances, it will be outnumbered, cornered and destroyed as was the Paris proletariat in the desperate June insurrection of 1848. Of this hopeless and heroic uprising Marx remarked: 'On the side of the Paris proletariat stood none but itself.' Without the leadership of the proletariat, that is, of the class whose position in the relations of production makes it the only class capable of carrying through the struggle for socialism, the other progressive classes will fall victim to the ideological illusions, political demands and forms of action which result from their specific situation in production relations.[5]

Engels raises the question of the lumpenproletariat in relation to this problem of class alliances in his 1874 Preface to *The Peasant War in Germany* (Engels, 1874, p. 645):

> But even the proletariat has not yet outgrown the parallel drawn with 1525. The class that is exclusively dependent on wages all its life is still far from forming the majority of the German people. This class is, therefore, also compelled to seek allies. The latter can only be found among the petty bourgeoisie, the *lumpenproletariat* of the cities, the small peasants and the agricultural labourers.

His remarks on the political efficacy of this class are as follows (ibid., p. 646):

> The lumpenproletariat, this scum of the depraved elements of all classes, which establishes its headquarters in the big cities, is the worst of all possible allies. This rabble is absolutely venal and absolutely brazen. . . . Every leader of the workers' who uses these scoundrels as guards or relies on them for support proves himself by this action a traitor to the movement.

Why are these elements not to be relied on? First, as a parasitic class, living off productive labour by theft, extortion and beggary, or by providing 'services' such as prostitution and gambling, their class interests are diametrically opposed to those of the workers. They make their living by picking up the crumbs of capitalist relations of exchange, and under socialism they would be outlawed or forced to work (see section 4 of this chapter for a fuller account of this point). Secondly, they are open to the bribes and blandishments of the reactionary elements of the ruling classes and the State; they can be recruited as police informers and the armed elements of reactionary bands and 'special' State forces.

The 'criminal classes', Marx and Engels argue, are the natural enemies of any disciplined and principled workers' movement. Ideologically and politically, they are incapable of taking a militant socialist position, and fall victim themselves, and threaten to lead elements of the workers, to the worst deviations of putschism, commandism, and arbitrary acts of violence, theft and intimidation. Their highest forms of political action are mob agitation and street fighting. As such, they represent at best the incidental material of anarchist bands, such as those established by Blanqui, which reject an organized relation to the workers' movement and seek political power through the *coup d'état*, independent of the struggles of the working class. Mob agitation and street fighting are primitive forms of political action. Modern revolution, in countries where large-scale capitalist production prevails, demands the mass seizure and control of the means of production by the workers. The factory, and the modern forms of distribution and communication, are the objective foundation of modern capitalist society and, therefore, the objective basis of proletarian power. Without the organized support of the proletariat, and that means proletarian leadership, an insurrection would be isolated, immobilized, starved and finally crushed by the forces of order.

Marx discusses two salient examples of the reactionary role of the lumpenproletariat. In the June Days the 'special' State forces, the Guardes Mobiles, were in the forefront of the suppression of the workers' rising. This same class formed the backbone of Louis Bonaparte's 'personal' political party, the Society of 10 December. Bonaparte, a declassé adventurer, relied upon his own kind. These passages of Marx are too well known to require quotation (see Marx, 1850, p. 155; 1853, p. 295).

Marx and Engels's strong language and their strong opposition to the criminal classes and the demi-monde, far from expressing an idiosyncratic moralism, stems from a definite theoretical-political point of departure.

(b) *The 'delinquent solution' and political action*

But, if Marx and Engels reject the criminal classes as a reactionary force, what of the 'individual' who is driven to crime? Surely, we see here a victim of the capitalist system, a product of forces beyond his control. As early as *The Condition of the Working Class in England in 1844*, Engels discusses the formation of criminals thus (1844, p. 163):

> The contempt for the existing social order is most conspicuous in its extreme form, that of offences against the law. If the influences demoralising the working man act more powerfully, more concentratedly than usual, he becomes an offender as certainly as water abandons the fluid for the vapourous state at 80 degrees, Réaumur. Under the brutal and brutalising treatment of the bourgeoisie, the working man becomes precisely as such a thing without violition as water, and is subject to the laws of Nature with precisely the same necessity; at a certain point freedom ceases.

In *Capital*, amongst many other passages indicating the effect of capitalist production on the worker, Marx discusses the effects of the employer's attempts to evade the Factory Acts by use of the relays system, and he remarks thus: 'The hours of rest were turned into hours of idleness, which drove the youths to the pot-house, the girls to the brothel' (1867, p. 291).

The majority of the poor wretches displaced by evictions and enclosures, by the Primitive Accumulation which separated the worker from the means of production, had little option but to become thieves, vagabonds and bandits, and as such they were mercilessly persecuted by the very class that had produced their downfall (ibid., p. 734):

> On the other hand, these men, suddenly dragged from their wonted mode of life, could not as suddenly adapt themselves to the discipline of their new condition. They were turned *en masse* into beggars, robbers, vagabonds. . . .
> Hence at the end of the 15th and during the whole of the 16th century, throughout Western Europe a bloody legislation against vagabondage.

Marx and Engels, although they constantly warned the workers' movement of the danger of the criminal classes, were far from moralizing with the bourgeoisie about the conditions which produced criminality, which filled the ranks of the criminal classes with recruits. They demonstrated that it was the very capitalist system, which the bourgeoisie put forward as the model of a just and virtuous society, that produced these threats to its own 'order', 'respectability' and 'property'.

Marx and Engels did not, however, accept the bourgeoisie's own estimation of the threat to 'society' represented by the criminal. The criminal career and the 'delinquent solution', however much enforced by the harsh necessities of capitalism, are not *in effect* forms of political rebellion against the existing order but a more or less reactionary accommodation to them. The professional criminal, like all other men, 'enters into definite relations that are . . . independent of their will'; he joins the ranks of the lumpenproletariat. Like it or not, a specific class position is forced upon him. The romanticization of crime, the recognition in the criminal of a rebel 'alienated' from society, is, for Marxism, a dangerous political ideology. It leads inevitably, since the 'criminal' is an individualist abstraction of a class position, to the estimation of the lumpenproletariat as a revolutionary force.

Crime is not only the business of professional criminals; other illegal actions, machine-breaking, industrial sabotage, the murder of landlords and officials by peasants, have a more obviously 'political' character. Marx and Engels remark thus about outbreaks of machine-breaking (1848, pp. 41–2):

> The proletariat goes through various stages of development. With its birth begins the struggle with the bourgeoisie. At first the contest is carried on by individual labourers, then by the workpeople of a factory, then by the operatives of one trade, in one locality, against the individual bourgeois who directly exploits them. They direct their attacks not against the bourgeois conditions of production, but against the conditions of production themselves; they destroy imported wares that compete with their labour, they smash to pieces machinery, they set factories ablaze, they seek to restore by force the vanished status of the workmen of the middle ages.

Industrial sabotage is a similar index of immediate reaction to harsh, gruelling and frustrating conditions of work. For Marx and Engels these were immediate and spontaneous forms of struggle; forms which are inadequate to transform conditions of production because they are directed toward immediate objects which result from a misrecognition of the real determinants of the workers' situation. It is the task of the workers' organizations and of the political theory of Scientific Socialism to transform such forms and ideologies of struggle. To glorify such primitive forms would be to fixate the workers' movement in its infancy.

In agrarian class societies, banditry, terrorism or the spontaneous peasant uprising are the immediate forms of struggle. Bandits appear time and again in popular mythology and police reports only to vanish again into prisons, into the service of the ruling class, or to be destroyed by the forces of order. Peasant uprisings effect their spontaneous justice and redistributions and are crushed. Both forms of struggle are quite normal incidents in the socio-political rebellion.[6] It is only with the development of capitalism, and later imperialism, and with the consequent development of nationwide political movements led by the proletarian vanguard, that peasant movements, linked with the struggle, forms of organization and politics of the proletariat, develop into a genuinely revolutionary political force. The case of China illustrates this point: it was only under the political leadership of the communists, who broke with the forms of organization and ideology of banditry and the spontaneous peasant uprising, that the social and political conditions of agrarian China could begin to be transformed as the result of a successful revolutionary war.

Thus the criminal 'individual', or spontaneous mass actions of an illegal character, are of interest to Marxism from the standpoint of political and ideological struggle alone. They are of interest only in so far as spontaneous mass action is the point of departure of a political critique and a political struggle which transforms it into an organized and theoretically-based politics.

(c) *Political 'crimes' and the State*

'Crime' is defined by State law and detected and punished by the State repressive apparatus. Marx regards the State as an instrument of class oppression; an instrument which intervenes in the class struggle on behalf of the ruling class and against the proletariat and its allies. The State intervenes in the class struggle on behalf of the ruling class and against the proletariat and its allies. The State intervenes in the class struggle with its ideological and repressive apparatus to break the power of the political movement of the workers by means of legal and extra-legal sanctions. One form of such State intervention is the stigmatization of political opponents of the bourgeoisie as 'criminals'. To stigmatize political opponents as 'common criminals' is to deny ideologically their *political* character and aims, to castigate them as bandits and adventurers. The effect of such ideological-repressive interventions, if successful, is to give the political movement a pre-political character.

Marx's response to this situation was complex. To glorify illegal struggle, to argue that the State is *only* the obedient creature of the ruling class, and to argue that all legal struggles, and all attempts to use the representative means and the political freedoms protected by State law, are a sham since the State is a *mere* expression of force, is to do the bourgeoisie's own ideological job for it. To cringe before legality and State power, on the other hand, to reject all forms of struggle proscribed by the State, is to cut the political movement off from the revolutionary road. At one time and another, trades unions, the free press and free public assembly have all been illegal forms of action, even in bourgeois 'democracies'. How does Marx resolve this dilemma, the dilemma of ultra-Leftism and reformism? Certainly not by a return to the Kantian differentiation between rational and empirical law. He does so by the application of a rigorous class and political position. Forms of struggle, legal and illegal, which define the relation of the proletarian movement to the class State, are determined solely on the basis of their efficacy, under determinate conditions, in the proletarian struggle for socialism.

A good example of Marx's position in this respect is his intervention in a specific case of political oppression, the Cologne Communist Trial. The Prussian government, in 1851–2, in the tide of repression following the defeat of the democratic revolutions of 1848, attempted to destroy its most effective opponents, the communists, by the exposure and prosecution of an international 'conspiracy' to overthrow the established order. A 'conspiracy' which proved the implication of the Communist League in plans for revolution by the fabrication of minutes and documents. Marx worked to expose the fraud, clear the name of the Communist League and assist the victims in their defence. Marx's wife Jenny, often considered falsely and unjustly to have been at heart a reactionary and ill at ease with her husbands' doings, wrote about Marx's efforts (J. Marx, 1852, p. 72):

> You can imagine how the 'Marx Party' is active day and night. . . . All the allegations of the police are lies. They steal, forge, break open desks, swear false oaths . . . claiming they are privileged to do so against Communists, who are beyond the pale of society!

The reasons for Marx's struggle were simple and entirely political; to counter police ideology about the Communist League and to attempt to check the repression of the movement. Marx's aim was clear, to preserve the political-legal conditions necessary for open communist agitation. Marx and Engels were always determined to use the legal freedoms available in the bourgeois State to the full in order to develop the workers' movement. The greatest possible political-legal freedom could only be of advantage to the workers' movement. Thus Marx and Engels constantly promoted the demands for universal suffrage, a free press, freedom for trades unions and the abolition of arbitrary and repressive laws.

4 Professional crime and production relations

In *Theories of Surplus Value*, vol. 1, Marx discusses the role of the criminal in production relations. This passage, 'The Apologist Conception of the Productivity of all Professions', is of great interest (Marx, 1969, pp. 387–8):

> A philosopher produces ideas, a poet poems, a clergyman sermons, a professor compendia and so on. A criminal produces crimes. If we look a little closer at the connection between this latter branch of production and society as a whole, we shall rid ourselves of many prejudices. The criminal produces not only crimes but also criminal law and in addition to this the inevitable compendium in which this same professor throws his lectures onto the general market as 'commodities'. This brings with it augmentation of national wealth, quite apart from the personal enjoyment which – as a competent witness Herr Professor Roscher, [tells] us – the manuscript of the compendium brings to its originator himself.
>
> The criminal, moreover, produces the whole of the police and of criminal justice, constables, judges, hangmen, juries, etc.; and all these different lines of business, which form equally many categories of the social division of labour, develop different capacities of the human spirit, create new needs and new ways of

satisfying them. Torture alone has given rise to the most ingenious mechanical inventions, and employed many honourable craftsmen in the production of its instruments.

The criminal produces an impression, partly moral and partly tragic, as the case may be, and in this way renders a 'service' by arousing the moral and aesthetic feelings of the public. He produces not only compendia on criminal law, not only penal codes and along with them legislators in this field, but also art, *belles-lettres*, novels, and even tragedies, as not only Mullner's *Schuld* and Schiller's *Rauber* show, but also (Sophocles's) *Oedipus* and (Shakespeare's) *Richard the Third*. The criminal breaks the monotony and everyday security of bourgeois life. In this way he keeps it from stagnation, and gives rise to that uneasy tension and agility without which even the spur of competition would get blunted. Thus, he gives a stimulus to the production forces. Whilst crime takes a part of the superfluous population off the labour market and thus reduces competition amongst the labourers – up to a certain point, preventing wages from falling below the minimum – the struggle against crime absorbs another part of this population. Thus, the criminal comes in as one of those natural 'counterweights' which bring about a correct balance and open up a whole perspective of 'useful' occupations.

The effects of the criminal on the development of productive power can be shown in detail. Would locks ever have reached their present degree of excellence had there been no thieves? Would the making of bank-notes have reached its present perfection had there been no forgers? Would the microscope have found its way into the sphere of ordinary commerce (see Babbage) but for trading frauds? Doesn't pratical chemistry owe just as much to adulteration of commodities and the efforts to show it up as to the honest zeal for production? Crime, through its constantly new methods of attack on property, constantly calls into being new methods of defence, and so is as productive as strikes for the invention of machines. And if one leaves the sphere of private crime: would the world-market ever have come into being but for national crime? Indeed, would even the nations have arisen? And hasn't the 'Tree of Sin been at the same time the Tree of Knowledge ever since the time of Adam?'

On the surface this passage appears to argue that crime has an important function in the economy, that it 'produces' many other occupations as the result of its own product and, that, in the manner of Durkheim, the criminal reinforces the bourgeois 'conscience collective'. To take the passage out of the context of the whole work, is, however, very misleading.[7] The passage is shot through with irony; the irony Marx so often uses to castigate the bourgeoisie. In this text Marx is ridiculing these vulgar bourgeois apologists who justify a 'profession' by its morality. This vulgar moralist conception of the economy divides society into the respectable and the idle, depraved, feckless and criminal. Marx teases these vulgarians with the proposition that the most upright citizens depend for their livelihood on the criminal classes.

The distinction between productive and unproductive labour in the bourgeois science of political economy is quite different; the distinction is made on the basis of the contribution of an occupation to the production of wealth, or value, variously conceived. Adam Smith, for example, uses two contradictory forms of differentiation: first, he attempts to argue that productive labour is labour which produces surplus value, but lacking the *concept* of surplus value he is unable to think the *phenomenon*. He therefore falls into a second, more ideological form of argument, that productive labour is labour which produces commodities (see Marx, 1969, pp. 155–74). Despite their failure to resolve the problem in a satisfactory manner, the theoretical political economists did attempt to give a rigorous and scientific answer.

The attitude of vulgar economics is quite different (Marx, 1969, pp. 174–5, my emphases):

> What particularly aroused these polemics against Adam Smith was the following circumstance.
>
> The great mass of so-called 'higher grade' workers – such as state officials, military people, artists, doctors, priests, judges, lawyers, etc. – some of whom are not only not productive but in essence destructive, but who know how to appropriate to themselves a very great part of the 'material' wealth partly through the sale of their 'immaterial' commodities and partly by forcibly imposing the latter on other people – found it not at all pleasant to be relegated *economically* to the same class as clowns and menial servants and to appear merely as people partaking in the consumption, parasites on the actual producers.

Marx establishes the distinction between productive and unproductive labour as follows (ibid., pp. 399–401, also my emphases):

> The result of the capitalist production process is neither a mere product (use-value) nor a *commodity*, that is, a use-value which has a certain exchange-value. Its result, its product, is the creation of *surplus-value* for capital, and consequently the actual *transformation* of money or commodity into capital – which before the production process they were only in intention, in their essence, in what they were destined to be. In the production process more labour is absorbed than has been bought. This absorption, this *appropriation* of another's unpaid

labour, which is consummated in the production process, is the *direct aim* of the capitalist production process; for what capital as capital (hence the capitalist as capitalist) wants to produce is neither an immediate use-value for individual consumption nor a commodity to be turned first into money and then into a use-value. Its aim is the *accumulation of wealth, the self-expansion of value, its increase*; that is to say, the maintenance of the old value and the creation of surplus-value. And it achieves this *specific product* of the capitalist production process only in exchange with labour, which for that reason is called *productive labour*.

Labour which is to produce *commodities* must be useful labour; it must produce a use-value, it must manifest itself in a *use-value*. And consequently only labour which manifests itself in *commodities*, that is in use-values, is labour for which capital is exchanged. This is a self-evident premise. But it is not this concrete character of labour, its use-value as such – that it is for example tailoring labour, cobbling, spinning, weaving, etc. – which forms its specific use-value for capital and consequently stamps it as *productive labour* in the system of capitalist production. What forms its *specific use-value* for capital is not its specific useful character, any more than it is the particular useful properties of the product in which it is materialised. But what forms its specific use-value for capital is its character as the element which creates exchange-value, abstract labour; and in fact not that it represents some particular quantity of this general labour, but that it represents a *greater* quantity than is *contained* in its price, that is to say, in the *value of the labour-power*. . . .

It follows from what has been said that the designation of labour as *productive labour* has absolutely nothing to do with the *determinate content* of the labour, its special utility, or the particular use-value in which it manifests itself. A singer who sells her song for her own account is an *unproductive labourer*. But the same singer commissioned by an entrepreneur to sing in order to make money for him is a *productive labourer*; for she produces capital.

Marx establishes a rigorous distinction between the two forms of labour: productive labour is labour which produces surplus-value.

These concepts enable us to investigate the various departments of professional crime and the role they play in production relations.

(a) *Theft*

The thief in capitalist society appropriates material products and means of exchange; in the act of theft he neither produces commodities, nor services, nor engages in commerce, nor financial speculation. He is consequently neither a productive nor an unproductive labourer, nor is he a capitalist, rather he is strictly parasitic on the labour and wealth of society. The thief steals from the members of all social classes and from all social institutions. His interdiction of the economic relations of society is ubiquitous; he intervenes in production and circulation. The modalities of employment of these appropriated resources are varied: the thief may steal either for his own direct consumption, or for exchange to provide means of exchange for the purchase of other commodities for his consumption, or, more rarely, to capitalize an enterprise of his own. Theft, whatever its source or function for the thief, always merely redistributes the existing material production or wealth and adds nothing to the stock of material production or wealth.

Extortion is similar in its economic character to theft. The pure beggar, unlike the thief, is parasitic only upon the consumption funds of other classes. The beggar who offers some pathetic token in exchange for a donation is little different in kind.

But if the thief is an economic parasite, are not the capitalist and the policeman also parasites? No, they are not. Whilst the capitalist is neither a productive nor an unproductive labourer his position is economically necessary in any economic system governed by capitalist relations of production. The capitalist system, based upon the separation of the worker from the means of production under conditions of private property, requires both wage labourers and capitalists as agents in its production process. The position of the capitalist is inscribed in the structure of capitalist production. The policeman, a State functionary, is necessary for the reproduction of capitalist social relations; he protects the property of capitalists and others, and secures certain of the conditions of labour discipline. The existence of the modern police force owes little to the exigencies of combating professional crime and was developed primarily as an instrument of political control and labour discipline. Capitalist economies require capitalists and policemen for their existence and reproduction, they do not require thieves. The thief is a parasite on the capitalist system of production, he has no specific position as an agent in it.

Theft is not an activity confined to capitalist societies. It is a feature of all modes of production with private property. However, the position of the thief in the various modes of production is very different. In feudal societies theft is analogous in its relation to the production process to other forms of parasitism. In feudal societies the activities of bandits and vagabonds are not different in character from the mode of appropriation of the surplus product and surplus labour-time by the ruling class; which relies for its economic basis on direct political-ideological appropriation and has no specific role in the process of production. Surplus labour, on the lord's demesne, is labour directly separate from the production of the labourer's means of subsistence and is forced upon him. The ruling class in feudal society is not an economically necessary agency; its appropriation is for its own consumption and it contributes nothing to production or reproduction. The State and the ruling class stand above a society of self-sufficient producers who control the means of production. The village, a self-sufficient unit of production, has no need of the State or ruling classes.[8]

In capitalist society the production of surplus value (the form the surplus product or surplus labour-time takes under conditions of free labour) occurs directly in the process of production, in the double character of labour. The capitalist in employing the use-value of the commodity labour-power, concrete labour, in combination with the means of production which he owns, obtains a product of a value greater than the cost of that labour-power and of the portion of constant capital which is transferred to the product. This is all strictly legal and above board. The worker sold his labour-power to the capitalist, for a wage determined by the average social cost of the reproduction of that commodity, in a free contract, and the capitalist has the full right to the use-value of that commodity. No extra economic extortion or injustice has taken place here.

The State in capitalist society appropriates a portion of this surplus-value from the capitalist class, and the taxes payed by labourers represent part of the means of subsistence (cost of labour-power) for which they sell their labour to the capitalist. The capitalist class, therefore, demands a measure of control of the State budget. Under feudal conditions the ruling class appropriate a portion of the surplus product directly from the producers; for the capitalist class under a feudal State this is an intolerable situation, akin to robbery, since they are threatened with an indeterminate extortion of their accumulation fund depending upon the rapacity and taste for consumption of the feudal class. This situation, one element of the conflict of two quite different modes of production, leads to the developing bourgeoisie overthrowing or capturing the feudal State.

Thus, theft under capitalist conditions is quite different from that under feudal conditions; the baron and the bandit are not entirely dissimilar in their relation to the process of production, the capitalist and the tax officer are quite different from the thief.[9]

To argue that private property *is* theft is an absurdity. This form of argument presupposes private property, bourgeois private-property right, as the natural form of relations between man and man. One can only steal another legal entity's property. Theft presupposes private property as a condition of its existence. To argue that private property is theft requires a conception of right and of the person in whom that right inheres which are effects of the ideological elaboration of property relations in political and legal philosophy.

But property is not a natural form of the relations between man and man (or between man and woman). Private property comes into existence in a definite form of social formation; it comes into existence with the appearance of classes, and with the appearance of the State as a guardian of class society. Primitive communism recognizes neither private property nor theft amongst the members of a particular kin-group; it recognizes only the transgression of kinship relations, and the form of relations between kin-groups, which are the relations of production and distribution in primitive communism. It recognizes only offences in respect of the rituals associated with kinship, of the rituals and mythologies which form the ideological superstructure which corresponds to this mode of production.[10] Property founded upon *appropriation* requires a definite ideological and repressive superstructure. For example, European feudal property corresponds to the ideological dominance of the Catholic church: 'This much, however, is clear that the middle ages could not live on Catholicism. . . . On the contrary it is the economic conditions of the time which explain why . . . Catholicism played the chief part' (Marx, 1867, p. 81n). In feudal societies there is a dislocation between production relations and property relations, between peasant production and the 'higher unity' of the State, which gives rise to this ideological dominance. In capitalist society there is no such dislocation since property relations are the direct product of production relations and no such ideological dominance. In developed communism the principle 'from each according to his ability to each according to his need' abolishes the very category of theft. To take from the stock of use-values distributed to a specific unit of consumption would be at best an inconvenience and would merit no more than general censure for inconsiderateness. To argue that property *is* theft is to be unable to think the specificity of the different forms of social relations. Thus, the analogy between the baron and the bandit is an *analogy*, and from one definite aspect, their relation to the production process.

(b) *Prostitution and illegal services*

The prostitute who sells for his/her personal support is an unproductive labourer, like the tutor or the lawyer who works on his own behalf. The prostitute who provides the same services for a wage in order to make money for an entrepreneur is a productive labourer, like the singer whose performances enrich a theatre-owner – both produce surplus-value which can function as capital.

Prostitution, we are told, is 'the oldest profession'; what therefore is different about prostitution in capitalist society? Nothing; capitalist relations pre-exist capitalist social formations. This is only confusing to those historicists who believe in a history of essentially unique 'epochs' rather than the Marxist analysis of the structure of different modes of production.

The same generalizations can be made about various forms of gambling and racketeering.

(c) *Criminal enterprises*

Illegal forms of capitalist production, for example, the production and sale of intoxicating liquors in the USA between 1920 and 1933, have certain specific differences from legitimate capitalist enterprises. The capital of the illegal enterprise has no legal title as property. Capital that is not legal property is a contradiction that sets very definite limits to its function as capital and which restricts the economic freedom of the illegal enterprise. The accumulation of capital in such enterprises is limited by their necessarily clandestine character, and this restriction enforces the conversion of such accumulated capital into strictly legal enterprises and the employment of various subterfuges to convert it into legal property.

Illegality has certain very specific effects in respect of the employment of wage labour. Such enterprises will generally recruit labour from the industrial reserve army and the lumpenproletariat. Such labour is not strictly 'free' labour, since it is driven into a collusive relation of common criminality with the employer and is subject to coercion. The rate of exploitation may be higher than in broadly comparable branches of capitalist production. The wage labourer in such enterprises has no measure of protection from the Factory Acts or the police, and is unable to form trades unions. Such labour is very unlikely to play any part in the class struggle or the workers' movement.

The outlaw capitalist has very distinct relations to his own class and to the State. He does not enjoy the protection of the State, he is unable to defend his interests politically, and he is open to immediate State closure and appropriation. The illegal capitalist must, therefore, defend his own 'property' and develop his own repressive apparatus. Where the widespread corruption of public officials and political representatives exists, outlaw capital may enjoy great security and great privileges, at a price.

In general criminal enterprises are absent from the central forms of capitalist production, from large-scale industry, and large commercial and financial enterprises. Criminal enterprises are economically marginal compared with the productive power of modern industry.

To return, in conclusion, to Marx's 'The Apologist Conception of the Productivity of all Professions'. The ironic character of the text should now be evident. To say the criminal 'produces' crimes is to use the term in a very different sense from Marx's scientific concept of production. The criminal does not produce the law or law enforcement; the existence of private property and class society give rise to these elements of the superstructure. The production of instruments of torture and of locks has been at no period a major branch of capitalist production. 'Practical chemistry', as Marx and Engels show in many other texts, owes far more to the textile industry and the manufacture of explosives than it does to fraud. Modern industrial chemistry, as Engels demonstrated, depends on the application of modern chemical science to industry. The criminal classes are a tiny fraction of the industrial reserve army, even in these days of 'full employment'. As for the criminals' services to bourgeois morality we have seen that the ideological forms of capitalist society, and of other social formations, correspond to the mode of production and not to the exigencies of outlawing the criminal. One would have to be a vulgar apologist of the bourgeoisie to discover in this text 'the Marxist theory of crime'.

Appendix

Other writings of Marx and Engels on law

This chapter is by no means an exhaustive account of Marx and Engels's positions on law and the class struggle. It concentrates upon those aspects of their work which are most relevant to the demarcation between Marxism and radical criminology. Important aspects of their positions on law neglected here are the following:

(a) *The class struggle and law*. See, Marx, 1867, chapter 10, 'The Working Day', where Marx deals with the effects of the English Factory Acts on the hours and conditions of labour, and the workers' struggle for the legal regulation of hours of work.

(b) *The law of contract, the wage-form and surplus-value*. See, Marx, 1867, chapter 12, 'The Transformation of the Value (and Respectively the Price) of Labour Power into Wages', where Marx demonstrates that the bourgeois legal rights of contract are an essential element of the wage-form, an essential ideological component of the production of surplus-value (ibid., pp. 539–40):

> The wage-form thus extinguishes every trace of the division of the working day into necessary labour and surplus labour, into paid and unpaid labour.

> Hence, we may understand the decisive importance of the transformation of value and the price of labour-power into the form of wages, or into the value and price of labour itself. This phenomenal form, which makes the actual relation invisible, and, indeed, shows the direct opposite of that relation, forms the basis of all the juridical notions of both labour and capitalist.

The bourgeois rights of contract are simultaneously the ideological condition of existence of the wage-form, and therefore, of exploitation, and at the same time the ideological effect of that form.

(c) *Law and the social formation.* The classic texts in this respect are: Marx, 1964a; Engels, 1884; 1876, part 1, chapters 9, 10 and 11.

Notes

1 We refer here to a general ideological tendency in the social sciences; a tendency far more marked in its widespread and spontaneous manifestations than in particular published works. It is the object of this chapter to counter this general tendency by reference to Marxism rather than to offer a specific critique of the writings of radical deviancy theorists.

2 See Jacques Rancière, 'Le Concept du critique et la critique de économie politique', in Althusser *et al.* (1965). The first two sections of this important paper have been translated in *Theoretical Practice*, nos. 1 and 2, 1971.

3 This position, which is similar in many respects to that of Godelier (1967) is clearly inadequate as a complete account of Marx's theory of the social formation. The 1859 *Preface* has certain tendencies toward relativism and factorialism in the relation of structure and superstructure. The author does not subscribe to Godelier's position or to these tendencies, but is constrained by the limitations of space from citing more scientific works of Marx. For a more adequate discussion of Marx's basic concepts of the social formation, see, Althusser (1970) in particular the essay, 'On the Materialist Dialectic'.

4 Della Volpe (1970) argues that the *Critique* is an example of Rousseau's 'anti-levelling egalitarianism'. But, sophistry and rhetoric apart, Della Volpe offers no proofs whatsoever that Marx's actual position in the *Critique* and his critical attitude to Rousseau are in 'contradiction'.

5 Anyone who doubts this exposition in favour of the economistic and sectarian interpretation current in sociology should consult two outstanding texts: Marx's discussion of the proposition in the Gotha Programme that, 'The emancipation of labour must be the work of the working class, relatively to which all other classes are *only reactionary mass*', see Marx (1875), and Engels's 1895 *Preface* to Marx's *The Class Struggles in France*, see Engels (1895).

6 For a good orthodox Marxist analysis of forms of pre-political rebellion in agrarian class societies, see Hobsbawm (1959).

7 This passage has recently been reproduced in this isolated manner in the

Marxist journal *Monthly Review* and under the most misleading title, 'The Productivity of Crime'. It is also reproduced, in like fashion, in the collection of Marx's writings edited by Bottomore and Rubel, 1963, see pp. 167–8.

8 See Marx (1964a).

9 This analysis is based upon, Etienne Balibar, 'Fundamental concepts of Historical Materialism', in, Althusser and Balibar (1970). However, it should be noted that the present text uses Balibar's analysis in a very partial and vulgarizing fashion.

10 For a systematic Marxist account of the social relations of 'primitive' societies, see Engels (1884), and Terray (1969).

9 Radical deviancy theory and Marxism: a reply to Paul Q. Hirst's 'Marx and Engels on law, crime and morality'

Ian Taylor and Paul Walton

We are somewhat mystified by Paul Hirst's attack on radical deviancy theory, and the idiosyncratic use of Marxism (allegedly as the true, and scientific, alternative). The comments below derive from our interest in both areas, but we do not claim – since this chapter is reactive rather than innovative – that they represent a resolution of issues which Hirst's essay raises.

In the first place, Hirst at no time names the 'radical deviancy theorists' against whom he constructs his polemic. We can think of no theorist of crime and deviancy in this country, and only two in the USA (John Horton and Tony Platt) who could be accused of the 'Marxism' in deviancy theory he sees to be prevalent. None of the other 'conflict' theorists of crime (for example, Howard Becker, Edwin Lemert or even the more 'political' Richard Quinney) borrow in any significant fashion from Marxism: they are all, to different extents, phenomenological in orientation. Naming names would not be important, except that in refusing to deal with concrete examples, Hirst's arguments tend to be erected against hypothesized rather than real positions. Now it is true that there are small groups of people in Britain and in the USA who are interested in developing something like a 'Marxist' approach to criminology, and Hirst's erudite, if rather assertive, article can be taken as a contribution in itself.

Second, and closely connected with Hirst's tendency to assume quite specific features in a 'general ideological tendency' within the social sciences, is Hirst's rather narrow conception of the problem of knowledge and interest. Hirst alleges that there is a total disjunction between the 'Marxism' under debate in 'the established social sciences' and the scientific Marxism of practice (which he then proceeds to describe). His Marxism flows out of the interplay of revolutionary theory and concrete 'practical' activity. This conception of Marxism as embodying a theory whose only object is the proletarian revolution and whose nature is that of a 'science' forgets that, in the analysis of social life, whilst the material basis can be clearly delineated scientifically, the way in which men see the world (and this includes social scientists, lawyers, ruling ideologists, etc.) is a problem of consciousness, and is not amenable to study with the perspectives of natural science. What many radical deviancy theorists, Marxists or otherwise, are attempting to do is to move criminology away from a focus on the 'criminality' of the poor, the pathologizing of 'deviant' behaviour into categories derived from biology, psychology or positivistic sociology, and to abolish the *distinction* between the study of human deviation and the study of the functioning of States, and ruling-class ideologies as a whole.

In short, many of these people are struggling towards a coherent theoretical position which, whilst not following Hirst in abolishing 'criminology and deviancy as a coherent object of study', insists that they are only coherent when the false distinctions between politics, economics, psychology, etc., are collapsed and their interpenetration revealed. This is nothing if not an exercise in theoretical consciousness: a problem Hirst sees to be soluble only in alliance with a certain (and very contentious) form of Marxism. Hirst, holding to a narrow view of science, wants to insist that 'crime and deviance are no more a scientific field for Marxism than education, the family or sport'. The objects of Marxist theory, according to Hirst, are 'specified by its own concepts: the mode of production, the class struggle, the state, ideology, etc.'. Hirst's view of Marxism coupled with his less than exhaustive list of the concepts utilized by Marx at various points in his work, leads him to reject the study of any aspects of social formations other than those which are likely to give rise to proletarian revolution.

The massive amount of work carried out by Marx, Engels, Lukacs, Gramsci, Reich, Habermas and Marcuse in combating bourgeois consciousness and bourgeois theorists does not stop short at the examination of the dissolution of capitalism, but is concerned also with the nature of liberation as a whole. Hirst's 'Marxism' would not allow examination of the question of sexuality, of the constraints and 'illnesses' (*sic*) induced, maintained and amplified by the bourgeois family, and of the problem of the 'education' and 'socialization' experiences under capitalism in general. The Marxism which we believe, contrary to Hirst's caricature, to be at the base of one developing tendency in deviancy theory, is a Marxism which would be concerned to take on, and reveal, the ideological nature of social science, and in that battle, to win people to the struggle against oppression in its various guises. To quote from the *later* Marx i.e. the period in which Hirst alleges that Marx was developing, exclusively, an Historical-Materialist framework for the analysis of social formations (Marx, 1859a, pp. 328–9, our emphasis):

> My investigations [into Hegel's philosophy] led to the result that legal relations as well as forms of state are to be grasped neither from themselves nor from the so-called general development of the human mind, but rather have their roots in the material conditions of life. . . . With the change of the economic foundation the entire immense superstructure is more or less rapidly transformed. In considering such transformations *a distinction should always be made* between the material transformation of the economic conditions of production, which can be determined with the precision of natural science, and the legal, political, religious, esthetic or philosophic – in short, ideological forms in which men become conscious of this conflict and fight it out.

At a time when increasing numbers of intellectuals, involved in the study of 'legal, political, religious, esthetic, and philosophic' questions, are coming to realize the interconnectedness of their concerns, indeed, are coming to see apparently personal (e.g. psychological and sexual) questions as requiring political and historical solutions – what is needed is not the rejection so much as the correction of these important tendencies.

Marx, in *The Communist Manifesto*, foresaw the situation of 'bourgeois' intellectuals in the following terms (Marx and Engels, 1848, p. 44):

> Finally, in times when the class struggle nears the decisive hour, the process of dissolution going on within the ruling class, in fact within the whole range of old society, assumes such a violent glaring character, that a small section of the ruling class cuts itself adrift, and joins the revolutionary class, the class that holds the future in its hands. Just as, therefore, at an earlier period, a section of the mobility went over to the bourgeoisie, so now a portion of the bourgeoisie goes over to the proletariat, and in particular, a portion of the bourgeois ideologists, who have raised themselves to the level of comprehending theoretically the historical movement as a whole.

Our suggestion is, then, that Hirst has damagingly misunderstood both the significance and seriousness of what he calls 'radical deviancy theory', and that this misrepresentation flows directly from his simplified view of the problem of consciousness and scientific knowledge: in brief, we believe that it is incorrect to see 'established social science' as a monolithic reification, in which no significant contradictions are developing.

Our third set of comments has to do more with the substance of Hirst's interpretation of what 'radical deviancy theory' is about. He writes:

> The romanticisation of crime, the recognition in the criminal of a rebel 'alienated' from society, is, for Marxism, a dangerous political ideology. It leads *inevitably*, since the 'criminal' is an individualistic abstraction of a class position, to the estimation of the lumpenproletariat as a revolutionary force.

It would require little 'science' and no imagination to erect a study of society which sees all opposition, however lumpen, as somehow progressive. But radical deviancy theory, at least as we see it, is guilty of no such sin. Of course it is true, as Alvin Gouldner has argued that the neo-Chicagoan school of sociology (the followers of Howard Becker) have tended to look at deviants rather in the same way as 1930s Stalinists tended to look on the proletariat itself (Gouldner, 1968). But present theoretical developments are directed *against* the *romanticization* of criminality, especially in the light of the social processes, peculiar to this particular period of capitalist crisis, the 'deviancy' of vast numbers of middle-class students and youth (the dissolution of the equation of poverty and pathology) and the politicization of some deviant groups themselves. In short, at present there is a self-consciousness about oppression and its immediacy.

Our real quarrel with Hirst, however, arises over the interpretation of Marx's writings on crime and deviancy: a question which is clearly not only of academic importance, but which has relevance also for the intellectuals who are working towards new theoretical positions, via a reading of Marx, and that section of the population who are feeling the brunt of oppression in the form of a criminal sanction. Writing of a different period, the Marx of Hirst's third period (the Historical-Materialist Marx) wrote (1859b):

> There must be something rotten in the very core of a social system which increases its wealth without decreasing its misery, and increases in crimes even more rapidly than in numbers. . . . Violations of the law are generally the offspring of the economical agencies beyond the control of the legislator, but, as the working of the Juvenile Offenders' act testifies, it depends to some degree on official society to stamp certain violations of its rules as crimes or as transgressions only. This difference of nomenclature, so far from being indifferent, decides on the fate of thousands of men, and the moral tone of society. Law itself may not only punish crime, but improvise it.

Now here, Marx, as in the best of modern deviancy theory, is pointing to social processes which give rise to misery and oppression for thousands of people under capitalism. To reject studies which reveal the nature and genesis of such oppression is to write off the possibility of demonstrating openly one aspect of the criminal nature of bourgeois society.

Lastly, Hirst seems to suffer from the illusion that there exist radical deviancy theorists who have discovered in Marx's text 'The Apologist Conception of the Productivity of all Professions' (Marx, 1969, pp. 375–6) the basis for a 'Marxist theory of crime'. Of course, no such people exist. It is apparent, as Hirst himself suggests, that when Marx says 'the criminal produces not only crimes, but criminal laws', etc., that the text is an ironic tirade at those who would regard all social activity as productive, in as much as for Marx the distinction between productive and non-productive labour, in his own work, hangs upon his theory of surplus value. Indeed, Hirst is correct in implying that Marx dismissed the lumpenproletariat precisely because it did not contribute towards this productive process but was parasitic upon it. But this text is important for other reasons. As Marx himself suggests: 'A criminal produces crimes. If we look a little closer at the connection between this latter branch of production and society as a whole, we shall rid ourselves of many prejudices' (ibid., p. 375). Marx's position here is that, if we regard *all* activity as productive or (in the language of modern social science) *functional* for the social system, then we are driven to see crime or criminal activity as functional too. Indeed, Marx quotes Mandeville's *Fable of the Bees* and suggests that Mandeville, in showing that every kind of activity is productive, had followed the ultimate logic of his position in arguing that: '[if] evil ceases, the society must be spoiled, if not totally dissolved' (Mandeville, 1714). As Marx suggests, 'Mandeville was, of course, infinitely bolder and more honest than the philistine apologists of bourgeois society' (Marx, 1969, p. 375). What Marx had seen, more clearly than the later functionalists such as Durkheim, was that viewing activities in functional terms drives one into the absurd position of seeing crime as a necessary feature of society. Of course, for Marx and us, it is not. That is the importance of this passage, and that is the importance of establishing, and struggling in theoretical practice, with functional, structural (in short, ideological), interpretations of social formations and establishing theoretically the potentiality of a classless, human and non-criminal society.

10 Radical deviancy theory and Marxism: a reply to Taylor and Walton

Paul Q. Hirst

Taylor and Walton's reply to my article 'Marx and Engels on law, crime and morality' is internally contradictory. On the one hand, they assert that the target of my 'polemic' does not exist. On the other hand, they spend a considerable amount of time defending the very approach they claim to be a figment of my imagination.

The authors of the reply have misrecognized the object and scope of the critique of radical deviancy theory in the essay. What is criticized in that essay is by no means a failing confined to radical deviancy theorists. It is a very general tendency in the social sciences which is particularly manifest in the field of deviancy. What is criticized in the essay is a specific form of an empiricism which considers that a theoretical problematic can be applied to externally 'given' real objects. It is a conception that theories are more or less convenient explanatory devices to be applied to given phenomena which are under attack.

In the essay an attempt is made to show that the object of a theoretical problematic, in this case Marxism, is an object internal to that problematic, that is, an object constituted within knowledge and which is not 'given' in the real. What is studied and what is explained by a theory cannot therefore be taken as a given, nor can the theory be applied to any 'object' we choose. This, it is claimed, is true of both ideological and scientific theories. The essay examines the three major problematics in which Marx worked, the Kantian, the Feuerbachian and the Historical Materialist, and it shows that these problematics specify different and incompatible objects within knowledge. The essay demonstrates that none of these problematics are applicable to the given conceptions of crime and deviance. In the essay it is indicated that in the contemporary sociology of deviance (and also we might add in the other 'sociologies of') the objects of study are not theoretically constituted objects but objects constituted prior to theory by practico-social ideologies. This is as true in the case of 'radical' deviancy theory as it is of 'conservative' deviancy theory. The paper indicates, and this is its main point, the empiricism inherent in the application of theoretical concepts to objects untheoretically given in social experience. It was in this general theoretical context that I criticized 'radical' deviancy theory and attempted to show that Marxist theory is incompatible in essence with what it is that deviancy theory takes as its object.

There is not one word in reply to this critique of empiricism in the text of Taylor and Walton. This is at first sight surprising, for it emerges from their reply that they have a very different conception of the nature of scientific knowledge. Taylor and Walton conceive knowledge, on the one hand, as a form of consciousness, as the experience of the social world by a subject, and on the other, as a positivist 'natural-scientific' description of given real phenomena.

Let us examine their first conception, of knowledge as social consciousness, as it emerges from their discussion of what radical deviancy theory is about. Taylor and Walton suggest that deviance in the conventional sense has ceased to be the object of the radicals. This reorganization in respect of deviancy theory is not a reorganization in knowledge, the displacements effected in existing ideological problematics by the advent of a new science and a new object, it is a transformation in the political and social consciousness of the deviancy theorist. In their estimation radical deviancy theorists, whether Marxist or not, are attempting (see p. 234):

> to abolish the *distinction* between the study of human deviation and the study of the functioning of States, and ruling-class ideologies as a whole.

The radical deviancy theorists the authors claimed to be figments of my imagination, have taken on life half-way through their text. The authors characterize the position of these hitherto inexistent beings thus (See p. 234) (my emphasis):

> The Marxism which we believe, contrary to Hirst's caricature, to be at the base of *one developing tendency* in deviancy theory, is a Marxism which would be concerned to take on, and reveal, the ideological nature of social science, and in that battle, to win people to the struggle against oppression in its various guises.

This, it must be noted, is not a call for the scientific critique of ideological positions. It appears that *all* social science is ideological and that the new position the authors call for is nothing but a politically different, although epistemologically equivalent, ideology which is counterposed to that prevailing in the established social sciences. Deviancy theory ceases to exist by transforming itself openly into an ideology with political objectives.

Deviance as an object is abolished by a socio-political consciousness which recognizes that deviance is not an objective and scientific question but a political and ideological one. Radical 'deviancy' theorists and the 'deviants' themselves are rejecting the ideological category of deviance which cloaks the operation of real oppression. This new consciousness on the part of the radical intelligentsia develops because its members are (see p. 235)

> coming to realize the interconnectedness of their concerns, indeed, are coming to see apparently personal (e.g. psychological and sexual) questions as requiring political and historical solutions.

This emerging new consciousness is the product of a changed political and social situation, in which the oppressed and their allies can recognize the connection between their immediate experience and wider political and historical forces (see p. 236)

> in the light of the social processes, peculiar to this particular period of capitalist crisis, the 'deviancy' of vast numbers of middle-class students and youth . . . and the politicization of some deviant groups themselves. In short, at present there is a self-consciousness about oppression and its immediacy.

Aside from the absurd equation of 'self-consciousness' and scientific knowledge, an equation which negates science, this position has several disturbing aspects. Taylor and Walton identify deviancy and oppression. I do not see how anyone can follow this position to its logical conclusion.

All societies outlaw certain categories of acts and punish them. The operation of law or custom, however much it may be associated in some societies with injustice and oppression, is a necessary condition of existence of any social formation. Whether the social formation has a State or not, whether it is communist or not, it will control and coerce in certain ways the acts of its members. The police force in our own society is not *merely* an instrument of oppression, or of the maintenance of the capitalist economist system, but also a condition of a civilized existence under the present political-economic relations. One cannot imagine the absence of the control of traffic or the absence of the suppression of theft and murder, nor can one consider these controls as purely oppressive. If Taylor and Walton do not disagree with this view, then we can only suppose they select the cause of the 'deviants' they support with some care. We presume they do not intend us to believe that they make common cause with professional thieves or cynical murderers. However, they offer us no clear theoretical basis on which they might base this separation.

Taylor and Walton would no doubt reply that the consciousness of the oppressed themselves is the criterion of the separation. The authors will claim that the operation of the laws is inextricably connected with the political struggles in our society and that the consciousness of the oppressed is an ideological form 'in which men become conscious of this conflict and fight it out' (Marx, 1859a, quoted by Taylor and Walton, see p. 235). If this is their view, then knowledge becomes purely a matter of partisanship. Knowledge becomes the world-outlook of a class, a group or an individual, and beyond this world-outlook there is nothing. This position reduces all knowledge to the consciousness and experience of a subject, be it a class, a group or an individual, and the subject's self-consciousness is a knowledge constituted from its own position in the world. With this kind of essentialism there can be no argument. No wonder the authors of the reply find it impossible to recognize the object of my critique or to understand the question I posed concerning the difference of objects: of objects in knowledge and objects in practico-social ideologies.

Let us now turn to the question of my 'simplified view of the problem of consciousness and scientific knowledge' (see p. 235) and the authors' own grossly simplified view of this 'problem'. The authors consider my conception of Marxism 'a theory whose only object is the proletarian revolution' (pp. 234–5) I do not see how one can read the essay in this way except to misread it. If the proletarian revolution were the 'only object' of Historical Materialism, then my separation of the former and Scientific Socialism would make no sense. My point was that the objects of Historical Materialism are the objects specified by its concepts and that Marxism is not a 'theory of society' which can be applied to any given range of phenomena within 'society'. I stressed that Historical Materialism is first and foremost a scientific general theory of modes of production. It cannot, therefore, be a theory the 'only object' of which is a specific form of political practice in a specific social formation.

Taylor and Walton couple this misreading of my position with the most amazing misreading of the 1859 *Preface*. They take me to task for forgetting that (see p. 234)

> in the analysis of social life, whilst the material basis can be clearly delineated scientifically, the way in which men see the world . . . is a problem of consciousness, and is not emenable to the perspectives of natural science.

If the authors were to read footnotes carefully they would find that I make my position clear on this very question (see p. 231, n. 3). I intended these remarks to refer to certain very real theoretical weaknesses in the 1859 *Preface*; 'certain tendencies toward relativism and factorialism in the relation of structure and superstructure'. Taylor and Walton seem to consider that a 'natural scientific' analysis of the economic structure is possible but that the superstructure is a matter for subjectivism. In the authors' reading the 'economic' in Marx's work is reduced to a domain of given economic facts and to material technique, and the superstructure is reduced to a domain of the consciousness of subjects. My remarks about the ' "Marxism" that forms the basis of debates in the established social sciences' were evidently not wide of the mark as far as Taylor and Walton are concerned (see p. 203). Marxism is reduced by the authors of the reply to a dualistic essentialism. It seems that we are to read Marx with the epistemological protocols of Descartes. The economic structure is a realm of matter and is amenable to the methods of the 'natural sciences'. The superstructure is a realm of consciousness and it requires different methods: methods internal to consciousness itself; methods of self-conscious reflection by subjects. Render unto Matter that which is Matter's and unto Spirit that which is Spirit's. This is a grotesque combination of vulgar positivism in the sphere of 'economics', and blatant subjectivism in the sphere of 'consciousness'.[1]

Whatever the positivist factorialist and relativist errors of the 1859 *Preface*, and, we might add, of *The German Ideology*, these positions of Taylor and Walton are incompatible with materialism. The authors' position represents an ideological-philosophical reprise of Marx's scientific concepts. Marx in the *Preface*, and in *The German Ideology* insists that the superstructure is not a realm of consciousness or 'ideas' in the classical, philosophical sense but is composed of material practices.

Marx's conception of the economic structure is not of a domain of given and essentially 'economic' facts. The 'economy', what it is that is 'economic', in Marx's general theory of modes of production is thought of as the effect of the structures of the different modes of production and of the specific articulations with the instances of the political and the ideological which are a necessary aspect of those structures. The economy is not given but is specified theoretically in Historical Materialism. Hence, the epistemological disjuncture between Marxism and factorialist theories of historical causation.[2]

It is amazing that the authors make no attempt to produce a rigorous, theoretical critique of my reading of the 1859 *Preface*. In this reading I make it clear that the superstructure cannot be reduced to the consciousness and experience of subjects, and this is the basis of my separation of the *Preface* and the 1844 *Manuscripts*. For Marx the constitution of subjects, their inscription as supports or agents in definite practices, is an effect of the structures of the social formation.

Just as the economy is not a given essence, so it is also the case that the subject is not an essential subject (Man) whose 'praxis' creates the social formation as its effect, but a subject-support whose character as a subject is an effect of the structure in which it functions as a support.

I do not deny that in 1859 Marx lacked the concepts to think the structure of the social formation in a scientific mode, that many of the fundamental elements of this theory were not developed until the production of *Capital*, and that Marx never developed an adequate philosophical reflection of his scientific discoveries. The 1859 *Preface* is open to a positivistic reading, this is a measure of the unevenness which characterizes all scientific work, but the problematic of Historical Materialism as a whole specifically excludes this positivist reading as a Marxist reading. It is a mis-reading precisely because it fails to read this unevenness, because it does not read symptomatically, because it does not read the text in the problematic.[3]

Taylor and Walton make use of certain inadequate and erroneous formulations of Marx to justify the importation of idealism into Marxism. Doubtless, their renderings unto Matter will be at best perfunctory; gestures preliminary to the worship of Spirit. This uncritical use of the *Preface* is made without so much as a gesture toward conceptual proofs of the validity of their position. It contrasts with my attempts, however partial, to give proofs of my reading in relation to the problematics in which Marx worked. The authors never question my method of analysis of texts, nor do they offer any credible alternative method. Their *ad-hoc* quotation of scraps of Marx's writings is merely arbitrary, but this arbitrariness is all too common. It rests on a failure to separate the author from the problematic in which he worked. It breeds a biblical fetishism of the Word; a fetishism of discourse as the speech in which a subject's essence is revealed to us. The separation of the subject and the text is anathema to the position Taylor and Walton hold. A generally subjectivist conception of knowledge must conceive the text as the objectified consciousness of a subject. Taylor and Walton's conception of Marxism is a conception which makes it what it is not; compatible with the subjectivist ideologies in the social sciences which are all to common in our day.

Notes

1 This combination is not surprising, positivism and subjectivism form a couple. Subjectivism is not challenged by positivism, which also has the category of subject at the centre of its epistemology.

2 See Althusser (1971, part 2, pp. 91–144) for a discussion of the disjuncture between Marxism and classical philosophies of history.

3 It should be noted that at no point in my essay did I claim that sciences are characterized by evenness; however, for Taylor and Walton, 'science' seems to mean an absolutely formalized system without the continuance of theoretical practice.

Bibliography

ADAMIC, LOUIS (1931), *Dynamite: The Story of Class Violence in America*, New York: Harper & Row.

ALBINI, JOSEPH L. (1971), *The American Mafia: Genesis of a Legend*, New York: Appleton-Century-Crofts.

ALLEN, FRANCIS A. (1964), *The Borderland of Criminal Justice*, University of Chicago Press.

ALTHUSSER, LOUIS (1970), *For Marx*, Harmondsworth: Penguin/Allen Lane.

ALTHUSSER, LOUIS and BALIBAR, E. (1970), *Reading Capital*, London: New Left Books.

ALTHUSSER, LOUIS, RANCIERE, J. and MACHERAY, P. (1965), *Lire le Capital*, Paris: Maspero.

AMERICAN FRIENDS SERVICE COMMITTEE (1971a), *Struggle for Justice*, Philadelphia: Hill & Wang.

AMERICAN FRIENDS SERVICE COMMITTEE (1971b), *Police on the Home Front (National Action/Research on the Military-Industrial Complex)*, Philadelphia: Hill & Wang.

ANDERSON, PERRY (1968), 'Components of the national culture', *New Left Review*, 50, July–August, 3–57.

ARENDT, HANNAH (1971), 'Thinking and moral considerations', *Social Research*, 38, 3, pp. 417–46.

BALBUS, ISAAC D. (1971), 'The concept of interest in pluralist and marxian analysis', *Politics and Society*, 1, February, pp. 151–77.

BARAN, PAUL A. and SWEEZY. PAUL M. (1966), *Monopoly Capitalism: An Essay on the American Economic and Social Order*, New York: Monthly Review Press.

BECKER, ERNEST (1968), *The Structure of Evil: An Essay on the Unification of the Science of Man*, New York: Braziller.

BECKER, HOWARD S. (1963), *Outsiders: Studies in the Sociology of Deviance*, New York: Free Press.

BECKER, HOWARD S., (ed.) (1964), *The Other Side: Perspectives on Deviance*, New York: Free Press.

BECKER, HOWARD S. (1967), 'Whose side are we on?' *Social Problems*, 14, 3, pp. 239–47.

BECKER, HOWARD S. (1968), 'Ending campus drug incidents', *Trans-action*, 5, April, pp. 4–5.

BECKER, HOWARD S. (1974), 'Labelling theory reconsidered', in PAUL ROCK and MARY MCINTOSH, eds, *Deviance and Social Control*, London: Tavistock Publications.

BECKER, HOWARD S. and HOROWITZ, IRVING L. (1971), 'The culture of civility', in H. S. BECKER, ed., *Culture and Civility in San Francisco*, Chicago: Aldine.

BENN, STANLEY I. (1967), 'Egalitarianism and the equal consideration of interests', in *J. Roland Pennock* and *John Chapman*, eds, *Equality*, New York: Atherton Press, pp. 61–78.

BERGER, PETER (1971), 'Sociology and freedom', *American Sociologist*, 6, 1, pp. 1–5.

BERGER, PETER and LUCKMANN, THOMAS (1967), *The Social Construction of Reality*, London: Penguin/Allen Lane.

BERGER, PETER and PULLBERG, STANLEY (1966), 'Reification and the sociological critique of consciousness', *New Left Review*, 35, pp. 56–71.

BIANCHI, HERMAN (1956), *Position and Subject-Matter of Criminology: Inquiry Concerning Theoretical Criminology*, Amsterdam: North Holland Publishing.

BIANCHI, HERMAN, SIMONDI, MARIO and TAYLOR, IAN, eds. (1975), *Deviance in Europe, Papers from the European Group for the Study of Deviance and Social Control*, London: Wiley.

BLACK, DONALD J. and REISS, ALBERT J. (1972), 'Police control of juveniles', in R. A. SCOTT and J. D. DOUGLAS, eds, *Theoretical Perspectives on Deviance*, New York: Basic Books, pp. 119–41.

BLACKBURN, ROBIN (1969), 'A brief guide to bourgeois ideology', in ALEXANDER COCKBURN and ROBIN BLACKBURN, eds., *Student Power*, Harmondsworth: Penguin.

BLUM, ALAN F. (1970), 'Theorizing', in J. D. DOUGLAS, ed., *Understanding Everyday Life*, Chicago: Aldine; also London: Routledge & Kegan Paul.

BLUMER, HERBERT (1937), 'Social disorganization and individual disorganization', *American Journal of Sociology*, 42, pp. 871–7.

BLUMER, HERBERT (1967), 'Threats from agency-determined research', in I. L. HOROWITZ, ed., *The Rise and Fall of Project Camelot*, Cambridge, Massachusetts: MIT Press.

BONGER, WILLEM A. (1936), *An Introduction to Criminology*, London: Methuen.

BOTTOMORE, T. B. and RUBEL, MAXIMILIEN, eds. (1963), *Karl Marx: Selected Writings in Sociology and Philosophy*, Harmondsworth: Penguin.

BOTTOMS, A. E. (1971), 'On the decriminalisation of the English juvenile court', paper delivered to the First Anglo-Scandinavian Seminar in Criminology, Borkesjø, Norway; extended version appearing in ROGER HOOD, ed., *Festschrift for Sir Leon Radzinowicz*, London: Heinemann, 1974.

BOTTOMS, A. E. (1973), 'Methodological aspects of classification in criminology', in *Tenth Conference of Directors of Criminological*

Research Directors, Strasbourg: Council of Europe.

BRITISH BROADCASTING CORPORATION (1961), *A Report on Some Audience Research Enquiries Connected with the Television Series 'Crime'*, London: BBC Audience Research Department VR/61/1.

CANNAN, CRESCY (1970), 'Deviants – victims or rebels?' *Case-Con*, no. 1.

CARSON, W. G. and WILES, P., eds, (1971), *Crime and Delinquency in Britain: Sociological Readings*, London: Martin Robertson.

CATTIER, MICHEL (1969), *La Vie et L'Oeuvre du Docteur Wilhelm Reich*, Lausanne: La Cité.

CHAMBLISS, WILLIAM J. (1974), 'The state, the law and the definition of behaviour as criminal or delinquent', in DANIEL GLASER, ed., *Handbook of Criminology*, Indianapolis: Bobbs-Merrill.

CHAMBLISS, WILLIAM J. and NAGASAWA, R. H. (1969), 'On the validity of official statistics', *Journal of Research on Crime and Delinquency*, January, pp. 71–7.

CHAPMAN, DENNIS (1968), *Sociology and the Stereotype of the Criminal*, London: Tavistock Publications.

CHOMSKY, NOAM (1967), *American Power and the New Mandarins*, New York: Pantheon Books.

CHRISTOFFEL, TOM, FINKELHOR, DAVID and GILBERG, DAN, eds., (1970), *Up Against the American Myth*, New York: Holt, Rhinehart & Winston.

CICOUREL, AARON V. (1968), *The Social Organisation of Juvenile Justice*, New York: John Wiley.

CLARK, RAMSAY (1970), *Crime in America*, New York: Simon & Schuster.

CLEAVER, ELDRIDGE (1968), *Soul on Ice*, New York: McGraw-Hill; also London: Cape, 1969.

CLOWARD, RICHARD and OHLIN, LLOYD (1960), *Delinquency and Opportunity: A Theory of Delinquent Gangs*, New York: Free Press.

COCKBURN, ALEXANDER and BLACKBURN, ROBIN, eds., (1969), *Student Power*, Harmondsworth: Penguin.

COHEN, ALBERT K. (1955), *Delinquent Boys: The Culture of the Gang*, Chicago: Free Press.

COHEN, ALBERT K. (1965), 'The sociology of the deviant act; anomie theory and beyond', *American Sociological Review*, 30, 1, pp. 5–14.

COHEN, ALBERT K. (1973), 'Political and ideological implications of the new deviancy theory', paper delivered to National Deviancy Conference, January 1973 (mimeo).

COHEN, STANLEY, ed., (1971), *Images of Deviance*, Harmondsworth: Penguin.

COHEN, STANLEY (1974a), 'Criminology and the sociology of deviance in Britain: a recent history and a current report', in PAUL ROCK and MARY MCINTOSH, eds., *Deviance and Social Control*, London: Tavistock Publications.

COHEN, STANLEY (1974b), 'A futuristic scenario for the prison system', in FRANCO BASAGLIA, ed., *The Crimes of Peace*, Turin: Einaudi.

COHEN, STANLEY and TAYLOR, LAURIE (1972), 'Contemporary British approaches in the sociology of deviance', unpublished paper delivered to the Society for the Study of Social Problems, New Orleans, USA, 26 August 1972.

CONNOR, WALTER D. (1972), *Deviance in Soviet Russia: Crime, Delinquency and Alcoholism*, New York: Columbia University Press.
COOPER, DAVID (1965), 'Violence in psychiatry', *Views*, 8, pp. 18–24.
COOPER, DAVID (1971), *The Death of the Family*, London: Allen Lane.
COULTER, JEFF (1974), 'What's wrong with the new criminology?', *Sociological Review*. 22, 1, pp. 119–35.
CRESSEY, DONALD R. (1936), 'Epidemiology and individual conflict: a case from criminology', *Pacific Sociological Review*, 3, Autumn, pp. 47–58.
CRESSEY, DONALD R. (1960), *Crime, Delinquency and Differential Association*, The Hague: Nijhoff.
CRESSEY, DONALD R. (1969), *Theft of the Nation: The Structure and Operations of Organized Crime in America*, New York: Harper & Row.
CURRIE, ELLIOTT (1973), *Managing the Minds of Men: The Reformatory Movement 1865–1920*, unpublished Ph.D. dissertation, University of California.
DAVIS, ANGELA (1971), *If They Come in the Morning*, New York: Third Press; London: Orbach & Chambers.
DAVIS, FRED (1967), 'Why all of us may be hippies some day', *Transaction*, 2, pp. 10–18.
DAVIS, KINGSLEY (1953), 'Reply to Tumin', *American Sociological Review*, 18, pp. 394–7.
DAVIS, KINGSLEY and MOORE, WILBERT (1945), 'Some principles of stratification', *American Sociological Review*, 10. pp. 242–9.
DELLA VOLPE, GALVANO (1970), 'The Marxist critique of Rousseau', *New Left Review*, 59, January–February, pp. 101–9.
DENTLER, ROBERT and MONROE, LAWRENCE J. (1961), 'Early adolescent theft', *American Sociological Review*, 28, October, pp. 733–43.
DEWEY, JOHN (1938), *Logic: The Theory of Inquiry*, New York: Henry Holt.
DOMHOFF, WILLIAM G. (1967), *Who Rules America?*, Englewood Cliffs, N.J.: Prentice-Hall.
DOMHOFF, WILLIAM G. (1970), *The Higher Circles: the Governing Class in America*, New York: Random House.
DOUGLAS, JACK D., ed. (1970), *Deviance and Respectability: The Social Construction of Moral Meanings*, New York: Basic Books.
DOUGLAS, JACK D. (1971a), 'Crime and justice in America', in J. D. DOUGLAS, ed., *Crime and Justice in American Society*, Indianapolis: Bobbs-Merrill.
DOUGLAS, JACK D. (1971b), *The American Social Order*, New York: Free Press.
DOUGLAS, J. W. B., ROSS, J. M., HAMMOND, W. A. and MULLIGAN, D. G. (1966), 'Delinquency and social class', *British Journal of Criminology*, 6, 3, pp. 294–302; reprinted in W. G. CARSON and P. WILES, eds. (1971).
DURKHEIM, ÉMILE (1958), *The Rules of Sociological Method*, trans. S. A. SOLOWAY and J. H. MUELLER, Chicago: Free Press.
DURKHEIM, ÉMILE (1960), *The Division of Labour in Society*, trans. GEORGE SIMPSON, New York: Macmillan; also Chicago: Free Press.
DUSTER, TROY (1970), *The Legislation of Morality*, New York: Free Press.
EDIE, JAMES M., (ed.) (1962), *What is Phenomenology?*, Chicago: Quadrangle Books.
EDWARDS, RICHARD C., REICH, MICHAEL and WEISSKOPF, THOMAS E. (1972),

The Capitalist System: A Radical Analysis of American Society, New Jersey: Prentice-Hall.

EMPEY, LAMAR T. and ERICKSON, MAYNARD L. (1966), 'Hidden delinquency and social status', *Social Forces*, 44, June, pp. 546–54.

ENGELS, FREDERICK (1844), *The Condition of the Working Class in England in 1844;* references here to (1950) Allen & Unwin ed., and (1969) Panther ed.

ENGELS, FREDERICK (1874), Preface to *The Peasant War in Germany*, in *Marx-Engels Selected Works*, vol. 2, London; Lawrence & Wishart, 1950; also Moscow: Foreign Languages Publishing House, 1951.

ENGELS, FREDERICK (1876), *Anti-Duehring*, reference here to London: Lawrence & Wishart ed., n.d.

ENGELS, FREDERICK (1884), 'The origin of the family, private property and the state', in *Marx-Engels Selected Works*, vol. 2, London, Lawrence & Wishart, 1950; also Moscow: Foreign Languages Publishing House, 1951.

ENGELS, FREDERICK (1895), Preface to *The Class Struggles in France 1848–50*, in *Marx-Engels Selected Works*, vol. 1, London; Lawrence & Wishart, 1950; also Moscow: Foreign Languages Publishing House, 1951.

ENGELS, FREDERICK (1942), *The Origin of the Family, Private Property and the State*, New York: International Publishers.

ENGELS, FREDERICK (1969), *The Condition of the Working Class in England in 1844*, Harmondsworth: Penguin.

ERIKSON, KAI T. (1965), *Wayward Puritans*, New York: John Wiley.

EWEN, STUART (1972), 'Charlie Manson and the Family: authoritarianism and the bourgeois conception of "Utopia": some thoughts on Charlie Manson and the fantasy of the *id*,' *Working Papers in Cultural Studies*, 3, pp. 33–45.

FEUERBACH, LUDWIG (1841), *The Essence of Christianity*, trans. GEORGE ELIOT, New York and London: Harper & Row, 1976.

FITZGERALD, MIKE and POOLEY, DICK (1975), *Prisoners in Revolt*, Harmondsworth: Penguin.

FLACKS, RICHARD (1967), 'The liberated generation', *Journal of Social Issues*, 23, pp. 52–75.

FLACKS, RICHARD (1970), 'Social and cultural meanings of the student revolt', *Social Problems*, 17, 3, pp. 340–57.

FREUD, SIGMUND (1957), *Civilisation and Its Discontents*, London: Hogarth Press; originally published, 1930.

GARAFOLO, RAFFAELE (1885), *Criminology*, Boston: Little, Brown.

GIBBONS, DONALD C. (1965). *Changing the Lawbreaker*, New Jersey: Prentice-Hall.

GLASER, DANIEL (1965), 'Correctional research: an elusive paradise', *Journal of Research in Crime and Delinquency*, 2, 1, pp. 1–8.

GLASER, DANIEL (1970), 'Victim survey research: theoretical implications', in ANTHONY L. GUENTHER, ed., *Criminal Behaviour and Social Systems*, Chicago: Rand McNally.

GODELIER, MAURICE (1967), 'System, structure and contradiction in *Capital*', in R. MILIBAND and J. SAVILE, eds., *The Socialist Register 1967*, London: Merlin Press.

GOFFMAN, ERVING (1961), *Asylums*, Harmondsworth: Penguin.

GOFFMAN, ERVING (1963), *Behavior in Public Places*, New York: Free Press.

GOLD, MARTIN (1966), 'Undetected delinquent behaviour', *Journal of Research in Crime and Delinquency*, 3, January, pp. 27–46.

GORDON, DAVID M. (1971), 'Class and the economics of crime', *Review of Radical Political Economics*, 3, 3.

GORDON, DAVID M. (1973), 'Capitalism, class and crime in America', *Crime and Delinquency*, 19, April, pp. 163–86.

GOULDEN, JOSEPH C. (1970), 'The cops hit the jackpot', *The Nation*, 23 November 1970, pp. 520–33.

GOULDNER, ALVIN (1962), 'Anti-minotaur: the myth of a value-free sociology', *Social Problems*, 9, Winter, pp. 199–213; reprinted in A. W. GOULDNER, *For Sociology: Renewal and Critique in Sociology Today*, London: Penguin/Allen Lane, 1973.

GOULDNER, ALVIN W. (1968), 'The sociologist as partisan: sociology and the welfare state', *The American Sociologist*, 3, May, pp. 103–16; reprinted in J. D. DOUGLAS, ed., *The Relevance of Sociology*, New York: Appleton-Century-Crofts, 1970; also in A. W. GOULDNER (1973).

GOULDNER, ALVIN W. (1970), *The Coming Crisis of Western Sociology*, New York: Basic Books; also London: Heinemann, 1971.

GOULDNER, ALVIN W. (1973), *For Sociology: Renewal and Critique in Sociology Today*, London: Heinemann.

GRAMSCI, ANTONIO (1970), *Prison Notebooks*, London: Lawrence & Wishart.

GRIFFIN, SUSAN (1971), 'Rape: the all-American crime', *Ramparts*, September, pp. 26–35.

HABERMAS, JÜRGEN (1970), *Knowledge and Human Interests*, trans. J. J. SHAPIRO, Boston: Beacon Press; also London: Heinemann, 1971.

HABERMAS, JÜRGEN (1971a), *Towards a Rational Society*, trans. J. J. SHAPIRO, London: Heinemann, 1971.

HALL, STUART (1973), 'A "reading" of Marx's 1857 Introduction to the *Grundrisse*', unpublished MS., Centre for Contemporary Cultural Studies, University of Birmingham.

HALMOS, PAUL (1970), *The Personal Service Society*, London: Constable.

HARVEY, DAVID (1973), *Social Justice and the City*, London: Edward Arnold.

HAYDEN, TOM (1971), *Trial*, London: Cape.

HEIDEGGER, MARTIN (1966), *Discourse on Thinking*, New York: Harper & Row.

HEIDEGGER, MARTIN (1967), *What is a Thing?*, Chicago: Henry Regnery.

HEMPEL, CARL G. (1952), 'Fundamentals of concept formation in empirical science', *International Encyclopaedia of Unified Science*, 2, 7, University of Chicago Press.

HESSE, HERMAN (1965), *Steppenwolf*, Harmondsworth: Penguin.

HINDESS, BARRY (1973), *The Uses of Official Statistics in Sociology*, London: Macmillan.

HIRSCHI, TRAVIS and SELVIN, HANNAN (1967), *Delinquency Research: An Appraisal of Analytic Methods*, New York: Free Press.

HOBSBAWM, ERIC J. (1959), *Primitive Rebels*, New York: Norton; also Manchester: University of Manchester Press, 1959.

HOME OFFICE (1968), *Children in Trouble*, London: HMSO, Cmnd. 3601.

HOROWITZ, DAVID (1969), *Empire and Revolution: A Radical Interpretation of Contemporary History*, New York: Random House.

HOROWITZ, DAVID (1971–2), 'Marxism and its place in economic science', *Berkeley Journal of Sociology*, 16, pp. 46–59.

HOROWITZ, IRVING L., ed. (1963), *Power, Politics and People*, New York: Oxford University Press.

HOROWITZ, IRVING L., ed. (1967), *The Rise and Fall of Project Camelot*, Cambridge, Massachusetts: MIT Press.

HOROWITZ, IRVING L. and LIEBOWITZ, MARTIN L. (1968), 'Social deviance, and political marginality: towards a redefinition of the relation between sociology and politics,' *Social Problems*, 15, 3, pp. 280–96.

HORTON, JOHN (1966), 'Order and conflict theories of social problems as competing ideologies', *American Journal of Sociology*, 71, pp. 701–13.

HUGHES, EVERETT C. (1958), *Men and their Work*, Chicago: Free Press.

HUMPHREYS, LAUD (1970), *Tearoom Trade*, London: Duckworth.

HYMAN, RICHARD (1973), *Strikes*, London: Fontana.

IGGERS, GEORG (1958), *The Doctrine of Saint-Simon: an Exposition. First Year 1828–1829*, trans. with notes and introduction, GEORG C. IGGERS, Boston: Beacon Press.

INGLEBY, DAVID (1970), 'Ideology and the human sciences: some comments on the role of reification in psychology and psychiatry', *The Human Context*, 12, 2, pp. 159–80.

INTERNATIONAL TIMES (1969), 'Who's Crazy?', *I.T.*, no. 66, 10–23 October.

IRWIN, JOHN and CRESSEY, D. R. (1962), 'Thieves, convicts and the inmate culture', *Social Problems*, 10, 2, pp. 142–55; reprinted in H. S. BECKER, ed. (1964), pp. 225–45.

JACKSON, GEORGE (1971), *Soledad Brother: The Prison Letters of George Jackson*, London: Cape.

JACKSON, GEORGE (1972), *Blood in My Eye*, New York: Random House; also London: Cape.

JEFFERY, C. RAY (1956), 'The structure of American criminological thinking', *Journal of Criminal Law, Criminology and Police Science*, 46, 5, pp. 658–72.

JENKINS, R. L. and HEWITT, LESTER (1944), 'Types of personality structure encountered in child guidance clinics', *American Journal of Orthopsychiatry*, 14, January, pp. 84–94.

JONES, JAMES A. (1971), 'Federal efforts to solve social problems', in E O. SMIGEL, ed., *Handbook on the Study of Social Problems*, Chicago: Rand McNally.

KANT, IMMANUEL (1929), *Critique of Pure Reason*, trans. NORMAN KEMPT SMITH, New York: Macmillan.

KANT, IMMANUEL (1948), *The Moral Law: Kant's Groundwork of the Metaphysic of Morals*, trans. H. J. PATON, London: Hutchinson.

KAPLAN, ABRAHAM (1964), *The Conduct of Inquiry*, San Francisco: Chandler.

KERR, CLARK (1961), *The Uses of the University*, New York: Anchor.

KITSUSE, JOHN I. (1963), 'Societal reactions to deviant behaviour: problems of theory and method', *Social Problems*, 9, Winter, pp. 247–56.

KITSUSE, JOHN I. and CICOUREL AARON V. (1963), 'A note on the uses of official statistics', *Social Problems*, 11, pp. 131–9.

KLARE, KARL E. (1971–2), 'The critique of everyday life, Marxism and the new left', *Berkeley Journal of Sociology*, 16, pp. 15–45.

KLARE, MIKE (1971), 'Bringing it back: planning for the city', in AMERICAN FRIENDS SERVICE COMMITTEE (1971b).

KNOWLES, JOHN (1970), 'US health: do we face a catastrophe?', *Look Magazine*, 2 June 1970, pp. 74–8.

KOLKO, GABRIEL (1962), *Wealth and Power in America*, New York: Praeger.

KOLKO, GABRIEL (1967), *The Triumph of Conservatism*, Chicago: Quadrangle Books.

KOLKO, GABRIEL (1969), *The Roots of American Foreign Policy*, Boston: Beacon Press.

KRISBERG, BARRY (1972), Review of Laud Humphreys's *Tearoom Trade*, *Issues in Criminology*, 7, Winter, pp. 126–7.

KUTCHINSKY, BERL (1971), 'Towards an explanation of the decrease in registered sex crimes in Copenhagen', *Technical Report of the Commission on Obscenity and Pornography*, vol. 7, Washington, D.C.: Government Printing Office.

KUTCHINSKY, BERL (1972), 'Sociological aspects of deviance and criminality', in *Perception of Deviance and Criminality; Collected Studies in Criminological Research*, vol. 9, Strasbourg: Council of Europe, pp. 9–102.

KUTCHINSKY, BERL (1975), *Pornography and Sex Crimes in Denmark: Early Research Findings*, London: Martin Robertson.

LAING, R. D. (1971), *The Politics of the Family*, New York: Pantheon.

LANDER, BERNARD (1954), *Towards an Understanding of Juvenile Delinquency*, New York: Columbia University Press.

LAUER, QUENTIN (1965), *Phenomenology: Its Genesis and Prospect*, New York: Harper.

LAW AND SOCIETY ASSOCIATION (1966–74), *Law and Society Review*, California: Sage Publications.

LEARY, TIMOTHY (1970), *The Politics of Ecstasy*, London: Paladin.

LEMERT, EDWIN M. (1951), *Social Pathology*, New York: McGraw-Hill.

LEMERT, EDWIN M. (1970), *Social Action and Legal Change: Revolution within the Juvenile Court*, Chicago: Aldine.

LEMERT, EDWIN M. (1972), *Human Deviance, Social Problems and Social Control*, 2nd ed., Englewood Cliffs, N.J.: Prentice-Hall.

LIAZOS, ALEXANDER (1972), 'The poverty of the sociology of deviance: nuts, sluts and preverts', *Social Problems*, 20, pp. 102–20.

LICHTMAN, RICHARD (1970–1), 'Symbolic interactionism and social reality: some Marxist queries', *Berkeley Journal of Sociology*, 15, pp. 75–94.

LOUCH, A. R. (1969), *Explanation and Human Action*, Berkeley: University of California Press.

LUKÁCS, GEORG (1971), *History and Class Consciousness*, Cambridge; Mass: MIT Press; also London: Allen Lane.

LYMAN, S. M. (1970), 'Red guard on Grant Street', *Trans-action*, 7, 6, pp. 21–34.

MCLELLAN, DAVID, ed. (1971), *Karl Marx – Early Texts*, Oxford: Basil Blackwell.

MCLELLAN, DAVID (1973), *Karl Marx: His Life and Thought*, London: Macmillan.

MCCLINTOCK, F. H. and AVISON, N. H. (1968), *The State of Crime in England and Wales*, London: Heinemann.

MANDEVILLE, BERNARD (1714), *The Fable of the Bees; or Private Vices, Publick Benefits*, London: J. Roberts; reference here is to Penguin ed., edited with an introduction by PHILLIP HARTH, 1970.

MARCUSE, HERBERT (1960), *Reason and Revolution*, Boston: Beacon Press.

MARCUSE, HERBERT (1964), *One-Dimensional Man*, Boston: Beacon Press; also London: Routledge & Kegan Paul.

MARCUSE, HERBERT (1969), *An Essay on Liberation*, Harmondwsorth: Penguin.

MARCUSE, HERBERT (1972), *Counter-Revolution and Revolt*, Boston: Beacon Press.

MARX, JENNY (1852), Letter to A. Claus, 28 October 1852, in *Marx-Engels Selected Correspondence*, Moscow: Foreign Languages Publishing House, n.d.

MARX, KARL (1842a), 'The proceedings of the sixth Rhenish parliament: debates on the freedom of the press and the publication of parliamentary proceedings', first published *Die Rheinische Zeitung*, 5–19 May 1842, trans. in D. MCLELLAN, ed. (1971), pp. 35–6.

MARX, KARL (1842b), 'Remarks on the latest Prussian instruction on the censorship', first published *Anekdote zur neuesten deutschen Philosophie und Publicistik*, ed., A. RUGE, trans. in D. MCLELLAN, ed. (1971), pp. 29–30.

MARX, KARL (1842c), 'Communism and the *Augsburger Allgemeine Zeitung*', first published *Die Rheinische Zeitung*, 16 October 1842, trans. in D. MCLELLAN, ed. (1971).

MARX, KARL (1842d), 'Proceedings of the sixth Rhenish parliament: debates on the theft of wood', first published *Die Rheinische Zeitung*, 25 October–3 November 1842; trans. in D. MCLELLAN, ed. (1971).

MARX, KARL (1844), *The Economic and Philosophical Manuscripts of 1844*, trans., M. MILLIGAN; reference here to 1967 ed., Moscow: Progress Publishers.

MARX, KARL (1850), *The Class Struggles in France 1848–50*, in *Marx-Engels Selected Works*, vol. I, London: Lawrence & Wishart, 1950; also Moscow: Foreign Languages Publishing House, 1951.

MARX, KARL (1853), *The 18th Brumaire of Louis Bonaparte*, in *Marx-Engels Selected Works*, vol. 1, London: Lawrence & Wishart, 1950; also Moscow: Foreign Languages Publishing House, 1951.

MARX, KARL (1859a), *Preface to a Contribution to a Critique of Political Economy*, in *Marx-Engels Selected Works*, vol. 1, London: Lawrence & Wishart, 1950; also Moscow: Foreign Languages Publishing House, 1951.

MARX, KARL (1859b), 'Population, crime and pauperism', *New York Daily Tribune*, 16 September 1859.

MARX, KARL (1867), *Capital*, vol. 1; reference here to 1961 ed., Moscow: Foreign Languages Publishing House.

MARX, KARL (1875), 'Marginal notes to the "Programme of the German Workers' Party" (Critique of the Gotha Programme)', in *Marx-Engels Selected Works*, vol. 2, London: Lawrence & Wishart, 1950; also Moscow: Foreign Languages Publishing House, 1951.

MARX, KARL (1950), 'Marginal Notes to the "Programme of the German Workers' Party" (Critique of the Gotha Programme)'; in *Marx-Engels Selected Works*, vol. 2, London: Lawrence & Wishart, 1950; also Moscow: Foreign Languages Publishing House, 1951.

MARX, KARL (1964a), *Pre-capitalist Economic Formations*, ed., E. J. HOBSBAWM, London: Lawrence &Wishart.

MARX, KARL (1964b), 'The state and the law', in T. B. BOTTOMORE and M. RUBEL, eds, *Karl Marx: Selected Writings in Sociology and Philosophy*, New York: McGraw-Hill.

MARX, KARL (1969), *Theories of Surplus Value*, vol. 1, Moscow: Foreign Languages Publishing House.

MARX, KARL (1971a), *A Contribution to the Critique of Political Economy*, London: Lawrence and Wishart.

MARX, KARL, (1971b), *Critique of Hegel's 'Philosophy of Right'*, ed, with an introduction by J. O'MALLEY, Cambridge University Press.

MARX, KARL (1973), *Grundrisse: Foundations for a Critique of Political Economy (Rough Draft)*, trans. with an introduction by Martin Nicolaus, Harmondsworth: Penguin.

MARX, KARL and ENGELS, FREDERICK (1848), *Manifesto of the Communist Party*, in *Marx-Engels Selected Works*, vol. 1, London: Lawrence & Wishart, 1950; also Moscow: Foreign Languages Publishing House, 1951.

MATHIESON, THOMAS (1974), *The Politics of Abolition*, London: Martin Robertson.

MATZA, DAVID (1964), *Delinquency and Drift*, New York: Wiley.

MATZA, DAVID (1969), *Becoming Deviant*, Englewood Cliffs, N.J.: Prentice-Hall.

MELVILLE, SAM (1972), *Letters from Attica*, New York: Morrow.

MESSINGER, SHELDON (1973), 'Some notes toward a discussion of the year 2000 and the problem of criminal justice', paper delivered at Conference of Criminal Justice, University of Chicago, 24 June 1973.

MICHAEL, JEROME and ADLER, MORTIMER (1932), *An Institute of Criminology and of Criminal Justice*, report of a survey conducted for the Bureau of Social Hygiene under the auspices of the School of Law at Columbia University, New York: Bureau of Social Hygiene.

MILIBAND, RALPH (1969), *The State in Capitalist Society*, New York: Basic Books.

MILLER, WALTER B. (1973), 'Ideology and criminal justice policy: some current issues', *Journal of Criminal Law and Criminology*, 64, 2, pp. 141–62.

MILLS, C. WRIGHT (1943), 'The professional ideology of social pathologists', *American Journal of Sociology*, 49, 2, pp. 165–80; reprinted in I. L. HOROWITZ, ed. (1963).

MILLS, C. WRIGHT (1959), *The Sociological Imagination*, New York: Oxford University Press.

MITCHELL, WESLEY C. (1927), *Business Cycles*, New York: National Bureau of Economic Research.

MOORE, WILBERT (1953), 'Comment on Kingsley Davis', *American Sociological Review*, 18, p. 397.

MOORE, WILBERT (1963), 'But some are more equal than others', *American Sociological Review*, 28, pp. 13–18.

MOORHOUSE, H. F. and CHAMBERLAIN, C. W. (1973), 'Lower class attitudes to property: aspects of the counter-ideology', unpublished MS., University of Glasgow.

MORRIS, NORVAL and HAWKINS, GORDON (1970), *The Honest Politician's Guide to Crime Control*, University of Chicago Press.

MUNDAY, B. (1972), 'What is happening to social work students?', *Social Work Today*, 3, 6, pp. 3–6.

MUNGHAM, GEOFF and PEARSON, GEOFF (1972), 'Radical action and radical scholarship', paper delivered to 11th National Deviancy Conference, University of York, 18–19 September 1972.

NAGASAWA, RICHARD H. (1965), 'Delinquency and non-delinquency: a study of status problems and perceived opportunity', unpublished MA thesis, University of Washington.

NAGEL, W. H. (1971). 'Critical criminology', *Abstracts on Criminology and Penology*, 2, 1, pp. 1–5.

NAIRN, TOM (1964), 'The anatomy of the Labour Party', *New Left Review*, 27, September–October, pp. 38–65.

NEIER, ARYEH and MARES, ALBERTO (1974), 'A program to cripple federal prisoners', *New York Review of Books*, 7 March 1974.

NEWTON, HUEY (1973), *Revolutionary Suicide*, New York: Harcourt, Brace.

NORTH, M. (1972), *The Secular Priests*, London: Allen & Unwin.

NUTTALL, JEFF (1970), *Bomb Culture*, London: Paladin.

NYE, F. IVAN, SHORT, JAMES F. and OLSEN, V. J. (1958), 'Socio-economic status and delinquent behavior', *American Journal of Sociology*, 23, January, pp. 318–29.

OGBURN, WILLIAM F. (1922), *Social Change*, New York: Viking Press.

O'NEILL, JOHN (1972), *Sociology as a Skin Trade*, London: Heinemann.

PARKIN, FRANK (1968), *Middle Class Radicalism*, Manchester University Press.

PEARCE, FRANK (1973), 'Crime, corporations and the American social order', in I. TAYLOR and L. TAYLOR, eds. (1973).

PEARSON, GEOFF (1972), 'Misfit sociology: a study in scholarship and, action', paper delivered to 11th National Deviancy Conference, University of York, 19 September 1972.

PHILLIPSON, MICHAEL (1973), 'Critical theorising and "the new criminology" ', review, *British Journal of Criminology*, 13, 4, pp. 398–400.

PIVEN, FRANCES F. (1971), 'Federal intervention in the cities: the new urban programs as a political strategy', in E. O. SMIGEL, ed. (1971).

PIVEN, FRANCES F. and CLOWARD, RICHARD A. (1972), *Regulating the Poor*, London: Tavistock Publications.

PLATT, ANTHONY M. (1969), *The Child Savers: The Invention of Delinquency*, University of Chicago Press.

PLATT, ANTHONY M. (1974), 'The triumph of benevolence: the origins of the juvenile justice system in the United States', in R. QUINNEY, ed. (1974).

PLATT, ANTHONY M. and COOPER, LYNN, eds. (1974), *Policing America*, Englewood Cliffs, N.J.: Prentice-Hall.

PLATT, ANTHONY M. and SKOLNICK, JEROME H. (1971), *The Politics of Riot Commissions 1971–1970*, New York: Macmillan.

PRESTON, WILLIAM, Jr. (1963), *Aliens and Dissenters*, Cambridge, Massachusetts: Harvard University Press.

QUINNEY, RICHARD, ed. (1969), *Criminal Justice in American Society*, Boston: Little, Brown.

QUINNEY, RICHARD (1970a), *The Social Reality of Crime*, Boston: Little, Brown.

QUINNEY, RICHARD, ed. (1970b), *The Problem of Crime*, New York: Dodd, Mead.

QUINNEY, RICHARD, ed., (1974), *Crime and Justice in America: A Critical Understanding*, Boston: Little, Brown.

RAINWATER, LEE (1967), 'The revolt of the dirty-workers', *Trans-action*, 5, 2.

RAPPAPORT, BRUCE and GARABEDIAN, PETER (1973), 'American socialism and criminological thought', unpublished paper presented at 1973 meetings of Pacific Sociological Conference, Scottsdale, Arizona.

RAY, GERDA (1973), 'Prisons are for punishment: early sentencing policies', unpublished paper, Center for the Study of Law and Society, University of California at Berkeley.

REICH, WILHELM (1946), *The Mass Psychology of Fascism*, New York: Orgone Institute Press; also London: Souvenir Press, 1972.

RENNER, KARL (1949), *The Institutions of Private Law and their Social Function*, London: Routledge & Kegan Paul.

RESLER, HENRIETTA and WALTON, PAUL (1974), 'How social is it?', in N. ARMISTEAD, ed., *Reconstructing Social Psychology*, Harmondsworth: Penguin.

ROCK, PAUL and MCINTOSH, MARY, eds. (1974), *Deviance and Social Control*, London: Tavistock Publications.

ROCK, PAUL and YOUNG, JOCK, eds. (1975), *The Myths of Crime*, London: Routledge & Kegan Paul.

ROSENBERG, DAVID (1972), 'The sociology of the police and sociological liberalism', unpublished MS.

ROSS, EDWARD A. (1901), *Social Control*, New York: Macmillan.

RUBIN, JERRY (1970), *Do It! Scenarios of the Revolution*, New York: Simon & Schuster.

RUDÉ, GEORGE (1964), *The Crowd in History: A Study in Popular Disturbances in France and England 1730–1848*, New York: Wiley.

SARTRE, JEAN-PAUL (1963), *Search for a Method*, trans. HAZEL E. BARNES, New York: Knopf.

SAVITZ, LEONARD (1970), 'Crime and the criminal', in A. L. GUENTHER, ed., *Criminal Behavior and Social Systems*, Chicago: Rand McNally; originally published in L. SAVITZ, *Dilemmas in Criminology*, New York: McGraw-Hill, 1967.

SCHAAR, JOHN H. (1970), 'Legitimacy in the modern state', in PHILIP GREEN and SANDFORD LEVINSON, eds., *Power and the Community: Dissenting Essays in Political Science*, New York: Vintage Press.

SCHEFF, THOMAS J. (1966), *Being Mentally Ill*, London: Weidenfeld & Nicolson.

SCHUR, EDWIN M. (1965), *Crimes Without Victims*, Englewood Cliffs, N.J.: Prentice-Hall.

SCHUR, EDWIN M. (1969), *Our Criminal Society*, Englewood Cliffs, N.J.: Prentice-Hall.

SCHUR, EDWIN M. (1973), *Radical Non-Intervention*, Englewood Cliffs, N.J.: Prentice-Hall.

SCHUTZ, ALFRED (1962), *The Problem of Social Reality – Collected Papers I*, The Hague: Nijhoff.

SCHUTZ, ALFRED (1963), 'Concept and theory formation in the social sciences', in M. NATANSON, ed., *Philosophy of the Social Sciences*, New York: Random House.

SCHWENDINGER, HERMAN and SCHWENDINGER, JULIA (1974), *The Sociologists of the Chair: A Radical Analysis of the Formative Years of North American Sociology 1883–1922*, New York: Basic Books.

SCHWITZGEBEL, RALPH (1964), *Street Corner Research*, Cambridge, Massachusetts: Harvard University Press.

SCOTT, ROBERT A. (1970), 'The construction of conceptions of stigma by professional experts', in J. D. DOUGLAS, ed. (1970).

SCOTT, ROBERT A. (1972), 'A proposed framework for analyzing deviance as a property of social order', in R. A. SCOTT and J. D. DOUGLAS, eds. (1972).

SCOTT, ROBERT A. and DOUGLAS, JACK D., eds. (1972), *Theoretical Perspectives on Deviance*, New York: Basic Books.

SEALE, BOBBY (1970), *Seize the Time*, Harmondsworth: Penguin.

SEDGWICK, PETER (1970), 'The problem of fascism', *International Socialism*, 42, February–March, pp. 31–4.

SEDGWICK, PETER (1972), 'Peter Sedgwick meditates on the acceptability of R. D. LAING', *The Listener*, 18 May 1972, pp. 646–8.

SELLIN, THORSTEIN (1938), *Culture Conflict and Crime*, New York: Social Science Research Council Bulletin no. 41.

SENNETT, RICHARD (1970), 'The brutality of modern families', *Transaction*, 7, 11, pp. 29–37.

SENNETT, RICHARD (1971), Review of R. D. Laing's *The Politics of the Family*, *New York Review of Books*, 3 October 1971, p. 40.

SIEGLER, M., OSMOND, H. and MANN, H. (1969), 'Laing's models of madness', *British Journal of Psychiatry*, vol. 115, p. 947.

SITUATIONIST INTERNATIONAL (1967), *Ten Days that Shook the University: The Situationists at Strasbourg*, London: Situationist International.

SKOLNICK, JEROME (1966), *Justice Without Trial*, New York: Wiley.

SKOLNICK, JEROME (1972), 'Perspectives on law and order', unpublished lecture delivered to the Inter-American Congress of the American Society of Criminology and the Inter-American Association of Criminology: Caracas, Venezuela, 19–25 November 1972.

SMIGEL, EDWIN O. ed. (1971), *Handbook on the Study of Social Problems*, Chicago: Rand McNally.

SOLIDARITY (n.d.), *The Irrational in Politics*, London: Solidarity pamphlet no. 33.

SPRADLEY, JAMES P. (1970). *You Owe Yourself a Drunk*, Boston: Little Brown.

STAFFORD-CLARK, D. and WINCH, P. (1970), 'Psychiatry', in BBC publication, *Morals and Medicine*, London: BBC, pp. 88–101.

STANG DAHL, TOVE (1971), 'The emergence of the Norwegian child welfare laws', paper presented to 1st Anglo-Scandinavian Research Seminar in Criminology, Borkesjø, Norway; revised, extended version forthcoming from Martin Robertson, London.

STINCHCOMBE, A. (1963), 'Institutions of privacy in the determination of police practice', *American Journal of Sociology*, 69, pp. 150–60.

SUTHERLAND, EDWIN H. (1940), 'White collar criminality', *American Sociological Review*, 5, pp. 1–12.

SUTHERLAND, EDWIN H. (1941), 'Crime and business', *Annals of the American Academy of Political and Social Science*, 217, pp. 112–18.

SUTHERLAND, EDWIN H. (1945), 'Is "white collar crime" crime?' *American Sociological Review*, 10, pp. 132–9.

SUTHERLAND, EDWIN H. (1949), *White-Collar Crime*, New York: Dryden Press.

SUTHERLAND, EDWIN H. and CRESSEY, DONALD R. (1960), *Principles of Criminology*, New York: Lippincott.

SYKES, GRESHAM (1961), *Crime and Society*, New York: Random House.

SYKES, GRESHAM (1973), 'The rise of critical criminology', unpublished paper, University of Houston, Texas.

SZASZ, THOMAS S. (1970), *The Manufacture of Madness: A comparative study of the Inquisition and the Mental Health Movement*, New York: Harper & Row.

TAPPAN, PAUL R. (1947), 'Who is the criminal?', *American Sociological Review*, 12, pp. 96–102; reprinted in M. WOLFGANG, L. SAVITZ and N. JOHNSTON, eds., *The Sociology of Crime and Delinquency*, New York; Wiley, 1962.

TAYLOR, IAN (1972), 'The criminal question in contemporary social theory', *The Human Context*, 4, 3, pp. 633–40.

TAYLOR, IAN and TAYLOR, LAURIE, eds. (1973), *Politics and Deviance: Papers from the National Deviancy Conference*, Harmondsworth: Penguin.

TAYLOR, IAN and WALTON, PAUL (1970), 'Values in deviancy theory and society', *British Journal of Sociology*, 21, 4, pp. 362–74.

TAYLOR, IAN and WALTON, PAUL (1971), 'Hey, mister, this is what we really do – some comments on vandalism in play', *Social Work Today*, 2, 10, pp. 8–9; reprinted in COLIN WARD, ed., *Vandalism*, London: Architectural Press 1973.

TAYLOR, IAN, WALTON, PAUL and YOUNG, JOCK (1973), *The New Criminology: For a Social Theory of Deviance*, London: Routledge & Kegan Paul.

TAYLOR, LAURIE (1972), 'The significance and interpretation of replies to motivational questions: the case of sex offenders', *Sociology*, 6, 1, pp. 23–40.

TAYLOR, LAURIE and WALTON, PAUL (1971), 'Industrial sabotage: motives and meanings', in STANLEY COHEN, ed., *Images of Deviance*, Harmondsworth: Penguin, pp. 219–45.

TERRAY, EMMANUEL (1969), *Le Marxisme devant le sociétés 'primitives'*, Paris: Maspero.

THERNSTROM, STEPHAN and SENNETT, RICHARD (eds.), (1969), *Nineteenth-century cities: Essays in New Urban History*, New Haven: Yale University Press.

THEVENAZ, PIERRE (1962), in JAMES M. EDIE, ed. (1962).

THIO, ALEX (1973), 'Class bias in the sociology of deviance', *American Sociologist*, 8, February, pp. 1–12.

THOMPSON, EDWARD P. (1968), *The Making of the English Working Class*, Harmondsworth: Penguin.

TROTSKY, LEON (1973a), *Problems of Everyday Life*, New York: Menad Press.

TROTSKY, LEON (1973b), *On the Freedom of the Press*, ed. V. KARALASINGHAM, Colombo: International Publishers.

TUMIN, MELVIN (1953a), 'Some principles of stratification', *American Sociological Review*, *18*, pp. 387–94.

TUMIN, MELVIN (1953b), 'Reply to Kingsley Davis', *American Sociological Review*, 18, pp. 394–7; 672–3.

TURK, AUSTIN T. (1969), *Criminality and Legal Order*, Chicago: Rand McNally.

VAN DEN BERGHE, PIERRE L. (1964), 'Functionalism and dialectics', *American Sociological Review*, 69, pp. 695–705.

VOLD, GEORGE B. (1958), *Theoretical Criminology*, New York: Oxford University Press.

WALD, GEORGE (1970), 'Corporate responsibility for war crimes', *New York Review of Books*, 25, 2 July 1970, pp. 4–6.

WALTON, PAUL (1972), 'Social reaction: deviant commitment and career – a critique', paper delivered to Conference on Ethnomethodology, Labelling Theory and Deviance, University of Edinburgh, 29 June 1972.

WALTON, PAUL (1973), 'The case of the Weathermen: social reaction and deviant commitment', in I. TAYLOR and L. TAYLOR, eds. (1973).

WALTON, PAUL (1974), 'Max Weber's sociology of law: a materialist critique', *British Journal of Law and Society*, 1, 3, forthcoming.

WALTON, PAUL and GAMBLE, ANDREW (1972), *From Alienation to Surplus Value*, London: Sheed & Ward; also Penguin, 1974.

WARD, LESTER (1883), *Dynamic Sociology*, New York: Appleton.

WARD, LESTER (1903), *Pure Sociology*, New York: Macmillan.

WARNER, W. L., MEEKER, M. and EELS, K. (1949), *Social Classes in America*, Chicago: Science Research Associates.

WARREN, C. A. B. and JOHNSON, J. M. (1972), 'A critique of labelling theory from the phenomenological perspective', in R. A. SCOTT and J. D. DOUGLAS, eds. (1972).

WARRINGTON, JOE (1973), 'A critique of R. D. Laing's social philosophy', *Radical Philosophy*, 5, pp. 10–16.

WEBB, LEE (1971), 'Back home: the campus beat', in AMERICAN FRIENDS SERVICE COMMITTEE (1971b).

WEINSTEIN, JAMES A. (1968), *The Corporate Ideal in the Liberal State 1900–1918*, Boston: Beacon Press.

WERTHMAN, CARL (1969), 'Delinquency and moral character', in DONALD R. CRESSEY and DAVID A. WARD, eds., *Delinquency, Crime and Social Process*, New York: Harper & Row.

WILLIAMS, WILLIAM A. (1961), *Contours of American History*, New York: World Publishing.

WILLIAMS, WILLIAM A. (1969), *The Roots of the Modern American Empire*,

New York: Random House.

WOLFE, ALAN (1973), *The Seamy Side of Democracy*, New York: David McKay.

WOLFGANG, MARVIN (1973), 'Developments in criminology in the United States; with some comments on the future', paper delivered to 5th National Conference of the Institute of Criminology, Cambridge, 5 July 1973.

WRIGHT, ERIK O. (1973), *The Politics of Punishment*, New York: Harper & Row.

YOUNG, JOCK (1970), 'The zookeepers of deviancy', *Catalyst*, 5, pp. 38–46.

YOUNG, JOCK (1971a), *The Drugtakers: The Social Meaning of Drug Use*, London: MacGibbon & Kee/Paladin.

YOUNG, Jock (1971b), 'The police as amplifiers of deviancy, negotiators of reality and translators of fantasy', in STANLEY COHEN, ed. (1971).

YOUNG, JOCK (1972a), 'The politics of deviance' unpublished paper, Symposium on Social Action, University College, Cardiff, 2 December 1972.

YOUNG, JOCK (1972b), 'Watney's hash: it's a smash, smash, smash', *Oz*, 45, p. 11.

YOUNG, JOCK (1972c), 'Romantics, Keynesians and beyond: a social history of the new deviancy theory', paper given at the 11th National Deviancy Conference, University of York, 18–19 September 1972.

YOUNG, JOCK (1972d), Review of TROY DUSTER'S, *The Legislation of Morality*, in *British Journal of Criminology*, Winter, 12, pp. 300–4.

YOUNG, JOCK (1973a), 'Drug use as problem-solving behaviour', in *Proceedings of the Anglo-American Conference on Drug Abuse*, London: Royal Society of Medicine.

YOUNG, JOCK (1973b), 'Student drug use and middle class delinquency', in ROY BAILEY and JOCK YOUNG, eds., *Contemporary Social Problems in Britain*, Farnborough, Hampshire: Saxon House.

YOUNG, JOCK (1973c), 'The hippie solution: an essay in the politics of leisure', in I. TAYLOR and L. TAYLOR, eds. (1973).

YOUNG, JOCK (1974a), 'New directions in subcultural theory', in JOHN REX, ed., *Contributions to Sociology*, London: Routledge & Kegan Paul.

YOUNG, JOCK (1974b), 'Mass media, drugs and deviance', in PAUL ROCK and MARY MCINTOSH, eds. (1974).

YOUNG, JOCK (1975), 'The myths of crime', in PAUL ROCK and JOCK YOUNG, eds. (1974).

YOUNG, T. R. (1971), 'The politics of sociology: Gouldner, Goffman and Garfinkel', *American Sociologist*, 6, 4, pp. 276–81.

ZANER, RICHARD M. (1970), *The Way of Phenomenology: Criticism as a Philosophical Discipline*, New York: Pegasus.

ZINN, HOWARD (1970), *The Politics of History*, Boston: Beacon Press.

Name index

Subject index

Routledge Social Science Series

Routledge & Kegan Paul London and Boston

68–74 Carter Lane London EC4V 5EL

9 Park Street Boston Mass 02108

Contents

Authors wishing to submit manuscripts for any series in this catalogue should send them to the Social Science Editor, Routledge & Kegan Paul Ltd, 68–74 Carter Lane, London EC4V 5EL

●*Books so marked are available in paperback*
All books are in Metric Demy 8vo format (216×138mm approx.)

International Library of Sociology

General Editor John Rex

GENERAL SOCIOLOGY

Barnsley, J. H. The Social Reality of Ethics. *464 pp.*
Belshaw, Cyril. The Conditions of Social Performance. *An Exploratory Theory. 144 pp.*
Brown, Robert. Explanation in Social Science. *208 pp.*
● Rules and Laws in Sociology. *192 pp.*
Bruford, W. H. Chekhov and His Russia. *A Sociological Study. 244 pp.*
Cain, Maureen E. Society and the Policeman's Role. *326 pp.*
Gibson, Quentin. The Logic of Social Enquiry. *240 pp.*
Glucksmann, M. Structuralist Analysis in Contemporary Social Thought. *212 pp.*
Gurvitch, Georges. Sociology of Law. *Preface by Roscoe Pound. 264 pp.*
Hodge, H. A. Wilhelm Dilthey. *An Introduction. 184 pp.*
Homans, George C. Sentiments and Activities. *336 pp.*
Johnson, Harry M. Sociology: *a Systematic Introduction. Foreword by Robert K. Merton. 710 pp.*
Mannheim, Karl. Essays on Sociology and Social Psychology. *Edited by Paul Keckskemeti. With Editorial Note by Adolph Lowe. 344 pp.*
Systematic Sociology: *An Introduction to the Study of Society. Edited by J. S. Erös and Professor W. A. C. Stewart. 220 pp.*
Martindale, Don. The Nature and Types of Sociological Theory. *292 pp.*
●**Maus, Heinz.** A Short History of Sociology. *234 pp.*
Mey, Harald. Field-Theory. *A Study of its Application in the Social Sciences. 352 pp.*
Myrdal, Gunnar. Value in Social Theory: *A Collection of Essays on Methodology. Edited by Paul Streeten. 332 pp.*
Ogburn, William F., and **Nimkoff, Meyer F.** A Handbook of Sociology. *Preface by Karl Mannheim. 656 pp. 46 figures. 35 tables.*
Parsons, Talcott, and **Smelser, Neil J.** Economy and Society: *A Study in the Integration of Economic and Social Theory. 362 pp.*
●**Rex, John.** Key Problems of Sociological Theory. *220 pp.*
Discovering Sociology. *278 pp.*
Sociology and the Demystification of the Modern World. *282 pp.*
●**Rex, John** (Ed.) Approaches to Sociology. *Contributions by Peter Abell, Frank Bechhofer, Basil Bernstein, Ronald Fletcher, David Frisby, Miriam Glucksmann, Peter Lassman, Herminio Martins, John Rex, Roland Robertson, John Westergaard and Jock Young. 302 pp.*
Rigby, A. Alternative Realities. *352 pp.*
Roche, M. Phenomenology, Language and the Social Sciences. *374 pp.*
Sahay, A. Sociological Analysis. *220 pp.*
Urry, John. Reference Groups and the Theory of Revolution. *244 pp.*
Weinberg, E. Development of Sociology in the Soviet Union. *173 pp.*

FOREIGN CLASSICS OF SOCIOLOGY

●**Durkheim, Emile.** Suicide. *A Study in Sociology. Edited and with an Introduction by George Simpson. 404 pp.*

Professional Ethics and Civic Morals. *Translated by Cornelia Brookfield. 288 pp.*

●**Gerth, H. H.**, and **Mills, C. Wright.** From Max Weber: *Essays in Sociology. 502 pp.*

●**Tönnies, Ferdinand.** Community and Association. (*Gemeinschaft und Gesellschaft.*) *Translated and Supplemented by Charles P. Loomis. Foreword by Pitirim A. Sorokin. 334 pp.*

SOCIAL STRUCTURE

Andreski, Stanislav. Military Organization and Society. *Foreword by Professor A. R. Radcliffe-Brown. 226 pp. 1 folder.*

Coontz, Sydney H. Population Theories and the Economic Interpretation. *202 pp.*

Coser, Lewis. The Functions of Social Conflict. *204 pp.*

Dickie-Clark, H. F. Marginal Situation: *A Sociological Study of a Coloured Group. 240 pp. 11 tables.*

Glaser, Barney, and **Strauss, Anselm L.** Status Passage. *A Formal Theory. 208 pp.*

Glass, D. V. (Ed.) Social Mobility in Britain. *Contributions by J. Berent, T. Bottomore, R. C. Chambers, J. Floud, D. V. Glass, J. R. Hall, H. T. Himmelweit, R. K. Kelsall, F. M. Martin, C. A. Moser, R. Mukherjee, and W. Ziegel. 420 pp.*

Jones, Garth N. Planned Organizational Change: *An Exploratory Study Using an Empirical Approach. 268 pp.*

Kelsall, R. K. Higher Civil Servants in Britain: *From 1870 to the Present Day. 268 pp. 31 tables.*

König, René. The Community. *232 pp. Illustrated.*

●**Lawton, Denis.** Social Class, Language and Education. *192 pp.*

McLeish, John. The Theory of Social Change: *Four Views Considered. 128 pp.*

Marsh, David C. The Changing Social Structure of England and Wales, 1871-1961. *288 pp.*

Mouzelis, Nicos. Organization and Bureaucracy. *An Analysis of Modern Theories. 240 pp.*

Mulkay, M. J. Functionalism, Exchange and Theoretical Strategy. *272 pp.*

Ossowski, Stanislaw. Class Structure in the Social Consciousness. *210 pp.*

Podgórecki, Adam. Law and Society. *About 300 pp.*

SOCIOLOGY AND POLITICS

Acton, T. A. Gypsy Politics and Social Change. *316 pp.*

Hechter, Michael. Internal Colonialism. *The Celtic Fringe in British National Development, 1536–1966. About 350 pp.*

Hertz, Frederick. Nationality in History and Politics: *A Psychology and Sociology of National Sentiment and Nationalism. 432 pp.*

Kornhauser, William. The Politics of Mass Society. *272 pp. 20 tables.*
Laidler, Harry W. History of Socialism. *Social-Economic Movements: An Historical and Comparative Survey of Socialism, Communism, Co-operation, Utopianism; and other Systems of Reform and Reconstruction. 992 pp.*
Lasswell, H. D. Analysis of Political Behaviour. *324 pp.*
Mannheim, Karl. Freedom, Power and Democratic Planning. *Edited by Hans Gerth and Ernest K. Bramstedt. 424 pp.*
Mansur, Fatma. Process of Independence. *Foreword by A. H. Hanson. 208 pp.*
Martin, David A. Pacifism: *an Historical and Sociological Study. 262 pp.*
Myrdal, Gunnar. The Political Element in the Development of Economic Theory. *Translated from the German by Paul Streeten. 282 pp.*
Wootton, Graham. Workers, Unions and the State. *188 pp.*

FOREIGN AFFAIRS: THEIR SOCIAL, POLITICAL AND ECONOMIC FOUNDATIONS

Mayer, J. P. Political Thought in France from the Revolution to the Fifth Republic. *164 pp.*

CRIMINOLOGY

Ancel, Marc. Social Defence: *A Modern Approach to Criminal Problems. Foreword by Leon Radzinowicz. 240 pp.*
Cain, Maureen E. Society and the Policeman's Role. *326 pp.*
Cloward, Richard A., and **Ohlin, Lloyd E.** Delinquency and Opportunity: *A Theory of Delinquent Gangs. 248 pp.*
Downes, David M. The Delinquent Solution. *A Study in Subcultural Theory. 296 pp.*
Dunlop, A. B., and **McCabe, S.** Young Men in Detention Centres. *192 pp.*
Friedlander, Kate. The Psycho-Analytical Approach to Juvenile Delinquency: *Theory, Case Studies, Treatment. 320 pp.*
Glueck, Sheldon, and **Eleanor.** Family Environment and Delinquency. *With the statistical assistance of Rose W. Kneznek. 340 pp.*
Lopez-Rey, Manuel. Crime. *An Analytical Appraisal. 288 pp.*
Mannheim, Hermann. Comparative Criminology: *a Text Book. Two volumes. 442 pp. and 380 pp.*
Morris, Terence. The Criminal Area: *A Study in Social Ecology. Foreword by Hermann Mannheim. 232 pp. 25 tables. 4 maps.*
Rock, Paul. Making People Pay. *338 pp.*
● **Taylor, Ian, Walton, Paul,** and **Young, Jock.** The New Criminology. *For a Social Theory of Deviance. 325 pp.*

SOCIAL PSYCHOLOGY

Bagley, Christopher. The Social Psychology of the Epileptic Child. *320 pp.*
Barbu, Zevedei. Problems of Historical Psychology. *248 pp.*
Blackburn, Julian. Psychology and the Social Pattern. *184 pp.*

●**Brittan, Arthur.** Meanings and Situations. *224 pp.*

Carroll, J. Break-Out from the Crystal Palace. *200 pp.*

●**Fleming, C. M.** Adolescence: Its Social Psychology. *With an Introduction to recent findings from the fields of Anthropology, Physiology, Medicine, Psychometrics and Sociometry. 288 pp.*

● The Social Psychology of Education: *An Introduction and Guide to Its Study. 136 pp.*

Homans, George C. The Human Group. *Foreword by Bernard DeVoto. Introduction by Robert K. Merton. 526 pp.*

● Social Behaviour: *its Elementary Forms. 416 pp.*

●**Klein, Josephine.** The Study of Groups. *226 pp. 31 figures. 5 tables.*

Linton, Ralph. The Cultural Background of Personality. *132 pp.*

●**Mayo, Elton.** The Social Problems of an Industrial Civilization. *With an appendix on the Political Problem. 180 pp.*

Ottaway, A. K. C. Learning Through Group Experience. *176 pp.*

Ridder, J. C. de. The Personality of the Urban African in South Africa. *A Thermatic Apperception Test Study. 196 pp. 12 plates.*

●**Rose, Arnold M.** (Ed.) Human Behaviour and Social Processes: *an Interactionist Approach. Contributions by Arnold M. Rose, Ralph H. Turner, Anselm Strauss, Everett C. Hughes, E. Franklin Frazier, Howard S. Becker, et al. 696 pp.*

Smelser, Neil J. Theory of Collective Behaviour. *448 pp.*

Stephenson, Geoffrey M. The Development of Conscience. *128 pp.*

Young, Kimball. Handbook of Social Psychology. *658 pp. 16 figures. 10 tables.*

SOCIOLOGY OF THE FAMILY

Banks, J. A. Prosperity and Parenthood: *A Study of Family Planning among The Victorian Middle Classes. 262 pp.*

Bell, Colin R. Middle Class Families: *Social and Geographical Mobility. 224 pp.*

Burton, Lindy. Vulnerable Children. *272 pp.*

Gavron, Hannah. The Captive Wife: *Conflicts of Household Mothers. 190 pp.*

George, Victor, and **Wilding, Paul.** Motherless Families. *220 pp.*

Klein, Josephine. Samples from English Cultures.

1. Three Preliminary Studies and Aspects of Adult Life in England. *447 pp.*
2. Child-Rearing Practices and Index. *247 pp.*

Klein, Viola. Britain's Married Women Workers. *180 pp.*

The Feminine Character. *History of an Ideology. 244 pp.*

McWhinnie, Alexina M. Adopted Children. *How They Grow Up. 304 pp.*

● **Myrdal, Alva,** and **Klein, Viola.** Women's Two Roles: *Home and Work. 238 pp. 27 tables.*

Parsons, Talcott, and **Bales, Robert F.** Family: Socialization and Interaction Process. *In collaboration with James Olds, Morris Zelditch and Philip E. Slater. 456 pp. 50 figures and tables.*

SOCIAL SERVICES

Bastide, Roger. The Sociology of Mental Disorder. *Translated from the French by Jean McNeil. 260 pp.*

Carlebach, Julius. Caring For Children in Trouble. *266 pp.*

Forder, R. A. (Ed.) Penelope Hall's Social Services of England and Wales. *352 pp.*

George, Victor. Foster Care. *Theory and Practice. 234 pp.*

Social Security: *Beveridge and After. 258 pp.*

George, V., and **Wilding, P.** Motherless Families. *248 pp.*

●**Goetschius, George W.** Working with Community Groups. *256 pp.*

Goetschius, George W., and **Tash, Joan.** Working with Unattached Youth. *416 pp.*

Hall, M. P., and **Howes, I. V.** The Church in Social Work. *A Study of Moral Welfare Work undertaken by the Church of England. 320 pp.*

Heywood, Jean S. Children in Care: *the Development of the Service for the Deprived Child. 264 pp.*

Hoenig, J., and **Hamilton, Marian W.** The De-Segregation of the Mentally Ill. *284 pp.*

Jones, Kathleen. Mental Health and Social Policy, 1845-1959. *264 pp.*

King, Roy D., Raynes, Norma V., and **Tizard, Jack.** Patterns of Residential Care. *356 pp.*

Leigh, John. Young People and Leisure. *256 pp.*

Morris, Mary. Voluntary Work and the Welfare State. *300 pp.*

Morris, Pauline. Put Away: *A Sociological Study of Institutions for the Mentally Retarded. 364 pp.*

Nokes, P. L. The Professional Task in Welfare Practice. *152 pp.*

Timms, Noel. Psychiatric Social Work in Great Britain (1939-1962). *280 pp.*

● Social Casework: *Principles and Practice. 256 pp.*

Young, A. F. Social Services in British Industry. *272 pp.*

Young, A. F., and **Ashton, E. T.** British Social Work in the Nineteenth Century. *288 pp.*

SOCIOLOGY OF EDUCATION

Banks, Olive. Parity and Prestige in English Secondary Education: a Study in Educational Sociology. *272 pp.*

Bentwich, Joseph. Education in Israel. *224 pp. 8 pp. plates.*

●**Blyth, W. A. L.** English Primary Education. *A Sociological Description.*

1. Schools. *232 pp.*
2. Background. *168 pp.*

Collier, K. G. The Social Purposes of Education: *Personal and Social Values in Education. 268 pp.*

Dale, R. R., and **Griffith, S.** Down Stream: *Failure in the Grammar School. 108 pp.*

Dore, R. P. Education in Tokugawa Japan. *356 pp. 9 pp. plates.*

Evans, K. M. Sociometry and Education. *158 pp.*

● **Ford, Julienne.** Social Class and the Comprehensive School. *192 pp.*

Foster, P. J. Education and Social Change in Ghana. *336 pp. 3 maps.*

Fraser, W. R. Education and Society in Modern France. *150 pp.*

Grace, Gerald R. Role Conflict and the Teacher. *About 200 pp.*

Hans, Nicholas. New Trends in Education in the Eighteenth Century. *278 pp. 19 tables.*

● Comparative Education: *A Study of Educational Factors and Traditions. 360 pp.*

Hargreaves, David. Interpersonal Relations and Education. *432 pp.*

● Social Relations in a Secondary School. *240 pp.*

Holmes, Brian. Problems in Education. *A Comparative Approach. 336 pp.*

King, Ronald. Values and Involvement in a Grammar School. *164 pp.*

School Organization and Pupil Involvement. *A Study of Secondary Schools.*

● **Mannheim, Karl,** and **Stewart, W. A. C.** An Introduction to the Sociology of Education. *206 pp.*

Morris, Raymond N. The Sixth Form and College Entrance. *231 pp.*

● **Musgrove, F.** Youth and the Social Order. *176 pp.*

● **Ottaway, A. K. C.** Education and Society: An Introduction to the Sociology of Education. *With an Introduction by W. O. Lester Smith. 212 pp.*

Peers, Robert. Adult Education: *A Comparative Study. 398 pp.*

Pritchard, D. G. Education and the Handicapped: *1760 to 1960. 258 pp.*

Richardson, Helen. Adolescent Girls in Approved Schools. *308 pp.*

Stratta, Erica. The Education of Borstal Boys. *A Study of their Educational Experiences prior to, and during, Borstal Training. 256 pp.*

Taylor, P. H., Reid, W. A., and **Holley, B. J.** The English Sixth Form. *A Case Study in Curriculum Research. 200 pp.*

SOCIOLOGY OF CULTURE

Eppel, E. M., and **M.** Adolescents and Morality: *A Study of some Moral Values and Dilemmas of Working Adolescents in the Context of a changing Climate of Opinion. Foreword by W. J. H. Sprott. 268 pp. 39 tables.*

● **Fromm, Erich.** The Fear of Freedom. *286 pp.*

● The Sane Society. *400 pp.*

Mannheim, Karl. Essays on the Sociology of Culture. *Edited by Ernst Mannheim in co-operation with Paul Kecskemeti. Editorial Note by Adolph Lowe. 280 pp.*

Weber, Alfred. Farewell to European History: *or The Conquest of Nihilism. Translated from the German by R. F. C. Hull. 224 pp.*

SOCIOLOGY OF RELIGION

Argyle, Michael and **Beit-Hallahmi, Benjamin.** The Social Psychology of Religion. *About 256 pp.*

Nelson, G. K. Spiritualism and Society. *313 pp.*

Stark, Werner. The Sociology of Religion. *A Study of Christendom.*
- Volume I. *Established Religion. 248 pp.*
- Volume II. *Sectarian Religion. 368 pp.*
- Volume III. *The Universal Church. 464 pp.*
- Volume IV. *Types of Religious Man. 352 pp.*
- Volume V. *Types of Religious Culture. 464 pp.*

Turner, B. S. Weber and Islam. *216 pp.*

Watt, W. Montgomery. Islam and the Integration of Society. *320 pp.*

SOCIOLOGY OF ART AND LITERATURE

Jarvie, Ian C. Towards a Sociology of the Cinema. *A Comparative Essay on the Structure and Functioning of a Major Entertainment Industry. 405 pp.*

Rust, Frances S. Dance in Society. *An Analysis of the Relationships between the Social Dance and Society in England from the Middle Ages to the Present Day. 256 pp. 8 pp. of plates.*

Schücking, L. L. The Sociology of Literary Taste. *112 pp.*

Wolff, Janet. Hermeneutic Philosophy and the Sociology of Art. *About 200 pp.*

SOCIOLOGY OF KNOWLEDGE

Diesing, P. Patterns of Discovery in the Social Sciences. *262 pp.*

●**Douglas, J. D.** (Ed.) Understanding Everyday Life. *370 pp.*

●**Hamilton, P.** Knowledge and Social Structure. *174 pp.*

Jarvie, I. C. Concepts and Society. *232 pp.*

Mannheim, Karl. Essays on the Sociology of Knowledge. *Edited by Paul Kecskemeti. Editorial Note by Adolph Lowe. 353 pp.*

Remmling, Gunter W. (Ed.) Towards the Sociology of Knowledge. *Origin and Development of a Sociological Thought Style. 463 pp.*

Stark, Werner. The Sociology of Knowledge: *An Essay in Aid of a Deeper Understanding of the History of Ideas. 384 pp.*

URBAN SOCIOLOGY

Ashworth, William. The Genesis of Modern British Town Planning: *A Study in Economic and Social History of the Nineteenth and Twentieth Centuries. 288 pp.*

Cullingworth, J. B. Housing Needs and Planning Policy: *A Restatement of the Problems of Housing Need and 'Overspill' in England and Wales. 232 pp. 44 tables. 8 maps.*

Dickinson, Robert E. City and Region: *A Geographical Interpretation 608 pp. 125 figures.*

The West European City: *A Geographical Interpretation. 600 pp. 129 maps. 29 plates.*

● The City Region in Western Europe. *320 pp. Maps.*

Humphreys, Alexander J. New Dubliners: *Urbanization and the Irish Family. Foreword by George C. Homans. 304 pp.*

Jackson, Brian. Working Class Community: *Some General Notions raised by a Series of Studies in Northern England. 192 pp.*

Jennings, Hilda. Societies in the Making: *a Study of Development and Redevelopment within a County Borough. Foreword by D. A. Clark. 286 pp.*

●**Mann, P. H.** An Approach to Urban Sociology. *240 pp.*

Morris, R. N., and **Mogey, J.** The Sociology of Housing. *Studies at Berinsfield. 232 pp. 4 pp. plates.*

Rosser, C., and **Harris, C.** The Family and Social Change. *A Study of Family and Kinship in a South Wales Town. 352 pp. 8 maps.*

RURAL SOCIOLOGY

Chambers, R. J. H. Settlement Schemes in Tropical Africa: *A Selective Study. 268 pp.*

Haswell, M. R. The Economics of Development in Village India. *120 pp.*

Littlejohn, James. Westrigg: *the Sociology of a Cheviot Parish. 172 pp. 5 figures.*

Mayer, Adrian C. Peasants in the Pacific. *A Study of Fiji Indian Rural Society. 248 pp. 20 plates.*

Williams, W. M. The Sociology of an English Village: *Gosforth. 272 pp. 12 figures. 13 tables.*

SOCIOLOGY OF INDUSTRY AND DISTRIBUTION

Anderson, Nels. Work and Leisure. *280 pp.*

●**Blau, Peter M.,** and **Scott, W. Richard.** Formal Organizations: *a Comparative approach. Introduction and Additional Bibliography by J. H. Smith. 326 pp.*

Eldridge, J. E. T. Industrial Disputes. *Essays in the Sociology of Industrial Relations. 288 pp.*

Hetzler, Stanley. Applied Measures for Promoting Technological Growth. *352 pp.*

Technological Growth and Social Change. *Achieving Modernization. 269 pp.*

Hollowell, Peter G. The Lorry Driver. *272 pp.*

Jefferys, Margot, *with the assistance of Winifred Moss.* Mobility in the Labour Market: *Employment Changes in Battersea and Dagenham. Preface by Barbara Wootton. 186 pp. 51 tables.*

Millerson, Geoffrey. The Qualifying Associations: *a Study in Professionalization. 320 pp.*

Smelser, Neil J. Social Change in the Industrial Revolution: *An Application of Theory to the Lancashire Cotton Industry, 1770-1840. 468 pp. 12 figures. 14 tables.*

Williams, Gertrude. Recruitment to Skilled Trades. *240 pp.*

Young, A. F. Industrial Injuries Insurance: *an Examination of British Policy. 192 pp.*

DOCUMENTARY

Schlesinger, Rudolf (Ed.) Changing Attitudes in Soviet Russia.

2. The Nationalities Problem and Soviet Administration. *Selected Readings on the Development of Soviet Nationalities Policies. Introduced by the editor. Translated by W. W. Gottlieb. 324 pp.*

ANTHROPOLOGY

Ammar, Hamed. Growing up in an Egyptian Village: *Silwa, Province of Aswan. 336 pp.*

Brandel-Syrier, Mia. Reeftown Elite. *A Study of Social Mobility in a Modern African Community on the Reef. 376 pp.*

Crook, David, and **Isabel.** Revolution in a Chinese Village: *Ten Mile Inn. 230 pp. 8 plates. 1 map.*

Dickie-Clark, H. F. The Marginal Situation. *A Sociological Study of a Coloured Group. 236 pp.*

Dube, S. C. Indian Village. *Foreword by Morris Edward Opler. 276 pp. 4 plates.*

India's Changing Villages: *Human Factors in Community Development. 260 pp. 8 plates. 1 map.*

Firth, Raymond. Malay Fishermen. *Their Peasant Economy. 420 pp. 17 pp. plates.*

Firth, R., Hubert, J., and **Forge, A.** Families and their Relatives. *Kinship in a Middle-Class Sector of London: An Anthropological Study. 456 pp.*

Gulliver, P. H. Social Control in an African Society: a Study of the Arusha, Agricultural Masai of Northern Tanganyika. *320 pp. 8 plates. 10 figures.*

Family Herds. *288 pp.*

Ishwaran, K. Shivapur. *A South Indian Village. 216 pp.*

Tradition and Economy in Village India: *An Interactionist Approach. Foreword by Conrad Arensburg. 176 pp.*

Jarvie, Ian C. The Revolution in Anthropology. *268 pp.*

Jarvie, Ian C., and **Agassi, Joseph.** Hong Kong. *A Society in Transition. 396 pp. Illustrated with plates and maps.*

Little, Kenneth L. Mende of Sierra Leone. *308 pp. and folder.*

Negroes in Britain. *With a New Introduction and Contemporary Study by Leonard Bloom. 320 pp.*

Lowie, Robert H. Social Organization. *494 pp.*
Mayer, Adrian C. Caste and Kinship in Central India: *A Village and its Region. 328 pp. 16 plates. 15 figures. 16 tables.*
Peasants in the Pacific. *A Study of Fiji Indian Rural Society. 248 pp.*
Smith, Raymond T. The Negro Family in British Guiana: *Family Structure and Social Status in the Villages. With a Foreword by Meyer Fortes. 314 pp. 8 plates. 1 figure. 4 maps.*

SOCIOLOGY AND PHILOSOPHY

Barnsley, John H. The Social Reality of Ethics. *A Comparative Analysis of Moral Codes. 448 pp.*
Diesing, Paul. Patterns of Discovery in the Social Sciences. *362 pp.*
●**Douglas, Jack D.** (Ed.) Understanding Everyday Life. *Toward the Reconstruction of Sociological Knowledge. Contributions by Alan F. Blum. Aaron W. Cicourel, Norman K. Denzin, Jack D. Douglas, John Heeren, Peter McHugh, Peter K. Manning, Melvin Power, Matthew Speier, Roy Turner, D. Lawrence Wieder, Thomas P. Wilson and Don H. Zimmerman. 370 pp.*
Jarvie, Ian C. Concepts and Society. *216 pp.*
Pelz, Werner. The Scope of Understanding in Sociology. *Towards a more radical reorientation in the social humanistic sciences. 283 pp.*
Roche, Maurice. Phenomenology, Language and the Social Sciences. *371 pp.*
Sahay, Arun. Sociological Analysis. *212 pp.*
Sklair, Leslie. The Sociology of Progress. *320 pp.*

International Library of Anthropology

General Editor Adam Kuper

Brown, Paula. The Chimbu. *A Study of Change in the New Guinea Highlands. 151 pp.*
Lloyd, P. C. Power and Independence. *Urban Africans' Perception of Social Inequality. 264 pp.*
Pettigrew, Joyce. Robber Noblemen. *A Study of the Political System of the Sikh Jats. 284 pp.*
Van Den Berghe, Pierre L. Power and Privilege at an African University. *278 pp.*

International Library of Social Policy

General Editor Kathleen Jones

Bayley, M. Mental Handicap and Community Care. *426 pp.*
Butler, J. R. Family Doctors and Public Policy. *208 pp.*
Holman, Robert. Trading in Children. *A Study of Private Fostering. 355 pp.*

Jones, Kathleen. History of the Mental Health Service. *428 pp.*
Thomas, J. E. The English Prison Officer since 1850: *A Study in Conflict. 258 pp.*
Woodward, J. To Do the Sick No Harm. *A Study of the British Voluntary Hospital System to 1875. About 220 pp.*

International Library of Welfare and Philosophy

General Editors Noel Timms and David Watson

● **Plant, Raymond.** Community and Ideology. *104 pp.*

Primary Socialization, Language and Education

General Editor Basil Bernstein

Bernstein, Basil. Class, Codes and Control. *2 volumes.*
1. *Theoretical Studies Towards a Sociology of Language. 254 pp.*
2. *Applied Studies Towards a Sociology of Language. About 400 pp.*

Brandis, W., and **Bernstein, B.** Selection and Control. *176 pp.*
Brandis, Walter, and **Henderson, Dorothy.** Social Class, Language and Communication. *288 pp.*
Cook-Gumperz, Jenny. Social Control and Socialization. *A Study of Class Differences in the Language of Maternal Control. 290 pp.*
● **Gahagan, D. M.,** and **G. A.** Talk Reform. *Exploration in Language for Infant School Children. 160 pp.*
Robinson, W. P., and **Rackstraw, Susan D. A.** A Question of Answers. *2 volumes. 192 pp. and 180 pp.*
Turner, Geoffrey J., and **Mohan, Bernard A.** A Linguistic Description and Computer Programme for Children's Speech. *208 pp.*

Reports of the Institute of Community Studies

Cartwright, Ann. Human Relations and Hospital Care. *272 pp.*
● Parents and Family Planning Services. *306 pp.*
Patients and their Doctors. *A Study of General Practice. 304 pp.*
● **Jackson, Brian.** Streaming: *an Education System in Miniature. 168 pp.*
Jackson, Brian, and **Marsden, Dennis.** Education and the Working Class: *Some General Themes raised by a Study of 88 Working-class Children in a Northern Industrial City. 268 pp. 2 folders.*
Marris, Peter. The Experience of Higher Education. *232 pp. 27 tables.*
Loss and Change. *192 pp.*

Marris, Peter, and **Rein, Martin.** Dilemmas of Social Reform. *Poverty and Community Action in the United States. 256 pp.*

Marris, Peter, and **Somerset, Anthony.** African Businessmen. *A Study of Entrepreneurship and Development in Kenya. 256 pp.*

Mills, Richard. Young Outsiders: *a Study in Alternative Communities. 216 pp.*

Runciman, W. G. Relative Deprivation and Social Justice. *A Study of Attitudes to Social Inequality in Twentieth-Century England. 352 pp.*

Willmott, Peter. Adolescent Boys in East London. *230 pp.*

Willmott, Peter, and **Young, Michael.** Family and Class in a London Suburb. *202 pp. 47 tables.*

Young, Michael. Innovation and Research in Education. *192 pp.*

● **Young, Michael,** and **McGeeney, Patrick.** Learning Begins at Home. *A Study of a Junior School and its Parents. 128 pp.*

Young, Michael, and **Willmott, Peter.** Family and Kinship in East London. *Foreword by Richard M. Titmuss. 252 pp. 39 tables.*

The Symmetrical Family. *410 pp.*

Reports of the Institute for Social Studies in Medical Care

Cartwright, Ann, Hockey, Lisbeth, and **Anderson, John L.** Life Before Death. *310 pp.*

Dunnell, Karen, and **Cartwright, Ann.** Medicine Takers, Prescribers and Hoarders. *190 pp.*

Medicine, Illness and Society

General Editor W. M. Williams

Robinson, David. The Process of Becoming Ill. *142 pp.*

Stacey, Margaret, *et al.* Hospitals, Children and Their Families. *The Report of a Pilot Study. 202 pp.*

Monographs in Social Theory

General Editor Arthur Brittan

● **Barnes, B.** Scientific Knowledge and Sociological Theory. *About 200 pp.*

Bauman, Zygmunt. Culture as Praxis. *204 pp.*

● **Dixon, Keith.** Sociological Theory. *Pretence and Possibility. 142 pp.*

● **Smith, Anthony D.** The Concept of Social Change. *A Critique of the Functionalist Theory of Social Change. 208 pp.*

Routledge Social Science Journals

The British Journal of Sociology. *Edited by Terence P. Morris. Vol. 1, No. 1, March 1950 and Quarterly. Roy. 8vo. Back numbers available. An international journal with articles on all aspects of sociology.*

Economy and Society. *Vol. 1, No. 1. February 1972 and Quarterly. Metric Roy. 8vo. A journal for all social scientists covering sociology, philosophy, anthropology, economics and history. Back numbers available.*

Year Book of Social Policy in Britain, The. *Edited by Kathleen Jones. 1971. Published annually.*

Printed in Great Britain by Unwin Brothers Limited
The Gresham Press Old Woking Surrey
A member of the Staples Printing Group